Rethinking Social Exclusion

Rethinking Social Exclusion

THE END OF THE SOCIAL?

Simon Winlow and Steve Hall

Los Angeles | London | New Delhi
Singapore | Washington DC

Los Angeles | London | New Delhi
Singapore | Washington DC

SAGE Publications Ltd
1 Oliver's Yard
55 City Road
London EC1Y 1SP

SAGE Publications Inc.
2455 Teller Road
Thousand Oaks, California 91320

SAGE Publications India Pvt Ltd
B 1/I 1 Mohan Cooperative Industrial Area
Mathura Road
New Delhi 110 044

SAGE Publications Asia-Pacific Pte Ltd
3 Church Street
#10-04 Samsung Hub
Singapore 049483

Editor: Chris Rojek
Editorial assistant: Gemma Shields
Production editor: Katherine Haw
Proofreader: Rose James
Marketing manager: Michael Ainsley
Cover design: Lisa Harper
Typeset by: C&M Digitals (P) Ltd, Chennai, India
Printed by: Replika Press Pvt Ltd

Library of Congress Control Number: 2013933560

British Library Cataloguing in Publication data

A catalogue record for this book is available from
the British Library

ISBN 978-1-84920-107-0
ISBN 978-1-84920-108-7 (pbk)

Contents

About the Authors

Simon Winlow is Professor of Criminology at Teesside University, UK. He is the author of *Badfellas* (Berg, 2001), and co-author of *Bouncers* (Oxford University Press, 2003), *Violent Night* (Berg, 2006) and *Criminal Identities and Consumer Culture* (Willan, 2008). He is also the co-editor of the recently published *New Directions in Criminological Theory* (Routledge, 2012) and *New Directions in Crime and Deviancy* (Routledge, 2012).

Steve Hall is Professor of Criminology at Teesside University, UK. He is the co-author of *Violent Night* (Berg, 2006) and *Criminal Identities and Consumer Culture* (Willan, 2008), and author of *Theorizing Crime and Deviance: A New Perspective* (Sage, 2012). With Winlow he is the co-editor of the recently published *New Directions in Criminological Theory* (Routledge, 2012).

Acknowledgements

We should begin by acknowledging a debt of gratitude to our colleagues in the Centre for Realist Criminology at Teesside University, UK. They have created a lively intellectual environment that has made the problems currently faced by Britain's University system a little easier to take. We would also like to thank Paul Crawshaw for his ongoing support and the skill and dedication he has shown in his direction of the Social Futures Institute at the university.

In the broader academic community we have been lucky enough to benefit from the support, encouragement and friendship of a number of hugely talented intellectuals. Among this group, we are particularly grateful to Georgios Antonopoulos, Rowland Atkinson, Pat Carlen, Elliot Currie, Walter DeKeseredy, Mark Featherstone, Jeff Ferrell, Keith Hayward, Simon Hallsworth, Dick Hobbs, John Lea, Bob Lilly, Ronnie Lippens, David Moxon, Georgios Papanicolaou, Larry Ray, Robert Reiner, Chris Rojek, Barry Smart, Colin Sumner, Steve Tombs, Sandra Walklate, Colin Webster, David Wilson and Majid Yar. Not that everyone on this list agrees with everything we say, but the fact that some disagree or only partially agree with us yet still support the dissemination of our arguments shows the true spirit of intellectual inquiry. We would also like to thank numerous postgraduate students who over the years have given us the constant stimulation and feedback we needed to develop our work.

Simon Winlow would like to thank Sara and Gabriel for... everything.

Steve Hall would like to thank his family Chrissie, Chris and Alex for putting up with him and his old mate Mike Randall for half a lifetime of encouragement.

1

Introduction:
Post-crash Social Exclusion

I muse upon my country's ills

The tempest bursting from the waste of Time

On the World's fairest hope linked with man's foulest crime.

Herman Melville, 'Misgivings'

Things cannot go on as they are...

We began writing this book in 2012, four years into the most severe financial crash in living memory. Our exposure to the profound human consequences of this event and its aftermath – via daily media coverage but also via our ongoing empirical work in areas of permanent recession in the north of England (Winlow, 2001; Winlow and Hall, 2006; Hall et al., 2008) – compelled us to reconsider the book's structure and content. The fallout from liberal capitalism's latest spectacular convulsion dragged the system itself from its background location in the analysis of social exclusion to centre stage. In many respects this book can be read as a preliminary theoretical analysis of liberal capitalism's social consequences, based in England, but, to a large extent, generalisable throughout the West. The analysis is also embedded in a global process. The huge growth in surplus populations in global cities (see Davis, 2007), when understood in the context of imminent crises in water, food, energy, finance and the generation and distribution of money (Heinberg, 2011; Keen, 2011; Hall, 2012b) and the permanent inability of capitalism to absorb these populations into its networks of production, exchange and consumption, makes social exclusion one of the most pressing issues we face at this point in our history. A sophisticated and updated analysis of social exclusion is therefore essential, and, with this book, we hope to make a small contribution to this endeavour.

In ways we hope will become clear, excluded populations, the conditions in which they find themselves and their cultural expressions should not be considered external to or separate from the organising logic of global neoliberalism. The stark realities of life in the slums of Jakarta or Rio are as indicative of the reality of contemporary global capitalism as life in the boardrooms of Wall Street, and the same might be said of the virtual implosion of state governance in the Congo or Somalia. We also believe that the considerable harms of social and economic marginality in the West, when placed alongside the apparent inability of contemporary liberal capitalism to provide secure and civilised forms of employment for former working-class populations, represent a serious and enduring problem. Of course these harms tarnish Western liberal democracy's preferred image of itself as inclusive, meritocratic, civilised and fair, but the accompanying accumulation of everyday miseries and dissatisfactions and the prevailing sense of *lack* will, as we shall see, have a profound political resonance as the twenty-first century unfolds.

By addressing the current nature and meaning of social exclusion and economic marginality we gain some insight into the future of civil society more generally. What becomes of 'the social' if growing numbers of people are cut adrift from its organising logic – its economic transactions, relations, customs, codes and cultural norms – *and* the tradition of political contestation about its future trajectory? To answer this question, we will occasionally wander off the well-trodden sociological and social policy paths to draw upon the resources of contemporary political theory, continental philosophy and theoretical psychoanalysis, and with these intellectual tools address the evolving nature of contemporary social life more generally. We will also investigate the current condition of the Symbolic Order (see glossary), that crucial network of meaning that makes the social world comprehensible and allows us to construct and maintain a viable system of elementary truths to which we must all subscribe, truths that make communication and politics possible.

Of course, if we are to think seriously about social exclusion, we must first establish whether, amid neoliberalism's destructive conflagration, the social is still there to be excluded from. Do we now, as some notable commentators have claimed, occupy a *post*-social world in which the structuring reality of public life and social institutions has been replaced by a milieu of atomised individuals struggling for finger-holds in fields of mere representation? If this is true, on what basis can individuals and groups be said to be 'excluded' from something that might not exist in the way we once understood it? This forces upon us a new context in which traditional questions, plus a few supplementary ones, need to be asked and a few preliminary answers provided. What is the power that drives this exclusion, and what is the status of the excluded in the eyes of this power? What might social exclusion mean for those categorised as 'the excluded', and what are the consequences of the exclusionary process for those who manage to remain connected to the social mainstream? In a more straightforward manner, what are the political, economic or social *functions* of exclusion? What do today's forms of social exclusion tell us about culture, economy, politics, subjectivity (see glossary) and the ways in which we constitute collective life in the contemporary post-political period?

In many respects, these rather basic questions have become lost amid a growing assortment of empirical studies that endlessly describe the realities of marginality, and frenetic yet ineffective policy work that has scoured the landscape of 'civil society' to find 'transformative solutions' to the problem of exclusion, or at least ameliorate its most harmful effects. In our view, however, we need to rethink the problem of exclusion from its philosophical and theoretical roots and open the field up to the types of critical analysis that can advance our understanding of the key issues involved and the connection of social exclusion to other socioeconomic processes that are reshaping our world. As one might imagine, this deliberate attempt to remove 'social exclusion' from its current academic and political location (as a 'problem' to be managed through 'policy', its harms reduced wherever possible) and subject it to a renewed theoretical critique requires a broad yet deep analysis that explores fields of enquiry that are usually regarded as marginal at best. The root of this renewed critique is social change, individualism and the loosening of social bonds in the post-political twenty-first century, a period during which the engine of historical progress appears to have stalled and liberalism's assumption of ceaseless, incremental, progressive economic and cultural evolution in relatively stable and benign social contexts was revealed as mere modernist myth-making. The act of admitting that this profound change *has* actually occurred allows anyone who does so to ask more revealing questions. What remains of the network of community obligations and interdependencies that defined modernity's civic and sociocultural life? What does the transformed nature of the city tell us about emerging forms of envy, social anxiety, insecurity and hostility, sometimes manifested in crime and violence (see Hall et al., 2008)? How might the withdrawal of the moneyed classes from public spaces and civic institutions – a retreat into gated and guarded compounds in order to avoid upsetting encounters with the pathologised 'real world' (see Atkinson and Smith, 2012) – be connected to the social processes that ensure the exclusion of the poorest and their consignment to specific areas of the city? As we hope readers will quickly appreciate, social exclusion is not simply a 'problem', an aberration in an otherwise progressive socioeconomic system, an ailment whose micro-causes and effects can be easily identified, isolated and 'fixed' by a sympathetic and benevolent governmental elite. Rather, the problem of 'social exclusion' reflects a broader 'problem of the social' during a period characterised by the restoration of liberal capitalism and its marketisation of the social world in the almost total absence of a political, economic or ideological alternative (Badiou, 2009). In this context, the principal issue becomes this: are we looking at social exclusion or the exclusion of the social from the most important domains of our lives?

The ultimate social impact of twenty-first century forms of embedded underemployment, worklessness and social redundancy have yet to be fully revealed. So far, the portentous signs thrown up by enduring global economic turmoil suggest that there is no simple remedy that might enable global capitalism to incorporate the rapidly growing global population or reconnect marginal populations in Western liberal democracies to the social mainstream by reintroducing stable and reasonably remunerative forms of employment. Put bluntly, how will capitalism continue to define itself as the most inclusive and productive economic system when growing numbers of people find it increasingly difficult to find the waged labour that might allow them to meet basic material needs and participate in the social and cultural activities that signify inclusion? And, given the increasingly acknowledged structural inconsistencies and practical limitations of global neoliberalism (Krugman, 2008; Stiglitz, 2010; Roubini, 2011), is it really possible to regard capitalism itself as the elixir of growth and progress in developing countries? Can it really 'civilise' failed states, or recover apparently lawless areas of the developing world (Wiegratz, 2010, 2012; Currie, 2011)?

In the chapters that follow, we will attempt to answer these questions and criticise the assumptions they reveal. We will look closely at the history of the capitalist project to represent a current reality in which the majority have been persuaded to stop seeking a genuine alternative or believing that such a thing is possible. We will analyse the fluctuations of volatile global markets and the serious outcomes of these fluctuations for everyday men and women, but we also hope to go a good deal further by asking, once again, why the marginalised do not rebel or self-organise in opposition. We are particularly keen to investigate the continued dominance, by means of the hegemony of consumerism, of capital over our everyday lives, cultures and institutions. To this end we will outline a theory of marginalised subjectivity that is markedly different from the dominant liberal concepts of the subject as the sovereign individual and the moral agent constituting its surrounding cultural norms and socioeconomic structures, or the 'subject as pliable object' constituted and normalised by external forces that are largely beyond its control or understanding.

Right-wing commentators are largely in agreement with the dominant neoclassical conception of a subject whose 'bad choices' and 'anti-social values and norms' ensure continued poverty and marginality. The liberal-left, often drawing upon symbolic interactionism and post-structuralism, counter this by claiming that the powerful demonise and stigmatise the economically excluded and label them with a broad range of negative characteristics. At its most extreme this becomes a process of 'othering', where the forbidding image of an uncivilised, feckless, dangerous and criminal other is projected upon the excluded subject, making its inclusion appear impossible. Whilst avoiding the right's dogmatic voluntarism and moralism, however, we are also keen to move beyond the liberal-left's equally doctrinaire notion that this symbolic 'othering' is the primary cause of social exclusion or indeed the issue that demands political attention.

Focusing primarily on social exclusion in Western liberal democracies, especially Britain and America, we will throughout this book attempt to identify the human costs of social exclusion. Whilst choice plays a role in individual responses – and even then we cannot understand choice without understanding the drives and desires that underpin it – we have no intention of portraying poverty and exclusion as the results of choices. There might be contexts in which choices are made, but, in the fourth year of a global economic downturn, we will not hesitate to offer measured doses of 'economic determinism' and 'ideology critique' when we address the roots of social inequality and exclusion. Poverty is not a lifestyle choice, and the cultures that develop in its shadow are rarely autonomous, rational and creative responses to immediate economic circumstances and cultural priorities that have been inherited from the past or imposed by neoliberalism's current processes.

However, in the mainstream academic and policy-making fields, the dominant intellectual tradition currently informing the analysis of social exclusion in Britain is not the radical liberalism of the neoclassical right (see glossary) or the postmodernist left (see glossary), but a more considered Fabian social democratic (or social liberal) approach. Many working in this tradition emphasise the significant improvements that were made to the lives of everyday people in the post-war years before the rise of neoliberalism in the 1980s. During this period the state regulated business practice to a much greater extent, provided a comprehensive welfare system, taxed wealth, controlled capital flows, used fiscal stimulus to promote growth, maintained control over key national industries, significantly narrowed the gap between rich and poor, and attempted to ensure the continuation of full employment for work-aged populations. We concede that for the British working classes this period of prolonged social improvement represents something of a 'golden age' (Bauman, 2000) and that a return to the politics of that era would indeed represent a significant improvement to the life chances of everyday working and non-working people. We also concede that other significant social benefits would follow in the wake of the return of a genuine social democracy. But despite all this, we cannot fully endorse the social democratic approach, and the reasons for our departure from the social democratic orthodoxy will become clear as the book progresses.

We should note, of course, that in today's dispiriting political climate, even to suggest that we should tax wealth to a greater degree, or that the state should make a commitment to full employment, is to invite popular derision. In the here and now, even the pragmatic Fabian social democrat is depicted as an unworldly idealist (Winlow, 2012a). Given the volatile and brutally competitive nature of global market activity tied to the unforgiving principles of comparative advantage and cost efficiency, and given capital's arcane financial mechanisms and web of tax havens, is the return of genuine social democracy possible? We must note that the social democratic compromise was possible only during a period of unprecedented and sustained economic growth at a historically high rate (Cairncross and Cairncross, 1992; Harvey, 2010; Wolff, 2010). Such a rate of growth is now reaching its objective limit (Heinberg, 2011; Hall, 2012b), which means that, as it slows down, the growth-dependent Keynesian economic platform necessary for social democracy to succeed cannot be reconstructed. In this unprecedented situation of enforced economic downsizing, can the raw, destructive power of the profit motive really be harnessed and set to work pursuing positive social ends? Despite the near collapse of the banking system, can we picture our current batch of political leaders abandoning the rhetoric of the free market and their perverse attachment to 'light-touch regulation' to once again pursue a genuinely inclusive socioeconomic project? If the beast in capitalism's cage can no longer be harnessed by a social democratic state, and there is no will amongst the establishment to do so, what are the implications for social exclusion?

At the risk of antagonising some of our peers, we should perhaps also consider the possibility that many in the social democratic mainstream who issue their call for 'real jobs' and the return of a comprehensive welfare system are secretly aware that their demands can no longer be met. Perhaps the most striking gap in social democratic thinking about social exclusion is that, in seeking to reintroduce the 'excluded' back into the civic mainstream, they are arguing for the reintroduction of resource-poor workers back into the very system of relentless socio-symbolic competition that expelled them in the first place. Social democratic discourses of inclusion are always shot through with the idea that expanding opportunities is the way back to an inclusive society. Are they not essentially arguing that the poor be given another shot at 'making it' within the system as it currently exists, rather than arguing for a fundamental reappraisal of the conditions under which social and economic justice can actually take place? Our goal here is to side-step this debate about the reintroduction of 'real jobs' and the intellectual injunction that we up-skill the poor and equip them with the drive to compete. Instead, we want to ask searching questions about the drivers that lead to the expulsion or marginalisation of the poor, and, more fundamentally, whether inclusion is possible at all in a capitalist economy currently experiencing a permanent reduction in its growth-rate and a seismic shift in the balance of global economic power.

Rather than figuratively patching up the poor with neatly organised CVs, new qualifications and a taste for entrepreneurial accomplishment, and then sending them out once again to do battle in the unforgiving and precarious advanced capitalist labour market, it might be more productive to address the source of social conflict and competition. Rather than attempting to push the poor back into the mainstream and hoping against hope that this time they might fare a little better, we must return to the types of critical realist (see glossary) analysis that allow us to see the reality of our world in a new light.

Instead of offering the usual account of workless populations who simply need to be 'included' by being given better chances to improve their own lot, we will attempt to offer a critical account of marginalised subjectivity (see glossary) that is deeper and more firmly located in its historical and socioeconomic locations. We will encourage the reader to think through what the unopposed and uninterrupted march of capitalism further into the twenty-first century will mean for social life and subjectivity. If it is true that minimally-regulated advanced capitalism contains within its core the fundamental cultural values of competitive individualism, atomism and functional self-interest, and that it drives new forms of economic creativity and efficiency whilst arranging the constant dissolution of the 'social' and the 'public', what does this mean for those who inhabit marginalised and impoverished social spaces? As the reader will soon gather, our goal is to shift academic consideration of social exclusion away from the dry and domesticated world of social policy into the realm of political and theoretical analysis. We do this not to dismiss or disparage social policy as a discipline, but in the hope that, by bringing the deeper context into stark relief, social policy can renew itself by feeding on a separate discourse founded on a recognition of the form and true magnitude of the 'policies' required to do anything concrete about the problem of social exclusion.

Economic futures

The rapidly growing economic power of countries such as China, India and Brazil in recent years is closely related to the huge growth of household debt that allowed Western populations to continue purchasing the goods produced in these low-wage economies in those heady days before the global crash of 2008. A number of neoliberal commentators and economic forecasters have suggested that the rise of these new players can have a significant bearing on the revival of the global economy in the post-crash era. Some maintain that, as workers in these economies gradually become capable of accessing more consumer goods, this new economic activity can fuel a global return to growth more generally across all continents. For the moment this seems doubtful; the financial crisis has slowed growth, which is impacting badly on the BRIC (Brazil, Russia, India, China) economies. They are still growing but at nowhere near the rate required to attain the level of development enjoyed by the West in the latter half of the twentieth century. Some liberal

commentators believe that the Easternisation of the global economy will precipitate a general shift away from the greed, avarice and short-termism now
infecting Western economic culture. On this vaguely 'new age' trajectory we will
move towards a more inclusive and ecologically-sensitive Eastern business culture built upon decorum, honour and long-term socioeconomic relationships.

However, the incautiously optimistic suggestion that we can identify the
shoots of a new benign capitalism growing in these developing countries
should give us pause for thought. We should consider the possibility that
these commentators are right, but for the wrong reasons (Žižek, 2008a).
China's economic ascent has not been aided by the democratic elections we
in the West consider absolutely vital to the continuation of Western civilisation. It
is now clear that capital can thrive in the absence of democracy, as it did during its early years in the West (see Losurdo, 2011; Hall, 2012a); in fact not
only can it thrive, but in the current climate it can out-compete the liberal
democratic West. In many ways, open elections and popular political attitudes can act as fetters restricting the onward march of capital. If we take this
point further, is it too outlandishly pessimistic to consider a future Western
capitalism in which the rights of liberal democracy and social welfare have
been suspended in order to compete with low-wage command-capitalist
economies? That is, that our political leaders abandon the pretence of elec-
tive democracy and move to ensure that capital continues unencumbered by
removing the chance that the electorate may make the wrong choices? Giorgio
Agamben (2005) has already drawn attention to the ability of the polity to
suspend these democratic entitlements in times of crisis, and there appears
to be a current in contemporary popular culture that accepts this suspension
as part of the postmodern state's mandate to ensure 'security' for 'the mainstream' in a postmodern world of manifold threats from as yet unidentified
internal and external foes (see Mythen and Walklate, 2006; Mythen et al.,
2009). At the time of writing, politicians in Britain were debating the removal
of existing legal restrictions that prevent the summary dismissal of workers,
and a similar debate is taking place across Europe as politicians battle to
drive national economies back to growth.

This might be just one small aspect of a much broader trend that removes
previously hard won legal entitlements from working populations to ensure
the wellbeing and continuity of capitalism itself. For instance, in the run-
up to the 2012 Greek election that was held as a popular response to the
bail-out package of further austerity and immiseration offered to Greece by
the Troika – the IMF, the European Commission and the European Central Bank – it was mooted by media commentators that elections should
have been suspended until order had been restored. These commentators
were advocating the suspension of democracy until the population could
be trusted to make the right decisions. They clearly believed that a popular
Greek rejection of the bail-out terms and the austerity package would mean
a Greek withdrawal from the Euro, and that this would trigger a series of

events that would destroy European monetary union and threaten economic recovery for many years to come. We have seen many military juntas and authoritarian political parties take charge of ailing nations under economic duress in the capitalist era, and we must not dismiss the possibility that the suspension of hard won rights and entitlements to ensure neoliberal capitalism's continuity is indeed a possible outcome of today's ongoing political and economic turmoil.

Capitalism is a highly adaptable economic system that has time and again proven its ability to mutate, especially when faced with major crises and growing popular opposition. Here we draw upon Žižek (2008a) as we claim that capitalism is an inhuman force that blindly seeks its own self-interest and continuation, totally inconsiderate of the human costs of its actions. As many noted theorists have recognised, capitalism is an abstraction with real effects. It is more than the mere sum of production, consumption and the accumulation and investment of profit. It has a reality that exists beyond our immediate social experience. It is not enough to say that those who operate in the system should ensure the application of ethics to everyday business practices. For us, the reality of liberal-postmodern capitalism should compel social analysts to abandon outdated conceptions of economic organisation and think again about what the free movement of capital means for twenty-first century social life.

Why do we need to 'rethink' social exclusion?

Against the political and economic backdrop described above, our goal is to encourage the reader to *rethink* social exclusion. But what does this mean? First, we suggest that the Western discourses that deal with social exclusion have become increasingly domesticated and non-dialectical. Despite all the research funding and spilt ink, there is little sense of forward motion in either theory or practice and little or no sign of the establishment of new truths relating to the lives of the marginalised. This is partly a reflection of the ways in which academic discussion about this crucial issue has been hamstrung by the degenerative research programmes of neoliberal governance and charitable trusts alike, aided and abetted by the attenuated critique of academia's elite research institutions.

The overarching problem in the field of social research is that the desire of funders to discover basic 'empirical facts', which are always restrictively themed and often pre-empted in the main objectives of the research programmes themselves, influences the theoretical and methodological frameworks of the social research that produces those facts. Social research becomes trapped in a vigilantly policed tautological loop, and thus the complexity of social life is rarely investigated with any honesty, fine detail or theoretical sophistication. In the act of producing data, researchers are treated rather like gun dogs, flushing out and retrieving game so that the hunter can pop it neatly into his bag and go home.

Further down the line when it comes to analysis, funders often encourage researchers to boil down their findings to basic bullet points and extract all 'superfluous' contextual, critical and theoretical discussion from the final reports. Mindful of the requirements of funders, researchers are forced to work well within their intellectual abilities – indeed, to abandon much of the theoretical complexity, political awareness and critique instilled in them throughout their undergraduate and postgraduate careers – as they dilute, miniaturise and tightly focus their critique, dig up basic empirical data and construct narrowband policy-friendly analyses that the rhizomatic politico-cultural network to which their financial benefactors belong might find useful. Research that threatens to construct a new contextualised idea relating to social exclusion is considered fundable only if the idea is likely to find some traction in existing political and media circles; a new theoretical framework, no matter how sorely needed, appears, quite frankly, out of the question.

The fundamental research objective remains clear, streamlined, steadfast and ubiquitous: how can we improve what already exists cheaply, effectively and, in the political sense, unobtrusively, calmly and safely? Any research project that challenges liberal-capitalism's conceit – that which already exists is permanent, basically good and in need of no more than a little tweak here and there to nudge us all back into the socioeconomic comfort zone – is considered biased, ideological, alarmist, unworldly and unusable, or some permutation thereof. Under no circumstances will it be funded.

With government-funded social research on poverty and marginality, the focus is strictly on the potential 'impact' of specific policy themes, ideas, practices and projects. What works in encouraging the poor to be more enthusiastic in their search for work? What are the likely outcomes of a new policy aimed at boosting the self-confidence of job applicants? Will IT skills and social networking help people to feel more included? Such research themes compel the researcher to define, describe and analyse the phenomenon of social exclusion in the narrow parameters laid out by the research question. Thus, apart from the occasional critical salvo that dares to draw from a broader and deeper context, the current academic 'discourse' on social exclusion is often little more than an accretion of the results of enforced mid-range policy analyses of issues selected by government agencies and funding bodies, contextualised in narrow theoretical paradigms based on the work of a small number of social theorists selected for their political safety, underlying reformist tendencies and indefatigable optimism.

The goal of encouraging the reader to *rethink* social exclusion is, firstly, to move beyond this official discourse and reanimate the field of social exclusion studies, to once again make it vivid and vital, filled with political contestation and theoretical ambition, and to open up a space where it once again becomes appropriate to construct new perspectives. Secondly, the act of *rethinking* the problem involves the clearing away of established ortho-doxies that clutter up the field and regiment the production of new data and theory. However, *rethinking* the problem involves more than simply criticis-ing established tropes and intellectual frameworks. It is about encouraging ambitious researchers to consider the possibility that the existing frame-works may not simply omit key truths but may in fact be systematically constructed impediments to truth, covering up potentially revealing perspec-tives on reality with ideological obfuscation. The process of *rethinking* must be driven by the intent to open up the field to a renewed critical analysis. *Rethinking* is to move beyond the stultifying world of policy production, handcuffed as it is to a liberal-capitalist parliamentary structure that refuses to countenance any alternative to the economic system it manages. It is to ask bold questions about ethics and justice, about what kind of world we want to live in, about what is practicable and possible in economic terms. It is to consider the future of our species and reflect on what will become of the social as we move more deeply into a post-political period of permanent, socially destructive economic turbulence (see Hall, 2012b). It is to stop liv-ing in fear of abstract theoretical discussion, to stop bowing to the academic priests of right and left liberalism and move beyond their established reper-toires to say something new and revealing.

Hard times

The current neoliberal austerity drive that has been the most common response to the economic crisis across the West is slowly transforming the assumptions we make about welfare provision for our poorest. The naked facts of the matter reveal that for many years countries such as Britain have moved away from productive endeavours in the real economy. The nation focuses instead on financial services while relying on the more mundane aspects of the service economy to provide the basic employment that might keep at least some of the post-industrial working classes out of dole queues and social security offices. In real terms incomes for a significant majority of working populations in Britain have dropped since the 1970s, and jobs are increasingly short-term and unprotected (see Harvey, 2010; Wolff, 2010; Southwood, 2011; Standing, 2011).

Despite the platitudes of mainstream politicians about the return of a post-crash industrialism, the underlying hope is to restart the economic jug-gernaut of global neoliberalism by re-inflating debt markets as a means of loosening purse strings and encouraging growth in consumer spending and subsequent bank lending and investment. There is absolutely no indication that this strategy might lead to growth in those forms of work that allow individuals and families a reasonable standard of living (Keynes, 2008; Krugman, 2012). Although the precise figure is shrouded in mystery, it has been suggested that there are upwards of 10.4 million working-age people out of work in Britain (ONS, 2009), and 5.4 million of those are claiming out-of-work benefits (ibid.). As Conservative politicians often remind us, such growth in welfare costs appears unsustainable, especially as there is currently no concerted attempt to revive production in the UK. Some nations prosper on the back of residual high-tech manufacturing, but when it comes down to the manufacture of everyday volume goods Western workforces in general continue to be 'priced out of the market'. Global corporations are of course no longer tied to particular nation states, and remain able to manoeuvre production facilities and the investment of productive capital around the globe, away from high-wage economies with restrictive tax and regulatory systems and towards developing countries and fragile democracies with desperate surplus populations. Unwilling to consider the post-Keynesian and redistributionist economic solutions now being mooted (see Keen, 2011), British politicians are left with the sole solution of driving down wages and cutting business regulations and taxes in an effort to persuade potential employers to set up production facilities in the UK. In this dismal context of post-politics and unforgiving neoliberal economics, is the social democratic call to return to manufacturing and the creation of 'real jobs' feasible?

The likelihood is that, without a root and branch reconstruction of the economic system, a return to full employment and economic participation is impossible. This has prompted us to address the future of welfare and the foundations of the *negative solidarity* that typifies postmodern popular attitudes toward taxation and welfare dependent individuals and households. How do politicians propose to address the problem of welfare in an era defined by a long-term global economic slowdown and rising underemployment? What political assumptions are made about the ability of workless and low-paid individuals, and how do these assumptions reflect the enduring 'economic liberal' view of the human being's value and place in the world? Is the standard conservative/neoliberal account of a British 'underclass' whose members are happy to remain welfare-dependent and have no desire to find work in any way reasonable, and if so, how might we explain – honestly and with neither moralistic condemnation nor naïve appreciation and optimism – the existence, beliefs, prospects and social position of such a socially excluded group? Once again, our hope is to dig beneath the surface of conservative, neoliberal and Fabian moralism to reveal what the grim reality of economic and social redundancy might mean for permanently marginalised people, and what it might tell us about our particular post-crash conjuncture and the future that lies just ahead.

Anxious accumulation

The economic turbulence of the 1970s provided the perfect opportunity for a hitherto marginalised school of economic theory to force itself to the centre stage. As neoliberal economic guru and functionary Alan Greenspan was to admit in an inquiry into the credit-crunch, the neoclassical economics of von Mises (2007[1949]), Hayek (2001[1944]; 2006[1960]) and Friedman (1980, 1993, 2002) appeared to merge with Ayn Rand's (2007a, 2007b) 'objectivism' – a populist political pseudo-philosophy rooted in the notion of value without labour, the socioeconomic functionality of selfishness and the virtual deification of the entrepreneur – to produce the new politics of neoliberalism. Greenspan, a fervent neoliberal and objectivist, had been Chairman of the Federal Reserve in the run-up to the financial crisis, which indicates just how far this ideology had penetrated into the institutional heart of capitalist political economy. Neoliberalism argued persuasively for an end to protectionism and a rapid move to a global free market in which entrepreneurs, workers, goods and capital could traverse the globe without governmental impediment. It proposed to cut taxes and encourage the entrepreneurship and investment that could return Western economies to growth. It believed that innovation and hard work should be nurtured and rewarded, and that the freedom of the people is best secured by ensuring that the mandate of the state is kept within strictly prescribed limits. The rediscovery of neoclassical economics and its attachment to the traditional themes of political conservatism met with huge political, intellectual and popular success, and, promulgated incessantly by an increasingly powerful and partisan mass media industry, propelled Western democracies into a new age.

For a short while this ideology was in its own terms so successful – despite the destruction of so many industrial areas and their social systems in the 'first world' – that many ceased to think of its central principles and practices as 'ideological' at all. Even though some individuals were disquieted by its socially destructive consequences, these principles were accepted by default by an electorally significant majority and went a long way to becoming installed as the 'common sense' at the very foundations of our society. Neoliberal restructuring was the 'tough medicine' we all had to take to cure the 'sick body' of the economy. It was this ideology that subtly encouraged the loosening of social bonds and advocated an increasingly self-interested, insecure and defensive sociability that profoundly affected the way that we approach living our lives together. Rather than seeing the poor and unemployed as unfortunate victims of circumstance and needful of state assistance, neoliberal culture instead encouraged individuals to view them with distrust, as self-interested, feckless, lazy and prone, for reasons of faulty genetics and sub-cultural values, to criminality and violence. After

the neoliberal incursion, if solidarity existed in relation to poverty, it existed
as a negative and factional solidarity based on the old Calvinist distinction
between the 'deserving' and the 'undeserving', in which the abstract interests
of 'taxpayers' had to be defended against the threats posed by the greedy
poor and their incessant petitions for state-sponsored welfare.

Voting for poverty

The global success of neoliberal politics from the late 1970s to the great
crash of 2008 has prompted a significant literature, which we will briefly
review later. But the question of why so many working and non-working
poor people voted for neoliberal political parties that articulated views and
created policies directly antagonistic to their class interests is worth dwelling
on for a moment. Firstly, do poorer people really vote for neoliberal parties
in significant numbers? It might be more reasonable to suggest that those
with a clear economic and political stake in the maintenance of the current
order are more likely to vote, and more likely to vote for neoliberal parties. In Britain the absence of genuine working-class representation at the
heart of the Labour Party and its policy ensures that growing numbers of
traditional Labour voters no longer see any point in voting for the party and
consequently abstain from voting altogether. Since the neoliberal triumph in
the late 1970s, the Labour Party has elected to move further to the right in
order to increase its appeal to those voters who still bother to vote, which,
at the same time, increased the number who are unlikely to vote. Quite
quickly, within a generation, the gap between our major political parties
shrank and the bland vista of our post-political present was upon us before
we knew it. All parties who populate this landscape – more arid even than
Beckett imagined in *Waiting for Godot* – are afraid to offer anything that
might animate those cynical and withdrawn but potentially very demanding
sections of the electorate who recognise that no matter who they vote for,
nothing really changes. The fundamental issue at stake here is that in many
respects voters from traditional working-class areas no longer have clear
political representation. Many do not recognise the combined neoliberalism and diluted Fabianism of Blair's 'third way' – a concept supplied to him
ready-made by liberal sociologist Lord Anthony Giddens – as in any way
related to or reflective of either their subjective or class interests. Today's
Labour politicians, groomed on a fast-track educational and research path
to power, do not speak to 'their world', 'their beliefs' or 'their attitudes'. To
a significant portion of the working class, contemporary Labour politicians
constitute part of the metropolitan middle class elite that looks down on 'the
likes of us' (Collins, 2005). The consequences of this clear lack of political
representation and leadership will be explored throughout the book, but
we should acknowledge immediately that, during the premierships of Blair

and Brown, Labour Party policy further embedded neoliberalism at the very heart of British politics and our national economy.

Perhaps the biggest indictment one can make of these Labour administrations is that the gap between rich and poor grew significantly on their watch (Hills and Stewart, 2005). Blair was perhaps Thatcher's most potent legacy, a populariser of ideological dogma who should be acknowledged as the standard-bearer of the post-political epoch, a shiny game-show host of a politician who presented the ideology of the market to the people as simple pragmatism, a socioeconomic framework that would ensure fairness and rising incomes for all. Blair did not speak to a history, a culture or a social class, and he did not speak the language of the traditional Labour Party or display any great consideration for its concerns with egalitarianism and social justice. Instead, he spoke to a new media-led politics of personal ambition, consumption and global markets while simultaneously appearing to maintain an old-fashioned 'social liberal' concern for the wellbeing of the poorest. Blair's premiership was a time in which the Labour party became, to quote Peter Mandelson – the former Business Secretary and key Blair aide – 'intensely relaxed about people getting filthy rich' (cited in Malik, 2012). The close relationship between the shrinking industrial working class and its precarious residuum – those trapped in insecure service employment and welfare – and the Parliamentary Labour Party was clearly at an end.

Despite the artificial credit-fuelled boom that underpinned the 'economic miracle' of the Blair years, working-class employment became increasingly precarious. The problems and harms of social exclusion embedded themselves in low-income neighbourhoods around the country. Genuinely oppositional politics had already been extinguished as neoliberal ideology incorporated the residual factions of the former working class into the remorseless individualisation process and interpersonal competition that constituted the cult of market performance. The cultural erasure of everything politically or ideologically external to liberal parliamentary capitalism removed the very framework that might have allowed for the development of an alternative politics based upon a revived ethic of egalitarianism. Instead, liberal capitalism overcame its categorisation as one of a range of competing economic systems to become the only conceivable economic system. In the very same move, it shed its ideological skin and took on the appearance of elementary economic pragmatism. The profound success of this move can be seen in the fact that even now, lodged as we are in a destructive vortex generated by what might be a permanent slowdown in economic growth and the failure of light-touch regulation, we remain ensnared in the logic of neoliberalism and incapable of constructing a realistic economic and political alternative.

What else can we say about the electoral successes of neoliberal political parties? How, precisely, do they keep getting into office when their policies benefit only a small percentage of the overall population? One might reasonably claim that the fundamental nature of class identity has changed quite considerably, and it has done so for the most part because of historic changes in the nature of capital accumulation. Basically, people today are much less likely to structure their identity in relation to a subjective sense of class belonging. Socioeconomic class might linger in the background, but it is increasingly disguised by the mutable field of culture and taste, with its porous and subjective social barriers. People these days are less tied to local traditions and cultures, less mindful of the lives, sacrifices, traditions and conventions of previous generations. For many young people, these restrictive and parochial considerations are something to escape from as the postmodern self is compelled to take on the task of Sisyphus and manufacture its own culturally astute identity (Winlow and Hall, 2006, 2009a). The contemporary postmodern subject strives for 'a life of one's own', and, for the moment at least, appears to see social bonds rooted in obligation and commitment as a straightjacket that erodes personal freedom. The dull normality of the everyday post-political present, systematically emptied of inspiring symbolism, appears to encourage the postmodern subject to balk at the very idea of dissolving the uniqueness of the self into a distressingly homogenised social group. In the political sphere the postmodern subject will not be swayed by calls to class loyalty or class interests. This subject is resolutely determined to make up its own mind in relation to ethico-cultural criteria that it believes are of its own choosing – in some cases of extreme postmodern solipsism, of its own unique and uninfluenced creation. This accelerates the dominant trend of voters moving away from the depth of policy and socioeconomic analysis towards the surface characteristics of political candidates, who of course are unique, creative and independent individuals who have chosen their own identities just like the voters have.

Other factions of the insecure and anxious post-industrial working class, perhaps less confident and less convinced of their own self-created uniqueness, grasp quite desperately at replacements for lost solidarity, identity and meaning in the narratives of nation that are so often trotted out by neoconservative politicians and commentators. In the USA especially, right-wing politicians have been remarkably successful in convincing the voting public that the nation's identity is inextricably bonded to liberal capitalism, and that any suggestion that the economy is subject to a greater degree of governmental regulation is 'unamerican', smacking of the inherent evils of defunct state communism (Frank, 2005, 2006). In this factional domain, it is almost as if the painfully free postmodern subject, no longer authorised and constituted as an individual by the collective fictions of the traditional Symbolic Order (see glossary), is attempting to grab hold of a mythical history in the vague hope that it might provide stability and fixity upon which some sense of clarity and belief can be developed (see Winlow and Hall, 2012a). Here, as long as the elite's representatives can maintain the seductive myth of the great national spirit – 'we're all in it together' – the working class voter will vote for a political party that continues to ensure that the elite are the ultimate beneficiaries of an economy whose neoliberal logic will further reduce the likelihood that workers will be able to sell their labour with a reasonable degree of continuity at a level able to support a reasonably civilised standard of living. They do this not because of stupidity but in order to address a complex form of subjective lack that neoconservative/neoliberal political partnerships promise to address with their clear focus on national identity, immigration controls and economic competitiveness.

These very basic points also inform the claim that, in an era that dismisses collective identities as a dead weight on individuality and freedom, the contemporary 'working-class' subject responds to exploitation and precariousness not by mobilising against the oppressor class but by attempting to join its ranks. The current inability of the postmodern subject to find utility, solidarity and common purpose in collective identities tends to prevent the establishment of new forms of political universality that have historically counteracted the destructive atomising effects of the cash nexus and sought a new reality built upon the ethics of cooperation and egalitarianism. The inability of the current political and economic conjuncture to encourage individuals to see their interests in relation to others of a similar socioeconomic position suggests that we now occupy an era of post-political biopolitics (see Chapter 5).

In terms of actual policy, there is very little difference between mainstream politicians; in essence, the cynic's cliché that 'they're all the bloody same' has become a reality. The general electorate must choose a candidate on the basis of some vague sense of who will benefit them personally. Political opposition to neoliberal excess and the brutal reallocation of money and assets from working populations to the super-rich – upwards of £13 trillion currently hidden away in global tax havens (Stewart, 2012b; see also Shaxson, 2012) – is expressed in the most attenuated and apologetic manner only by the political opponents that liberal capitalism itself appoints. Because there is no longer an organised political opposition, because the left has abandoned any conception of class struggle or an egalitarian future – or even a social democracy in which the huge gap in wealth and power can be seriously truncated – to focus exclusively on defending the human rights and arranging the piecemeal 'social inclusion' of marginalised identity groups, capitalism itself exists for ordinary voters as pure *doxa*, the common belief of what is and always will be. Indeed, such is the certainty of its permanent reign, even the word 'capitalism' had largely fallen out of use in political and academic circles. For the liberal-postmodern subject, existing in the absence of a politics that seeks to offer an account of subjective hardships, injustices, anxieties and rage, the social field of ceaseless struggle for symbolic and cultural capital becomes naturalised and the subject accepts – and then embraces and clings to – the myth of meritocracy. Their own inner torment, their enduring sense of lack and their fear of economic and cultural irrelevance compels them to throw themselves anew into capitalism's competitive struggle for social distinction. Until real politics returns, the very idea of transforming the other into a true neighbour, cleansing the realm of politics of its corruption or creating a new reality built upon social justice seems impossible, even ridiculous. The compensation, the safety barrier that prevents the plunge over the edge into total nihilism and despair, is the hope that the self might one day make the journey from exploited to exploiter. Such hope is presented daily by the mass media as liberal capitalism's great attraction, and today's subjects plot their journeys to 'inclusion' and eventual safety up the league table of contemporary consumer culture.

The point here is to encourage the reader at this early stage not simply to focus on the relative successes of the right but also to bear in mind the failures of the left. In Britain, the old socialist and social democratic discourses that created a labour movement capable of winning significant improvements in the lifestyles and entitlements of everyday working men and women were crushed by the rapid rise of neoliberalism, which used the open, competitive global market as the brutal instrument of social disruption and reconfiguration. In the eyes of those who voted for her, especially those members of the reasonably affluent and upwardly mobile working class, Thatcher won the argument about economic management in the 1980s (see Jenkins, 2007; Vinen, 2010). For her, the era of Keynesian demand management, with its panoramic welfare state, was dead. Using the mass media to ram home the message of TINA – 'there is no alternative' – the national economy could recover and move forward only if neoliberal politicians could reduce the size of the state, sell off public utilities, abandon ailing manufacturing industries and tackle the militancy of the labour unions that were reducing the efficiency of British business and holding the national economy to ransom. The seductive dream of a new era of neoliberal prosperity won the day, and it did so at least in part because those on the left misunderstood the nature of their adversary, abandoned their core values and capitulated to those who argued for a renewed Fabian reformism, a centre-leftist narrative that, dressed up in fashionable liberal-postmodernist verbiage, accepted the new economic reality and focused on defending the rights of marginalised social groups forced to struggle for an existence within it.

Some notes on the structure of the book

We have tried to sketch out a basic outline of what is to come in the preceding pages, but it is perhaps useful to provide a brief chapter outline before the book begins in earnest. In Chapter 2 we engage with the dominant European discourse on social exclusion. We outline key principles and try to identify the intellectual evolution of the field. In Chapter 3 we address the North American analysis of 'the underclass', and pay particular attention to the neoclassical model of human subjectivity (see glossary) usually associated with the political right. In Chapter 4 we begin to offer an original theoretical account of the problem of contemporary social exclusion. This begins with an analysis of the current condition of political economy and labour markets and, in Chapter 5, moves on to consider more directly the contemporary political context. Chapters 6 and 7 offer a creative engagement with two of the dominant ideas in what we might call 'social exclusion studies'. In Chapter 6 we explore the idea that the contemporary poor continue to constitute a reserve army of labour, and in Chapter 7, we attempt to move beyond Bauman's claim that the poor are excluded as a result of their inability to engage with the cultures of consumerism. In Chapter 8 we begin to address the problem of social exclusion using the intellectual tools of transcendental materialism (see glossary). Rather than simply offer an abstract discussion of the absent centre of political ontology, we begin our analysis by looking at the growth of what we might call post-social space, the new commercialised areas of the city that appear entirely devoid of the symbolic substance usually associated with really existing social life. In Chapter 9 we extend this discussion and try to outline clearly what the historic decline of symbolic efficiency means for the lives of the poorest. Much of our analysis across these chapters is quite polemical and seeks to banish the unrealistic optimism that prevents the social scientific analysis of social exclusion advancing from its present position. But our analysis is not blindly pessimistic. Instead, we hope to encourage the development of ultra-realist approaches to the study of social exclusion; an approach that captures with honesty the debilitating problems and social divisions of the contemporary post-crash world, and refuses to be held back by the liberal left's timeless romance of organic egalitarianism and resilient community life in the West's most impoverished areas. But despite what might be regarded by some as a bleak assessment of post-politics and the enduring power of global capitalism and its supporting ideology, we close the book with a note of optimism. It is, after all, possible to create a more just and equitable world if we wish to. In Chapter 11 we extend our analysis of Žižek and Badiou in order to give some sense of how change might develop and what it might look like. All that remains to be said is 'welcome to the book'. We hope you find value in our brief contribution and that you can recognise a deeper honesty and hope underneath the bleakness that often characterises the surface of our project.

2

Social Exclusion:
The European Tradition

When I give food to the poor, they call me a saint. When I ask why the poor have no food, they call me a communist.

Dom Helder Camara, 2009

Les exclus

The phrase 'social exclusion' has for some time been at the centre of popular and social scientific debates about the composition of late capitalist societies. But what precisely is 'social exclusion'? Students of social science will not be too surprised to hear that academia has yet to reach a unanimous agreement. However, we can identify a range of key themes and issues. This chapter will discuss these themes and issues to provide a foundation for the more critical material to be presented later in the book.

For many contemporary social scientists, the 'socially excluded' are not simply the latest manifestation of the residuum, the lumpen proletariat, the disreputable poor or the 'criminal underclass'. While there appears to be a degree of continuity in the production of marginalised and disreputable populations throughout Western history (Pearson, 1982; Welshman, 2007), the rise of a new form of entrenched post-industrial poverty and marginality during the 1980s presented a range of novel challenges that reflected the transformation of society and the global capitalist economy upon which it currently rests (see also Runciman, 1990; Westergaard, 1992). The phrase 'social exclusion' represents a process that actively *excludes* rather than simply marginalises the poor, a shift that has refocused the academic gaze on to declining levels of social cohesion and rising levels of social segregation in urban areas. Here, not only poverty or unemployment are at stake but the inability of the 'socially excluded' to access ostensibly 'normal' and routine services and aspects of our shared cultural life. The implication is that this inability produces significant knock-on effects in economically poorer areas. The accumulation of negative social and political dynamics along with specific dispositions and cultural characteristics that corrode social cohesion and hamper work and income prospects are said to exacerbate and entrench segregation (Wilson, 1996). On the other hand, some commentators (see for example, Pain, 2000; Pantazis, 2000) have highlighted the ways in which the negative labelling of particular neighbourhoods produces a range of perceptual effects that reinforce divisions between 'good' and 'bad' or 'safe' and 'unsafe' sections of the city. These commentators also acknowledge that these aggressive labelling processes can be 'realised' as they inform the inhabitants' construction of their own identities, which in turn produces yet further problems for the marginalised populations (Wacquant, 2007, 2009).

Given the long history of socio-spatial segregation in Western cities, readers might find it slightly odd that it is now regarded as such a novel issue in the study of contemporary social exclusion. Engels (2009) painted a particularly vivid picture of the realities of social segregation in early industrial Manchester, and the seminal work of the Chicago School explored ethnic enclaves during the 1920s and 1930s (see Bulmer, 1986; Hayward, 2012a, 2012b for discussions). We will discuss spatial segregation in more detail in Chapter 8, but for now we can simply note that in Britain the segregation observed by Engels had by the mid-twentieth century largely ceased to exist. Britain's post-war social democratic welfare state was driven by a desire to include marginalised populations and to draw the poor into industrial capitalism's productive system (Bauman, 2000). Building programmes provided better housing for the poor and new public spaces were established, which encouraged all to engage in civilised social life. Of course, neighbourhoods still possessed an obvious class character, but there was no clear sense of segregation or of the boundaries and borders that now inform our subjective experience of contemporary post-industrial British cities (Peach, 1999; Marcuse and van Kempen, 2000, 2002; Dorling and Rees, 2003; Meen et al., 2005).

The transformations that have taken place in American cities are slightly different to those experienced in Britain (see Peach, 1999; Sugrue, 2005; Beckett and Herbert, 2009). Race and ethnicity have played a more important role in the cultural and spatial evolution of American cities. Throughout the industrial period some urban ghettos were populated entirely by Black Americans. However, as Wacquant (2001, 2007) claims, many of the key characteristics of the Black ghetto changed quite considerably as the twentieth century progressed. He argues that this can be best understood as a shift from industrialism's 'communal ghetto' to the post-industrial 'hyperghetto'. For Wacquant (ibid.), this transformation has had profound consequences for inhabitants of such spaces. The rise of the post-industrial hyperghetto suggests fundamental shifts in forms of governance and the attitudes to the poor held by the state and the rest of the population. Of course, enclaves of other low-income ethnic groups were also present in the city (see for example Jargowsky, 1997; Hartigan, 1999, 2005), but it is the experience of Black Americans that is fundamental to our understanding of post-industrial poverty and exclusion on that continent. The death of traditional forms of working-class employment and the flight from the city of the more affluent working-class and middle-class populations have clearly exacerbated the problems faced by poor Black Americans, and these changes have also served to make segregation more extreme (Massey and Denton, 1993; Wilson, 1996; see also Abramson et al., 1995).

There are many other issues to consider in relation to urban segregation, but at this stage it is enough to acknowledge that, for Britons, segregation has very much returned and is central to our understanding of the contemporary city (see for example Atkinson and Flint, 2004; Atkinson and Helms, 2007; Minton, 2012). Material and non-material barriers have been erected around various commercial and residential spaces policed by a range of public and private entities. CCTV cameras and other exclusionary surveillance technologies are now ubiquitous, and urban spaces are also encoded with symbols used to either attract or ward off specific social groups. The modern civic ideal of free, open and civilised communion in shared public space has been either commodified and fragmented or abandoned altogether (Davis, 2004; Judt, 2010; Hatherley, 2011; Minton, 2012).

The meaning of 'social exclusion'

The phrase 'social exclusion' appears to have developed first in France (Hills et al., 2002; see also Levitas, 1998), and from the outset it possessed two defining characteristics. The first was that it was primarily concerned with the transformation of social life and the consequences of socioeconomic and cultural change for particular sections of society. The lives of the excluded were wrenched out of joint by a historical transformation that disrupted the certainties of modernity and threw us into a new postmodern world of cultural fluidity, social fragmentation and economic insecurity. This is not to say that the study of social exclusion has been narrowly concerned with small groups of people and the particular problems they face as a result of rapid and disruptive social change. European academic theorists of post-industrial poverty and inequality are aware that these crucial forms of change were also affecting *whole societies* in various ways. The second defining characteristic of the social exclusion discourse is that it distinguishes itself from the parallel 'underclass' debate that was reshaping the social analysis of post-industrial poverty in America. The American 'underclass' debate was concerned less with social and economic change – although there are important exceptions (see, for example, Marable, 1993; Gans, 1993; Wilson, 1996; Wacquant, 2007, 2009) – and more with the fields of culture, socialisation and the individual choices and propensities of the poor. In dismissing the collective experience of socioeconomic change and focusing on 'pathologi-cal' decision-making processes, the 'underclass' discourse reintroduced to the debate the calculative utilitarian subject of neoclassical economics (see Murray, 1984). These two key characteristics of the social exclusion dis-course deserve closer inspection.

As the debate about social exclusion developed during the late 1980s and early 1990s it took on a notably critical approach to the rapid social change that defined these decades. The 1980s were of course a crucial his-torical watershed, and perhaps the most important aspect of the change that occurred relates to the rise of neoliberalism and the establishment of a new economic and political orthodoxy markedly different from the social democratic politics of the post-war period (Harvey, 2007; Glynn, 2007; Judt, 2010, 2011). The social exclusion discourse begins with the claim that the end of Fordist industrialism and its relatively stable communities fun-damentally altered the nature of poverty and social marginality, generating a situation in which the social bonding process that encouraged people to commit themselves to collective forms of identity was somehow failing in the new 'postmodern' period. The relationship between the industrial work-ing class and the formal economy had changed, and the ability of people to find industrial work with a reasonable wage and degree of tenure declined (Bauman, 1998b). Traditional forms of employment were severely reduced, and some sections of the post-industrial working class seemed incapable of adapting their skills to meet the complex demands of a new and highly competitive labour market.

A number of commentators (see for example Bauman, 1998a, 2000; Young 1999) argued that the state and civil society no longer appreciated the benefits of fully integrating marginalised populations into the social mainstream. Others suggested that the norms, values, attitudes, tempera-ments and beliefs that had once provided a crucial integrative function in the industrial world were being dissolved or remodelled by political and ideological forces, or by the new economic realities of the post-industrial global order. Rather than encourage the formation of communities and soli-darity, the social climate of postmodernism appeared to corrode these things by encouraging an atomised form of individualism and social competition (Bauman, 2000, 2007a, 2007b, 2011; Winlow and Hall, 2006, 2009a). For many of those involved in the developing discourse on social exclusion, these and other changes ensured that poverty and social marginality in the post-modern period would be different from industrial-modern poverty in impor-tant ways. This was not simply a matter of the general decline of absolute poverty in the West and the rise of a pervasive and recontextualised 'relative deprivation' (Young, 1999), nor the rise of a new 'possessive individualism' (see McPherson, 1964) that encouraged the subject to engage in an increas-ingly fraught battle for social recognition. These general social trends were important, but not the whole story. Instead, the social exclusion discourse focused on the complex and multidimensional forces that constituted and reproduced a 'class' of people who could no longer access the forms of work that were accompanied by the full benefits of social membership. They were disbarred and cast adrift from a normal, mainstream social existence. Making sense of these trends and identifying and explaining associated issues became the key focus of the European social exclusion discourse.

As we mentioned earlier, this discourse was also from the outset concerned with the concentration of such people in *social space* and its consequences. Crucially, the spatial segregation of the poorest in particular parts of the city tended to impact negatively upon access to state services. For many years sociologists had known that the quality of the formal education provided to young people from low-income families played a considerable role in shaping their biographies and employment trajectories (Brown, 1995; Whitty, 2001; Bynner and Parsons, 2002). In Britain, public education remains free at the point of provision, but this does not mean that the quality of education provided is roughly equal. Middle-class parents tend to be more involved and ensure that their children find their way into those schools that appear to perform better in terms of student achievement. The concentration of poor pupils in particular parts of the city combines with other problems to ensure meagre achievement and progression into post-16 education. In Britain, poverty remains inextricably connected to poor educational outcomes (see Raffo et al., 2009), a key indicator of poor outcomes in adulthood (Hobcraft, 2000).

As our knowledge of the consequences of spatial segregation increased, growing numbers of researchers and theorists risked a discussion of the cultural forms that developed within these segregated areas and how they might contribute to the continued marginality of inhabitants. This new awareness of the importance of socialisation and culture reflected a growing willingness among European scholars to engage with the parallel discussion of the American 'underclass'. There was to hand a growing body of empirical data that dealt with the nature of family life, neighbourhood influences and the social reproduction of gender roles, attitudes, beliefs and cultural norms among the post-industrial poor (Hobcraft, 1998, 2000; Winlow, 2001). Even though thinkers as radical as Gramsci (1971) had shown awareness of ways in which the poor can collude in their own oppression, European academics tended to avoid what they saw as the victim-blaming that often accompanied analyses of individual decision-making and marginalised 'cultures of poverty' in the American 'underclass' literature. Instead, they attempted to make connections between neoliberal governance, global economic change and their formative impact on the cultural environment of excluded neighbourhoods (Wacquant, 2007, 2009). As the discourse moved forwards, intellectual differences began to open up. Perhaps the most important trend to identify here is the move of many social liberals away from an analysis of the socially deleterious effects of deep structural and processual shifts in culture, political economy and capital accumulation and towards a critical assessment of governmental policy targeted at the poorest; social exclusion was framed quite restrictively as a 'social management' issue. We discuss the political and ideological reasons for this in more detail later in the chapter.

The discourse on European social exclusion established itself as a legitimate and important area of study during the 1980s and 1990s. While the veracity of the concept was continually debated and the usual definitional debates raged on, the discourse remained a useful meeting place of sorts, a field in which academics, policy analysts and political activists could come together to debate the transformation of social life and new forms of poverty and social division. In academia, the discussion of social exclusion was dominated by sociologists and those working in the field of social policy, but urban analysts, criminologists, political scientists and geographers also pitched in. Certainly, the discourse became more policy-orientated as time wore on. Those interested in policy-orientated analyses of social exclusion became somewhat separated from those more interested in addressing the complexities of subjectivity (see glossary) and culture or analysing macro-level political economy. For all concerned, social exclusion was an urgent problem that necessitated serious governmental intervention, but approaches differed quite markedly. The policy analyst's task was to search for variables and causal relationships that might be addressed by targeted government initiatives, and to otherwise assess the efficacy of social policy aimed at improving the lot of the poor. For those more interested in a broader sociological analysis, the key drive appeared to be a fundamentally intellectual one: they wanted to understand and explain why the poor were poor. Empirical researchers contributed to this endeavour by providing evidence of the realities of life in marginalised neighbourhoods (see for example McAuley, 2007; Wacquant, 2007; Pitts, 2008; Hall et al., 2008; Briggs, 2011). Despite the sociological obsession with 'objectivity', most research in this latter tradition was actually motivated by ideology. These sociologists felt that social exclusion was wrong and they hoped that their work might make some contribution to alleviating the predicament of the excluded.

However, most of these sociologists also tend to be deeply apprehensive about even the slightest suggestion of wholesale socioeconomic change or even serious political intervention and regulation. They hoped that their work would be picked up by social policy experts and thus contribute to the project of gradually reforming the system as it is. Other sociologists appeared to simply hope that their work contributed in some way to the advance of their discipline and the ever more refined ways in which sociologists might understand the poor and their problems. The overall effect was to subjugate sociological analyses under the strict pragmatic demands and attenuated politics of the social policy field. Sociologists who wanted to rack up as many publications as possible in order to further their careers had to be careful and quite subtle about how they criticised the socioeconomic system of which they were a direct beneficiary. As Žižek (2002) has claimed, some liberal-leftist academics engage in an interminable critique of capitalism and the neoliberal state while at the same time subconsciously hoping this form of political economy will endure so they can continue to mount their critique while avoiding real social conflict and preserving their elevated social position.

As the passions and catastrophes of the twentieth century gave way to the pragmatism and obligatory liberalism of the twenty-first century (see Hall, 2012a), we saw a telling alteration of the trajectory of the sociological discourse on social exclusion. This adjustment signified the triumph of the broader cultural and political forces that had ensured the abandonment of the broad left's commitment to social justice, egalitarianism and political transformation. This was a product of the abandonment of the socialist vision and the rise of left liberalism, part of the triumph of liberal ideology more broadly across the political spectrum. In a similar way, neoliberalism, the right-wing variant of liberalism, infiltrated and reconfigured traditional conservative politics during the 1980s and 1990s. The one-nation Toryism that contributed to the post-war welfare consensus has almost disappeared from the contemporary British Conservative party and the political landscape (Hickson, 2009; Vinen, 2010). On the left, Blair's New Labour project represented a turn away from the traditional class politics of the Labour party and a growing concern with the relation between meritocracy and the identity politics of liberal multiculturalism. Blairism was keen to distance itself from the trade union movement and working-class culture in general. It hoped to appeal to a broader demographic interest in aspiration, social mobility and rising levels of wealth. The traditional fight for social justice need not be deliberately confrontational and it need not involve a conflict between the working class and the wealthy elite. Instead, the global 'free' market and new political and technocratic ways of managing it would improve living standards for all, making conflict redundant. Blair was, however, mindful of the suffering of the poorest and perhaps the political leader who contributed most to dragging social exclusion from a peripheral academic concern to the centre of British politics and policy-making. He established the Social Exclusion Unit in 1997 and liberally sprinkled speeches with reference to this new but regrettable phenomenon. We will not offer a critique of Blair's policies of social exclusion here (instead see Levitas, 1998). However, we should note that his desire to liberalise the economy and allow the market to provide specific welfare services, while at the same time expanding state spending and attempting to facilitate meritocracy and social mobility, was touted as 'the third way' (see Giddens, 1998, 2007), a new approach to statecraft and social management that took the commitments of social democracy seriously while at the same time radically altering labour politics by freeing up the capitalist market from deep-rooted regulatory control. Blair's premiership, like Clinton's presidency across the

Atlantic, clearly indicated a major transformation in mainstream leftist and social democratic politics. The left had moved to the centre ground to embrace a range of new concerns that surpassed the old ideologically driven political conflicts of the twentieth century.

Many left liberals do not publicly align themselves with Blairism or even the 'third way'. They often see themselves as far too radical to endorse any mainstream political figure. But what is 'left liberalism'? In basic terms it is the seemingly progressive political discourse that accompanies neoliberalism's unleashed market forces. Contemporary left liberals appear fully integrated into parliamentary capitalism while simultaneously being vociferous advocates of 'equality of opportunity' in legal, social and cultural relations. They seek to extend the rights of marginalised and underprivileged individuals or cultural groups in an overall project of social justice. For example, they demand that legislation is introduced to ensure men are not privileged over women in the labour market. However, the assumption that we can address the problem of exclusion by expanding the legal entitlements of individuals and cultural groups appears fundamentally flawed to those on the left who still advocate the traditional concerns of community and solidarity. This strategy treats each individual as a self-interested monad, entirely separated from others. The rights discourse is fundamentally defensive rather than progressive. It says 'this far and no further'. Left liberalism has little time for old leftist concerns with structural social justice, a concept that represents an entire class of wage-labourers, consisting of many otherwise disparate individuals and cultural groups, fighting to improve conditions for all. Here the traditional collective project of social justice is driven not to *defend* individuals and cultural groups from elite power and arrange fair competition, but to *disempower the elite* and rearrange socioeconomic relations on a more cooperative basis. So, while left liberals might fight to ensure that women have the same employment rights as men, to traditional leftists this can often seem like an argument for the right of women to be exploited in the same ways and to the same level as men. In a finite, competitive and volatile labour market, empowering one group simply means displacing others, undercutting wages and colluding in the elite's classic 'divide and rule strategy', which was dismissed as a cliché at the same time as it became a starker reality. The basic political distinction is that traditional leftists question the justice of existing socioeconomic arrangements, whereas left liberals instead appear more or less to accept the world as it is, focusing instead on incremental reform through the legal system and a continuous discourse on citizens' rights while still maintaining their image as the strident critics of all that is oppressive and unfair.

To this end, left liberals place great emphasis on the constant reform of a legal system that to others might seem inherently biased and corrupt. They believe that the poor and the marginalised should have the legal right to access better education and be protected from the discrimination often practised by employers, state institutions or powerful individuals. Unlike more traditional leftists, they do not argue for the incisive social and political change that might ensure 'really existing' equality of political power, economic participation and material conditions of existence. As liberals, they tend to assume that any attempt to establish really-existing equality by overthrowing incumbent elite power will result in the greater oppression of totalitarianism (Žižek, 2001; Hall, 2012a), and therefore the best that can be done is to provide incremental legal reform that might encourage citizens to discontinue discriminatory practices. In short, left liberals want to give the excluded every chance to move up and join the social mainstream, while also respecting their right to be culturally and individually different. They tend to avoid any consideration of the internal life of the subject, and instead proceed on the basis that all are equally 'rational' and mentally equipped to build a life for themselves. Thus, all that is needed to create a new and inclusive sociability is a pragmatic welfare framework that protects the vulnerable and allows people to educate themselves and find their way into employment, and an accompanying system of legal and cultural intervention that prevents the construction and application of negative and discriminatory stereotypes that demonise the poor and marginalised.

Left liberals do not entirely neglect the underlying economy and its social relations. Some argue that the government must do more to alleviate the suffering of the 'socially excluded' and to encourage the return of dependable and reasonably well-paid forms of work to areas of permanent recession (Webster et al., 2004; Shildrick et al., 2010). However, absent from the general discourse is any consideration that the initial production of the socially excluded is itself entirely unjust, an inevitable product of a deeply corrupt and obscene global market economy that discards all who cannot be turned into a source of surplus value and revenue. Nor is there any deep appreciation of the nature of postmodern capitalism's global economic system and the structural inequalities that are its unavoidable and functional by-products, or any conception that it is possible to build a better world, a world with social justice, fairness and equality at its core. This desire to defend the poorest ex post facto by means of welfare and law, supported by the charitable institutions of civil society, is a theme we will return to in Chapter 5, but we will preface that discussion with a preliminary observation.

The greater part of left-liberal academic analysis of social exclusion has abandoned any conception of class struggle. We will argue that a return to this concept, aided by a more sophisticated conception of class and its cell-like constitutive and reproductive process (see Hall, 2012a), has much to offer the discourse on social exclusion as the underlying structural economic convulsions signalled by the recent global financial crash continue to drive rising inequalities, joblessness and political malfeasance. Left liberals, intent on being seen as more 'sophisticated' even though this self-affirmed superiority seems to have led to nebulous ideas and ineffective politics, usually view such concepts as 'reductionist' and 'essentialist', a rather vulgar hang-over from naïve twentieth-century modernism (Winlow, 2012a). Rather than encouraging the excluded to become a class *for itself*, a class capable of being a collective agent for genuine social change, most left-liberal academics assume the endless continuation of liberal capitalism, its market economy and its shifting cultural plurality and identity. Some in fact concur with classic liberals and conservatives, believing that each individual is naturally self-interested and competitive, and therefore capitalism, as an economic system based on profit-seeking and exploitation, is a distasteful inevitability whose 'animal spirits' can only be domesticated and civilised, although to what extent is unclear. In this way, left liberals appear to see their role as custodians, casting an ever-vigilant eye over the market and the neoliberal state to ensure that the conduct of actors remains within socially acceptable limits.

Of course, if this view contains any truth, we must conclude that these liberal defenders of propriety fell into a deep sleep during the years of liberal capitalism's restoration (see Badiou, 2002, 2009; Harvey, 2007). It is perhaps more reasonable to claim that left liberalism is now more fully integrated into the system of parliamentary capitalism than it ever has been, yet, oddly, despite their fuller integration their critique is often ignored, and their policy suggestions constantly diluted and compromised. Even when they are listened to, their intervention merely serves momentarily to prevent the worst excesses of a system that will inevitably produce yet more harms. If left liberals are critics of parliamentary capitalism, it might be worth considering whether they are the official critics that parliamentary capitalism itself appoints to ensure that all critique continues to takes place on what has been revealed to be the barren field of post-political liberalism.

Before moving on to explore more fully how this left-liberal narrative is located at the core of contemporary analysis of social exclusion, we should perhaps acknowledge that we are not fundamentally against the central tenets of liberalism; freedom, justice, equality, democracy and so on. Who could be against such things? Rather, we claim that the dominant liberal discourse has co-opted these words and stripped them of their traditional meaning and political impact. After two centuries of liberalism, we feel that liberal politics is now incapable of realising these ideals (see Žižek, 2008a; Losurdo, 2011) and tacitly yet actively seeks a range of compromises even in their conception. In the wake of another global crisis of capitalism we see staggering inequalities and injustices (Beaumont, 2011; Treanor, 2011; Butler, 2012; Stewart, 2012a, 2012b), which have not been prevented by the panorama of legal entitlements that constitute the post-1948 human rights discourse. The 'equality' of contemporary liberal capitalism is a negativity that grants the subject nothing more than the 'avoidance of mistreatment' at the hands of the powerful (Badiou, 2002) and the right to compete freely for his or her own personal profit. This attenuated form of 'justice' ensures that the most

successful are allowed to retain the vast bulk of their wealth, a fair reward for
their skills and efforts, while those who have failed to accumulate the various
accoutrements of a consumerised life are consigned to the margins, with no
one to blame but themselves, to be comforted by the promise that good liberals
are out there working ceaselessly to arrange their re-inclusion at some later date.
In the meantime, individuals must help themselves with 'support' from the
state and civil society. One very good reason why all this inclusionary activity
seems to bear little fruit on society's margins is that liberals are also duty-
bound to maintain a modernist form of individual freedom, at the disavowed
core of which, as we will discuss in Chapters 6 and 8, is the *negative liberty*
that tacitly encourages the individual to avoid any real obligation to others.

A growing proportion of twenty-first century social exclusion analysis
appears to be more interested in the ways in which powerful and influential
social groups construct images of the poor as profligate, lazy, immoral and
dangerous. Liberals approach the danger of the 'stereotype' with a broad-
spectrum antibiotic, simply denying that all universal forms and categories
exist. However, just as this helps to protect the victims – although not very
effectively if popular discourse is anything to go by – it does a better job of
protecting the oppressors; very little interest is now paid to the realities of
social exclusion or its roots in a global capitalism reproduced on behalf
of the increasingly oligarchic global ruling class by corrupt politics, economic restructuring, hegemonic ideology and rapidly diffusing consumer
culture. The attachment left-liberal academics often have to postmodernist
accounts of boundless cultural diversity and individual differences tends to
verify the assumption that all empirical research addressing the reality of
advanced marginality is always already deficient in some important respect.
In a desire to avoid generalisation these left liberals tend to give up attempting to explain the reality of post-industrial poverty and instead focus on the
social and managerial responses to what they don't understand.

The deep underlying causes of social exclusion are thus off-limits, or in
some extreme cases where pure phenomenological, symbolic interactionist
or social constructionist discourses are drawn upon, reduced to a mere outcome of labelling and demonisation. As academics working in this area were
keen to show, labelling and stereotyping of the new urban poor had significant consequences. Ideological discourses that emanated from somewhere
on the political right shaped popular interpretations of the causes of poverty,
and these popular attitudes tended to feed back as justifications for right-
wing public policy. Over the past 30 years a majority of the political-media
classes and the population at large agreed that the best way to tackle poverty
was to task the poor with relieving their own circumstances: the 'socially
excluded' must be either threatened or cajoled into extracting themselves
from welfare and into legitimate work. Those who refused to comply were
to be policed by an increasingly expansive and intrusive criminal justice
system. The often complex and multidimensional negative characterisation

of the urban poor tended to feed back into a general cultural climate of pervasive fear and condemnation that positioned the socially excluded as an internal enemy rather than the social group most in need of social and governmental assistance.

A good deal of the material generated by this developing concern with the aggressive labelling of the poorest has value. However, it is our view that European social exclusion researchers and theorists have in recent years taken their eye off the ball with regard to the ways in which social exclusion is fundamentally underpinned by the structures, processes and values of liberal-capitalist political economy and the social and cultural consequences for the poorest. With one or two notable exceptions (for example Wacquant, 2007, 2009), there has been a move away from macro-level critical analysis and towards micro-analyses of socio-spatial manifestations of social exclusion and policy responses. We hear a great deal about the ways in which particular parts of the city and their inappropriately demonised inhabitants generate fear in the broader population. We hear about the ways in which these processes of 'othering' relate to the social policy agendas of the neoliberal state. We also hear about how male residents of excluded neighbourhoods are targeted by police and subjected to a much higher incidence of 'stop and search' before being criminalised, incarcerated and ushered towards a biographical cycle that moves them from the ghetto to the prison and back again (Fitzgibbon, 2007; Wacquant, 2009). Of course, much of this material has aided our understanding of the lives of the poorest and the dismal cycles in which they are trapped. However, this protective and fundamentally nominalist liberal discourse systematically glosses over the fact that the sudden removal of hostile labelling processes would relieve none of the multidimensional structural pressures – whose nexus is located deeply in the logic of the financialised global economy – that put the excluded where they are and continue to bear down upon them to reproduce their abject socio-economic position. As we shall see as the book's argument unfolds, neither would it on its own reconstitute the politics of solidarity.

Another vital issue neglected by mainstream liberal-left discourses is the incorporation of the majority of individuals into consumer culture and its global media circuits. This tends to be portrayed as profoundly 'democratic', a site for the free construction of identity, a gift from liberal-capitalism that conveniently disconnected the individual from the symbolic games of status traditionally monopolised in the real world by the wealthy and the privileged. Now, in a world saturated by the mass-manufactured symbolic objects of affordable luxury, all can adorn themselves with the rich social symbolism of the consumer market; and creatively, too, fashioning unique identities as they rummage through the sign-object system. However, the dark side of consumer culture has been hopelessly – and one could even argue systematically – avoided by liberal-left academia and politics over the past 30 years (Hall et al., 2008). The open field of self-expression that animates consumer markets

exacerbates the subjective insecurities and hostile social divisions that result
from incessant social comparison and competition (Winlow and Hall, 2006,
2009a; James, 2008, 2010). It is a profound mistake to assume that consumer capitalism is reflected only in the activities of the huge corporations
that control our high streets. Even the anti-consumerism of retro and other
do-it-yourself 'scenes', with their focus on charity shops and recycling, are
fully integrated into a market that constantly seeks to disturb established
hierarchies and styles in order to drive forwards new innovations in consumption trends. In Britain, the aggressive critique of 'chavs' directly relates to the field
of consumerism and the fight for social distinction and recognition. 'Chavs'
are, first and foremost, those who use consumer symbolism tastelessly (see
Hayward and Yar, 2006). If enough cash comes their way, they will embrace
in a naïve manner the symbolism of corporate advertising and adorn themselves with designer labels, or head out in search of unrestrained hedonistic
experiences (see Nightingale, 1993; Hallsworth, 2005; Hall et al., 2008;
LeBlanc, 2009). Of course, in committing themselves so completely to shallow consumer signification they ignore the edicts issued by liberal cultural
elites who believe themselves to be far too discerning to simply buy into the
advertising propaganda of corporate behemoths (Winlow and Hall, 2006,
2009a). The correct way for the liberal consumer to consume is to disregard
mass symbolism and instead pick one's way through the field in search of
idiosyncratic items that appear to suggest quirky personal tastes and resolutely 'individual' choices. One should construct for the self the image of the
thoughtful and critical consumer who will not be cajoled into buying items
simply because they have been heavily promoted by advertising campaigns.
Of course – and as we have shown elsewhere and in much more detail (ibid.;
Hall et al., 2008) – this purportedly critical consumer is fully integrated into
the circulation of capital, actively fulfilling a crucial role as the *condottiere*
of popular tastes, driving forward consumer markets from the vital position
of 'the street'. Only signals from the street can provide the constant movement and differentiation required to avoid the bland homogeneity and uniformity that would be consumer capitalism's death knell (Frank, 1998; Hall
and Winlow, 2007). That the individual can enter a mass market retailer in
order to choose an outfit, yet still retain the conceit of self-creation, should
be taken as an indication of the completeness of the incorporation of the
active subject into consumer ideology. In the consumption of 'organic' or
'fair-trade' products, even the guilt and hope of the discerning liberal consumer is built into the commodity itself.

As the master signifier of individuality is implanted in a popular culture
devoid of alternative sources of status and identity and pressed into the service of a competitive social hierarchy, both subjective incorporation and
dynamic movement are guaranteed. The tasteful consumer of a brand such
as Burberry, for example, must fight to distinguish the self from those tasteless *nouveau riche* consumers who hail from the lower orders (see Bourdieu,

1987). If both are now able to afford Burberry branded consumer items, a new distinction must be created in order to ensure the continuation of social hierarchy and assuage anxieties about social status; a sociocultural 'arms race' of positional goods begins (see Heath and Potter, 2006), drawing upon the traditional liberal culture of competitive individualism to maintain the immense input of human energy required to keep the market moving (Hall, 2012a). The prices of particular brand names are no longer enough to maintain a sense of cultural distinction. The problem for corporations like Burberry is that they must negotiate the tricky task of maintaining the exclusive brand image that is so attractive to consumers while at the same time racking up enough volume sales to ensure financial success and continuity. This problem is exacerbated by the flood of fake branded goods onto the market from developing economies in the east (McCartney, 2005; Phillips, 2007; Yi-Chieh, 2011). The result is the development of new complexities in marketing, promotion and public relations that encourage the growth of new forms of cultural distinction that seek to separate the tasteful self from the tasteless other (see Moore and Birtwistle, 2004; Bruce and Kratz, 2007). The fundamental point to bear in mind here is that these attempts to construct apparently new cultural hierarchies, to demonstrate cultural competence at least in part by encouraging others to see the cultural incompetence of others – a consumerised variant of *amour propre*, Rousseau's hostile form of ego-building on the downfall of the other – are indicative of the new realities of postmodern economic life, the ubiquity and seductive allure of consumer culture and its ability to invent new symbolic modes of social exclusion whilst incorporating the majority of individuals into its general symbolic order.

However, the cultural condemnation directed at the poor for wearing the wrong kinds of clothes or the right kinds of clothes wrongly, displaying the wrong attitudes to work and crime or inhabiting run-down neighbourhoods beset with a broad range of social problems by those struggling to maintain or achieve elite status is still not the main obstruction the poor face as they attempt to create a reasonably satisfying and rewarding life. The core problem is their fundamental inability to find reasonably remunerative work in the diminished and highly unstable labour markets that characterise areas of embedded poverty (Webster et al., 2004; Shildrick et al., 2010). This basic inability reflects the stark fact that, in the age of neoliberalism's 'global Minotaur' in which global flows of trade and capital have been reversed to relocate most labour-intensive production to the East and intensify the need for consumption in the West (see Varoufakis, 2011), neoliberal capitalism no longer needs a mass industrial workforce in the West to maintain profitable manufacture and investment (Rifkin, 1995; Granter, 2009; see also Beck, 2000). The individual 'choice' that is of so much concern to American underclass theorists is often, in reality, a choice between two ways of being poor: working in an exploitative and unsatisfying service job, or being welfare dependent.

One model of marginalised subjectivity (see glossary) focuses on the individual's perception of being hated and feared by those who populate the social mainstream and the way it is fully incorporated into the subject's self-image. This model has led to a renewed theoretical focus on self-ful-filling prophecies and the ways in which the poor apparently accept themselves as worthless, dishonourable and potentially criminal. Other analysts of social exclusion disagree with this view, arguing that the West's poorest citizens possess the political awareness and cultural power to resist these labels, or to invert them so that the individual can find a subjective benefit in embracing and re-contextualising the mainstream's negative judgement. In Britain for example, some authors have suggested that poor populations resist the negative 'chav' label by reclaiming the symbol to create an alternative and positive image of the 'chav' identity (Martin, 2009). Here, the (stereotypically) poor and uneducated 'chav' is accredited with the ability to understand the nature of the negative label and creatively construct a counterculture that celebrates and subverts the semiotics of the initial negative label. However, to us these theories and others associated with them have had their day. As the book develops we will try to offer the reader a realistic alternative to these basic models of socially excluded subjectivity.

To move forward we will offer an account of social exclusion that has both the subject and the nature of postmodern capital accumulation at its heart. We want to position marginalised subjectivity in a transformative historical conjuncture that has disrupted the certainties of the traditional symbolic order, destroyed traditional class structures and grounded forms of identity to encourage a culture of cynical 'capitalist realism' (see Fisher, 2009; Winlow and Hall, 2012b). We do not believe the problems of social exclusion can be solved simply by playing about with language, challenging stereotypes or forcing state institutions to discontinue prejudicial practices. We do not believe that marginalised subjectivity is constituted and reproduced chiefly in relation to neoliberal governmentality and the negative characterisations of the poor that are so common in contemporary culture. We will also avoid any real engagement with policy analysis. This is not because we are entirely dismissive of the ability of social policy to address the various problems associated with contemporary poverty. Rather, it reflects our desire to equip students with some of the theoretical tools that might allow them to grasp the abject reality of social exclusion and the very real harms associated with socioeconomic redundancy and marginality. We are neither 'liberals' nor particularly 'objective' sociologists. We do not see it as our task endlessly to describe the objective conditions and problems of the poor, and how some of them can be alleviated by micro-policies. Sociology's current *negative critique* can be complemented by the philosophical *positive critique* that encourages us to investigate beyond the borders of this world and to think about what *is* and what *might be* (see also Rancière, 2004). As we have suggested above, our political commitment is to a far greater degree of socioeconomic equality than that which currently exists. Rather than engage with policy debates about how we might turn off the tap of negative stereotyping or better enable the poor to be more ambitious and competitive, we are more concerned to tread a theoretical path that begins with the painful recognition that only a fundamental shift in the nature of global political economy can create the underlying conditions in which we can solve the problem of extreme inequality and postmodern social exclusion. Students must revisit the indisputable fact that contemporary capitalism is at its heart profoundly competitive. Because competition is systemic and functional and the much-vaunted 'morality' that many liberals posit at the core of our culture is little more than a restraint that sublimates competition into socially acceptable forms, inequality is inevitable. Social exclusion is thus not some sort of aberration that appears because the system is not being properly managed by its moral agents. Only the *extent* of social exclusion can be altered by liberal-parliamentary politics and social policy, but, in this current age of global economic reversal, not by very much.

3

Social Exclusion: The US Tradition

US individualism and the underclass

In the US, urban segregation is clearly quite extreme (see Massey and Denton, 1989; Davis, 2004; Wilkes and Iceland, 2004; Sugrue, 2005). The large former industrial cities of the Rust Belt have seen significant net reductions in their populations as a result of outward migration, which has occasionally left large tracts of the cities abandoned (Davis, 2004; Sugrue, 2005; Farley et al., 2007). Those who do not possess the economic and social resources to join the flight from urban blight and shrinking employment opportunities have found themselves increasingly cut off and poorly served by metropolitan and state administrations forced to cope with shrinking budgets. However, the problems faced by these largely abandoned populations are not restricted to shoddy public services and non-existent labour markets. Their segregation also shapes the nature of the threats and dangers they face on an everyday basis as legitimate job opportunities disappear and illegitimate job opportunities come to predominate (Frey, 1995; Eitle, 2009). Despite the much discussed great American crime decline (see for example Zimring, 2006), crime levels, especially violent crime, remain unconscionably high in these abandoned zones (Matthews et al., 2001; Harrell, 2007). The harms inflicted on these populations and the daily problems they face in creating for themselves reasonably safe and civilised lives reflect their marked segregation in dead and decaying parts of the city (Davis, 2004).

It makes sense to begin a discussion about the rise of an urban 'underclass' in the USA in conjunction with the rise of neoliberalism. Many commentators equate the rise of US neoliberalism within the transformative presidency of Ronald Reagan, who took office in 1981. However, the seeds that grew into Reaganomics were planted much earlier. Even though many of the USA's cultural values are conservative, in its politics and economics it is the archetypal classical liberal nation, still revering the historic constitution that planted classical liberalism's values at the centre of US life. The Bill of Rights, for example, firmly incorporated Locke's principles of limited government and the centrality of property and free trading rights into its dominant ideology, the wellspring of its glossy self-image as 'the land of the free'. The modern US state also reflects the experience of the founding fathers and later ancestors as immigrants, forced to flee their homelands in order to escape both religious persecution and restrictive socioeconomic circumstances. The mythology of freedom that developed when the USA consolidated its disparate parts as a nation-state and secured its independence was, despite the atrocities and harms that accompanied this turbulent period and its aftermath (see Zinn, 2005), to have far-reaching effects. In particular, the focus on the *sovereignty of the individual* is the Master Signifier (see glossary) that underlies much that US politics takes for granted these days.

US domestic politics should be understood in relation to a struggle between the individual and the state, which flattens and immobilises the true social dialectic to create an undialectical struggle that stalls history (Bosteels, 2011; Hall, 2012a). This stirs up a lot of social discord with no real forward movement but succeeds in its main aim of sustaining the belief that any large-scale collective action is the inevitable road to totalitarianism. It is usually taken for granted that the principal role of the state is to defend the interests and freedoms of the individual. The actions the state should take in order to secure these interests and freedoms are the substance of the USA's mainstream political discourse. However, this clear and unwavering focus on the individual means that this flattened and historically inert dialectic between the individual and the state has failed to develop an alternative politics that might challenge the prevailing order of things. The freedom of the individual from state intervention remains sacrosanct, despite a preponderance of evidence suggesting that a greater emphasis on such collective intervention and the principle of social justice is the only possible means of confronting the 'special liberty' of late-capitalism's oligarchs (Hall, 2012a), addressing the myriad harms caused by the ongoing economic and urban crises and giving grounds for some of the real optimism needed to inhibit the growing sense that the USA's best years have already passed (Galbraith, 1999; Keynes, 2008; Krugman, 2012. See also Wilkinson and Pickett, 2009; Lansley, 2012).

Twentieth century US politics placed a heavy emphasis on what Berlin (2002) calls 'negative freedom'. In this conception, the individual's freedom is secured by ensuring that the mandate of the state is restricted as much as possible. Taxes are kept as low as is practicable, and the individual is free to purchase services as they see fit. The state provides only those services that obviously require state management (this used to mean military, punishment and security services, but all of these services have been subject to marketisation in recent years; see Singer, 2007). Here the 'freedom' resides in the ability of the individual to determine for herself her cultural and religious identity and the nature and extent of her economic and social activity. The subject is essentially 'freed' from the control of external cultural and governmental influences. Berlin's (2002) conception of 'positive freedom' suggests that the state intervenes to disturb the sanctity of individualism and implements a series of programmes that enable the individual to *become* free. Here freedom is an achievement, a position that can be reached only when the individual is in possession of its basic prerequisites. From this perspective, the freedom from state interference is of no consequence if the individual lacks the means to secure food, shelter, education and so on. In practical terms this might mean the state provides education services, healthcare and a welfare system geared towards alleviating immediate suffering while simultaneously encouraging self-sufficiency.

This 'positive freedom' has been notable by its absence for long stretches of the USA's political history, but not all US political parties have ignored collectivist and integrationist policies (see Frank, 2005, 2006). Indeed, the rise and relative success of the American socialist left during the first two decades of the twentieth century revealed a strong inclination amongst working men and women to abandon the conceits of American individualism and embark upon a potentially transformative politics of universality (see Lasch, 1973; Kimeldorf, 1999). During the 1930s, Roosevelt's 'New Deal' claimed that it was possible to create a new social-liberal politics of active state intervention and 'positive freedom' (see Brands, 2009). Roosevelt's interventionism was of course a response to the harms of the Great Depression, a seismic economic event that indicated quite clearly the ability of reckless speculation and profiteering to wreck the lives of ordinary men and women (Galbraith, 2009). While there is debate over the extent to which Roosevelt was fully committed to interventionist welfare politics – it should be noted that he also sought to liberalise trade and control unions during his time in office (see Zinn, 2003) – it is certainly true that his tenure challenged the prevailing orthodoxies of US politics and briefly moved beyond the inert undialectical tension between state and individual.

Roosevelt's willingness to push the state into the market, to deploy Keynesian fiscal stimulus and to develop and systematise work programmes and new forms of social welfare, and to create governmental instruments capable of restraining the expansion of the market into all aspects of life, were a marked departure from the policies of the presidents who preceded him (Schlesinger, 2003; Smith, 2009). During his tenure the USA moved from the widespread desperation of the Great Depression to take its place as the premier global superpower at the end of the Second World War. Roosevelt's presidency is widely believed to have been one of the most important and successful of all time but, despite this, his liberal interventionism largely failed to be carried forward by the Democrat presidents who followed him. Across the Atlantic at the close of the war the Conservative Prime Minister Winston Churchill declared his intention to build 'a land fit for heroes'. The first Labour Government, headed by Clement Atlee, attempted to give Churchill's vague rhetoric some concrete shape and put it into practice, building a brand new welfare state that included free healthcare, free education, unemployment benefits and pensions for all citizens (see Harris, 2004; Judt, 2010, 2011). The Keynesian economic management and social democratic welfare interventionism of this government succeeded in establishing the conventions and expectations of British politics for the next 30 years. In practical political terms, Roosevelt's legacy was less enduring. In a nation whose mainstream cultural foundation is resistant to any form of socialism, no new consensus on welfare and employment was established, and, after its pivotal role in the historic Allied victory in 1945, the USA began a gradual return to the foundational model of laissez-faire classical liberalism bequeathed by the Founding Fathers.

Right across the political spectrum of US life the individual is sovereign. No power should attempt to impose itself on the individual's right to make personal decisions relating to religious practice, cultural identity, biographical trajectory or economic trading. The state should restrain itself to those activities that protect the sovereign individual and thus guarantee the well-being of the nation. In a nation partly founded on a rebellion against taxation, it is unsurprising that many ordinary US taxpayers view tax as a profound injustice – the imposition of the will of the state at the expense of the individual (see Galbraith, 1999 for a critique). It is the responsibility of the state to restrict tax-gathering activities as much as possible, yet, paradoxically, at the same time fund the military and security services to protect citizens from internal and external threats to their safety. Unlike many Europeans, many US citizens do not appear to consider any particular service beyond the military and law enforcement to be the responsibility of the state. It can often appear as if the greater US public has only limited concerns about the involvement of the market in education, health and policing. How can we understand the US people's marked distrust of the state? How and why has the orientation to negative freedom taken such a strong hold on American politics? These questions are of profound importance to our understanding of the cultural and political forces behind social exclusion in the USA. We can begin to answer them by addressing the basic building blocks of utilitarian philosophy.

What is utilitarianism?

Utilitarianism is generally considered to be an integral part of the eighteenth-century European Enlightenment. Jeremy Bentham's rather straightforward conception of the common good as 'the greatest happiness for the greatest number' is perhaps the best known contribution to this field of study, but during this same period many other liberal intellectuals were constructing a range of other ideas that contributed to the philosophy of utilitarianism. Hume, Locke and Mill are the most notable, and here we will provide a quick digest of their philosophical positions as a means of framing our discussion of liberal approaches to subjectivity (see glossary), welfare and the problem of the post-industrial US 'underclass'.

The obvious starting point is Bentham's claim that maximised happiness should be the measure of right and wrong and the key concern of the modern state (see Mill and Bentham, 2000; Schofield, 2009). This concern with the creation of human happiness can often encourage readers to respond positively to its message. Surely the creation of the greatest happiness for the greatest number is a noble calling for the modern state? Others have of course identified the less obvious negativity of the statement: what happens if one is not part of the 'greatest number'? Can't this statement advocate new forms of government that seek to advance the interests only of the majority, often at the expense of minorities? Of course, the most pressing problem is the dominant character of the majority; what if the majority are actively and prejudicially against all minorities whose lifestyles do not conform to the dominant self-image?

However, Bentham undercuts the problem of cultural differences and tensions by constructing a very crude, Universalist depth-psychology that posits human beings as essentially homogeneous. The starting point for understanding his approach to state-building is to outline this rudimentary model of human subjectivity, which rests on what he calls the *hedonistic calculus* (ibid.). Like other liberal intellectuals writing at the time, Bentham believed that by nature all human beings are desirous of pleasure and fearful of pain. They will attempt as much as possible to increase the sum total of happiness in their lives, and they will do so by avoiding those activities that might result in unhappiness. Bentham's crucial intervention is that the hedonistic calculus of men and women equips them with a clear method of evaluating activities and their potential consequences. We are, at root, both hedonistic and rational creatures fully capable of mentally working out the likelihood of pleasurable or painful outcomes and contrasting the purity and duration of potential pleasures with the intensity of associated potential pains. So, the nature of the pleasures that might result from ignoring the alarm clock, arising late and then phoning your workplace and informing them that you're sick, before spending the day at leisure, are judged in relation to the pains that might result from this course of action. In most cases, our hedonistic calculus allows us to see that the pleasures of a brief repose are fairly shallow in comparison to the potential pains – such as the loss of wages, respect and status – that might result should our deception be discovered.

Bentham famously extended this logic to the rapidly developing field of organised criminal justice; it was the state's duty to ensure that punishments for crimes outweighed the potential pleasure that might accrue to the criminal. Criminals must immediately be mindful that significant pains might result from their activities, but, crucially, the punishment should not be so harmful as to reduce the 'happiness of the greatest number'. In this respect he is often viewed as a reformer, encouraging modernity to abandon outmoded barbarism for a more even-handed and incremental system of punishments. However, this basic psychology behind Bentham's philosophy had also been common currency during the tumultuous years that preceded the drafting of the American constitution and the Bill of Rights. The conception of the sovereign individual capable of rationality and calculation in relation to the future consequences of their immediate social activity pervaded the philosophical and economic discourses of the Enlightenment.

The philosophy of liberalism is one of the most important outcomes of the Enlightenment. Its key architect was John Locke. His depiction of the human subject is slightly different from that offered by Bentham, and it also differs in important ways from the much earlier model of subjectivity offered by Descartes, whose work appears to have been a significant influence on Locke's development of philosophical liberalism. The Lockean subject is essentially self-interested and self-aware, and driven by the desire to improve its own wellbeing in the same way as Bentham's subject. However, Locke pays more attention to the importance of the environment and social influences upon the development of the adult self. The subject is essentially a *tabula rasa*, a blank slate upon which the social inscribes its influence. He is keen to acknowledge the influence of education in the creation of the social self, and he therefore offers an integrated image of the subject that foregrounds reason, self-interest and self-awareness, while at the same time acknowledging the role of the social in giving form and significance to these drives.

It is worth mentioning that Locke offers a labour theory of value, but one that is very different from the much better known theory offered by Karl Marx. Locke acknowledges that the labour applied to objects adds value to commodities, and the value that is given to the commodity is related to the nature of the labour applied and the effort expended in its production. Locke then goes on to elevate the abstract ownership of property above the grubby business of everyday manufacture and trade. Like other liberals of the time, he believed in natural rights, and one of these natural rights was the right to accrue and protect one's property. He believed that the state has no business intruding upon the rights of individuals to secure their own interests through the ownership and trade of property. The rise of a money economy allowed for the natural use-derived limits that exist on the consumption of material goods to be breached and the unfettered accumulation of wealth to be pursued; for Locke, to the betterment of all. Problems can arise when the accumulation of property in a money economy is no longer limited by the ability of individuals to produce and use commodities themselves, but he believed that limited government should manage these problems while remaining mindful of its commitment to the defence of natural freedoms.

Both Bentham and Locke subscribed to the idea of a social contract. Their interpretation of the creation of this contract differs from that offered by Hobbes, Rousseau and others, but their quintessentially liberal interpretation proved particularly important in the creation of the American constitution and the establishment of American liberalism. To be brief, authors working in this tradition begin with a mythical time of natural law, a time before any form of cultural authority or state power existed. In this state of nature, the individual is entirely free from interference and the restrictions of law. The individual may then follow basic hedonistic urges and pursue pleasure without fear of sanction. However, in such a situation, the individual is subject to the selfish pleasure-seeking behaviours of others, and we descend into a violent Hobbesian (2008[1651]) 'warre of all against all'. In this chaos, no one's interests are served and a civilised society cannot develop. In order to be free from violent chaos, the result of extreme freedom of drive, sovereign individuals construct a social contract that creates the rules to which all must comply. This is always a compromise. Individuals relinquish elements – exactly how much is always uncertain and situation-specific – of their natural freedom to a central authority so they might live a life of order and relative stability. Here we must acknowledge the distinction between power and authority (see Arendt, 1969); the former is founded on force whilst the latter is always the product of consensual agreement.

A state now exists to arbitrate disputes and to construct and enforce laws. For the early liberals, the state is a necessity that creates order, which is good, but, in order to do so, it must restrict some freedoms, which is bad. Therefore it should possess only a limited mandate and restrict its activities as much as possible. The government must acknowledge the true nature of its role and resist the urge to increase its power over and above the authority given to it and avoid unnecessary legislation. As we have seen, most liberals believe that sovereign individuals are capable of calculating the consequences of their actions and in the main naturally working towards the general happiness. This belief was allied to the *benevolentism* that viewed the individual as largely good-natured and sociable (Eagleton, 2009), which means that the state should exist only to restrict occasional expressions of hedonistic excess that might harm others. To the greatest extent possible the natural laws of life, liberty and the defence of property should not be interfered with. It is here that we can begin to see the close relationship between early philosophical liberalism and the founding principles of the American state. Locke in particular is cited as a key intellectual influence in the construction of the Declaration of Independence and the eventual constitution, in particular the Bill of Rights. Locke, Bentham and other early English liberals did not believe it was the responsibility of government to equip the citizenry with the basic capacity to pursue the positive freedoms required to live comfortable and civilised lives.

The other key issue we must consider in relation to the lasting influence of liberalism in the USA relates to capitalism, free markets and economic practice. The USA is of course the contemporary home of capitalism. Capitalism arose first in Europe, but it is the USA that latterly came to symbolise a true and unequivocal commitment to economic freedom and the sanctity of personal accumulation; all individuals have the right to accumulate wealth and, in a free and open market, trade property with anyone willing to pay the price. One can detect the influence of the classical European economists quite clearly in the development of the American concept of freedom. The natural right of each individual to pursue their own economic interests, enshrined in the Bill of Rights, in many ways became the indisputable moral good and fundamental inalienable right that shaped the twentieth-century USA's self-image. Classical-liberal and neoclassical economics were built upon the premise that markets are self-regulating and will find a natural equilibrium if left to their own devices. Despite the fact that the USA's rapid development in the late nineteenth century was built on state planning and protectionism, today's neoclassical economists still believe that too much regulation impedes enterprise, obstructs economic growth and unnecessarily intrudes upon the inalienable right of individuals to pursue their economic interests (Friedman, 1993, 2002).

We will not describe classical and neoclassical economics in detail at this juncture, but we must acknowledge that their orientation towards a free and unregulated market became deeply unpopular after poorly-regulated financial speculation led to the Wall Street Crash of 1929. In Europe, Keynes (2008[1936]) developed a very different model of economic management, which began from the premise that markets are inherently unstable and require significant governmental regulation. Keynesian economics defined the period 1945–79 in most industrialised nations. Even in the USA, the free market economics of Smith, Ricardo, Malthus and Mill became slightly unfashionable. Nixon, even as he was being persuaded by the monetarist economics of Friedman and others, still famously acknowledged 'we're all Keynesians now'. He was referring primarily to the Keynesian approach to tackling fiscal crises – that is, to restrict government spending during boom times and increase it during times of crisis – but this brief comment is quite telling. It was almost as if Keynes had won the economic argument in the liberal USA despite the fact that, during Nixon's time, monetarism and free market economics were growing in popularity and were to eventually become a totem for the political right. Classical liberal economics lingered on, nurtured, modified and developed by the neoclassical economists and those of the monetarist Chicago School (Harcourt, 2010). It appeared to refine its argument and gradually develop its strength as it waited for its opportunity to return to the very heart of US political and economic life.

Economists such as Milton Friedman, who developed modern monetarist economics at the Chicago School, were essentially radical libertarians who believed that all forms of state regulation impede growth and economic development. They used the work of the early liberals as their base, and assumed the fully rational, self-interested sovereign individual discussed above. The work of the Chicago School won widespread acclaim in academic circles, but for the most part it did not translate into public policy until the 1980s. From then on, it became by far the most important intellectual current in academic economics and dominated global economic policy. The dominance of revived and slightly modified neoclassical liberal economics – now known as neoliberalism – was such that it ceased to be considered simply as one of many possible economic models and became the only conceivable model for governments struggling to cope in rapidly deindustrialising Western liberal democracies.

Even during the brief period in which US governments maintained a commitment to interventionist economic management, economic liberalism continued to cast its shadow. For us, this is a reflection of the enduring ideological potency of classical liberal symbolism in twentieth-century US society. Processes of economic globalisation, and the machinations of geopolitical power, have ensured that this symbolism is now gaining traction across the globe. In the USA, even during times in which economic liberalism had been proven fundamentally flawed and socially destructive, there existed in the background a drive towards libertarianism, towards protecting the economic freedom of the individual and reducing the role of government still further, all pitched in relation to the fundamental ethical principal of freeing the sovereign individual from the 'tyranny' of unnecessary external control (see Friedman, 1980, 1993). It is a primary notion, a Master Signifier that can always be called upon as a response to an economic or political crisis, its content adjusted to fit with the cultural and political climate of any epoch. In US culture this shibboleth and the conditions it lays down are always presented as the vital prerequisites for freedom (Friedman, 1980).

However, despite the accompanying assumption that economic liberalism will increase wealth and freedom for all US citizens, its revival in the form of neoliberalism over the past three decades has benefited only those at the very top of US society whilst, for the first time in the history of US industrialism, the real wages of the majority have declined (Harvey, 2007; Wolff, 2010). The security state that has grown on the ideological bedrock of the 'war against terror' has also diminished the freedom of the majority, which threatens the ethical heart of the liberal project (Hallsworth and Lea, 2011). The rise of neoliberalism during the 1980s should be understood as a return to the logic of early unregulated capitalism with an unrelenting ideological accompaniment and the support of history's most powerful and interventionist militarised state. What we see from the 1980s onwards is the restoration of the US equivalent of the *ancien régime*, not a historical and dialectical movement towards progressive social outcomes (see Badiou, 2002, 2009).

The attempts made by post-war economists of all political persuasions to present the academic discipline of economics as a science is a further extension of this process, an attempt to erase ethico-political processes that might seek to regulate economic activity or make the economy work for a much broader section of the population. Management of the economy, we are told, should be left to the experts. For the most part, these experts, for instance Alan Greenspan, simplify and reduce the economic actor to the rational subject of early liberalism and admit to being driven by deep libertarian beliefs rather than reflexive intellectual enquiry (Friedman, 1980). As the global economic crash of 2008 indicated quite clearly, many influential academic economists failed fully to appreciate and account for the 'animal spirits' (Keynes, 2008) that can grip markets and drive 'irrational' systemic market activity. As we will show later, there is no fundamental 'science' of economics. Economics is always *political* (Chang, 2011), and all economic decisions have social, cultural, psychological and ethical outcomes. The reduction of the academic discipline of economics to the status of an abstract mathematicised science – little more than sophisticated macro-accountancy – that undercuts politics is a move that should be criticised for its obvious ideological content as well as its recently calamitous results.

Our point here is to position economic liberalism not as a progressive evolutionary form with no functional rivals but a fundamental *Idea*, which can be returned to time after time across history, especially during crises that appear in periods when the economy is being regulated by political authorities that classical liberals as a matter of principle do not like. In different epochs the *Idea* will present itself in different ways, but the deep principle – an economised libidinal drive masquerading as an ethical value and a political right – remains the same. That drive is fixated on the eternal reproduction of a porous socioeconomic hierarchy that allows social mobility to a position of extreme wealth for a tiny few hyper-successful entrepreneurs, technocrats, bankers and corrupt politicians, and the protection of that wealth stored as money and liquid assets. The economic exclusion of those consigned to the bottom of this hierarchy is an inevitable product of the system as it remains true to its fundamental classical liberal principles. Social liberalism, the political variant that attempts to ameliorate the brutality of exclusion by means of progressive taxation, state intervention and welfare, is, despite the recent financial catastrophe, currently in danger of losing once and for all the ideological and political battle.

We should consider here the basic presupposition of liberal economists: that the fundamental role of economics is to create wealth, not to arrange its fair and even distribution. The obvious philosophical considerations that accompany the sanctification of wealth creation are noticeable by their absence. How do liberal economists and politicians view their social role? They see themselves as guardians of the *Idea* and public servants who create the frameworks that encourage market economies to grow and work more efficiently, creating wealth that will guarantee jobs and trickle down to the poor. However, the main point pertinent to our discussion of social exclusion is that, whether they sit on the left or right side of the liberal fence, they certainly *do not* see themselves as the inspirational agents of structural change and alternative futures. Moreover, many amongst the excluded, in their own politically inarticulate yet emotionally arousing way, know this fine well.

Liberal interpretations of the underclass

In the last chapter we claimed that European debates about social exclusion developed in marked distinction from parallel debates about the establishment of a new post-industrial 'ghetto underclass' in the USA. The main character of US approaches to understanding the new poverty of the neoliberal period is deeply indicative of its cultural roots in philosophical and economic liberalism. Before we examine the claims made about the underclass by liberal commentators and social analysts, we should make it clear that not all US analysts of post-industrial poverty and exclusion display a commitment to liberalism. William Julius Wilson (1987, 1996; Wilson and Traub, 2007), perhaps the most notable commentator on the ghetto poor in America, is a committed social democrat. There are also many other writers who identify the importance of structural factors in the creation of post-industrial poverty. We are not claiming that all US analysts of contemporary poverty are rabid libertarians who have no interest in the roots of the urban crisis in fundamental changes that have taken place in the economy and in politics. Instead we suggest that mainstream *political* and *popular cultural* responses to contemporary urban poverty reflect a fundamental commitment to forms of liberal analysis. The responses of both Republican and Democrat Presidents since the early 1980s display a clear fidelity to a model of liberal subjectivity and a desire to intervene in the problem of embedded urban poverty only with a view to shaping the decision-making processes of the sovereign individual. This rather stark fact should encourage us to accept that, despite active dissent in the fringe, a classical-liberal ideological hegemony exists in US politics and popular culture. The nation dare not let go of this ideological foundation; the promise that the USA is the place where the individual can work hard to accumulate wealth without too much interference has attracted the generations of immigrants who have made the nation what it is. The political spectrum of US mainstream politics has always been rather narrow, but it seems that all American politics now must take place on the field of liberalism: the extreme right-wing economic liberalism, allied with remnants of conservative culture, of the Republicans on one side, and the eternally apologetic and compromised 'third way' social liberalism of the post-Clinton Democrats on the other.

Despite the complexity and insight offered by some of the sociological work that has addressed the entrenched problems of poor populations across the USA, since the 1980s this work has for the most part been ignored by neoliberal political administrations. For these politicians, sociology is a politically biased field of study and therefore its findings are always suspect, whereas economics is 'scientific' and therefore its models demand respect. We should also say that political liberalism is not simply a US malady. It is now firmly established in many European countries, shaping national social policy and shared economic policy. We are of course offering a rather simplified comparison between general approaches in Europe and the USA, but it is a division that makes sense in general conceptual terms.

For many left-liberal social scientists in Britain and the USA, Charles Murray is evil incarnate. His work has been mocked, pilloried and subjected to the kinds of intemperate invective rarely heard in the genteel world of academia. Despite the fact that his claims about the establishment and nature of a growing urban underclass have been repeatedly dismissed by mainstream social scientists, he continues to give many analysts of poverty and social exclusion nightmares. In truth his work fully justifies much of this critique, but we must acknowledge that outside of the university Murray's work has had considerable influence among policy-makers in Europe and the USA. Murray was certainly not a figure of fun in Reagan's Republican Party, Thatcher's Conservative Party and Blair's New Labour Party. Although his name is mentioned less in political and policy circles these days one can still detect his influence. Like it or not, Murray raised questions about poverty and welfare that continue to shape domestic policy in post-industrial Western countries. His work clearly struck a chord with those on the political right; in fact, one might reasonably claim that Murray simply articulated sentiments that had been common in right-wing liberal circles and had at least some purchase in popular culture for generations. Murray's work resonated with ordinary working people who had taken a right-wing turn since the late 1990s and suspected that their tax revenues were being wasted indulging the lifestyles of the profligate poor. Since the 1980s neoliberal ideology has attacked traditional anti-utilitarian aspects of working-class culture to implant the values of individualism, competition and accumulation at the heart of England (Winlow and Hall, 2006; Hall et al. 2008). The result was a new culture of self-interested pragmatism that viewed the more sympathetic traditional working-class attitudes to the poor as weak and unworldly. Increasingly the poor were seen as a drain on tax resources and the economic vitality of the nation. Cossetting the poor with generous welfare was counterproductive in that it reproduced a 'culture of dependency'; what they needed was some tough love. The post-industrial poor must recognise that this lonely, brutal neoliberal world driven by unforgiving economic competition, in which individuals can rely only on themselves, is simply the latest manifestation of the timeless and natural human condition. Only when the poor are made to appreciate that innovation, effort and sacrifice are necessary to relieve their stricken circumstances can the country begin to rid itself of the blight of embedded, intergenerational poverty and the tax burden that results from it.

Murray's admirably straightforward thesis about welfare and poverty appeared to catch the popular and political mood perfectly, inspiring those already predisposed to laissez-faire liberalism while it alienated all those who remained faithful to an ailing and shrinking left. Now, in 2012, almost 30 years after Murray wrote *Losing Ground* (Murray, 1984), the global economy is in a deeper phase of crisis and his harsh libertarian approach to welfare has returned to inform popular and political debates about unemployment, crime, welfare and the family. In Britain, a potential triple-dip recession and falling tax receipts have precipitated a heated discussion about the continued viability of modern welfare entitlements. Our ostensibly pragmatic political leaders tell us that cuts must be made somewhere, and once again the arguments about the waste supposedly inherited in outmoded bureaucratic welfare systems, most clearly made by Murray in the 1980s, reverberate around the mediascape. So, while Murray was certainly not the first to offer a passionate critique of modern welfare systems (see for example Tocqueville, 1997; Hayek, 2001[1944], 2006[1960]; Friedman, 2002), we will use Murray's thesis as a means of encapsulating the core concerns of liberal approaches to urban poverty in America.

Charles Murray is a right-wing political scientist who has for most of his career been employed by conservative and libertarian political think-tanks and policy groups rather than universities. He burst onto the political scene in 1984 with *Losing Ground*, in which he claims that welfare programmes in America were patently not working. Welfare spending continued to rise during the 1970s, but poverty remained unsolved. For Murray the reasons for this were perfectly straightforward. The American welfare system rewarded laziness and removed incentives that would otherwise encourage people to find paid employment. Paying people not to work was wrong-headed. It encouraged slothfulness, indolence, welfare dependency and degenerate forms of culture that broke apart the traditional family and led to crime. Civilised America's desire to help the deserving poor was creating a new group of undeserving poor that were tearing up their part of the social contract, draining the state and eroding traditional sociability and morality. As he claims, 'we tried to provide more for the poor and produced more poor instead. We tried to remove the barriers to escape from poverty, and inadvertently built a trap' (1984: 9). The aspect of Murray's moralistic critique of the new poor that attracted most attention related to Aid to Families with Dependent Children (AFDC), a welfare payment established by Roosevelt's administration and aimed at widows forced to raise children without the support of a breadwinning husband. For Murray, this payment encouraged illegitimacy and the fragmentation of the traditional family unit, and consequently denied children raised in such households the presence of a crucial male role-model; crucial for boys, anyway, but it was boys who were causing most of the trouble. Murray claims that by the 1950s it was clear that most claimants were not widows and that many had never been married. It was also clear that the lack of a supportive husband did not prevent the female parent from having yet more children who were to be 'reared at government expense'. In this case, as in others, the state's desire to help the poor encourages individuals to make choices that result in continued welfare dependency and the erosion of marriage and the traditional heterosexual nuclear family.

In *Losing Ground*, Murray displays his intellectual debt to the early English liberals. He talks of a basic calculus that structures decision-making for the poor and non-poor alike, but acknowledges that poor people often fail to have the resources to plan for the long-term, therefore the decisions they reach are often quite different to those reached by people who are not poor. He extends this logic into the field of crime control. Murray's basic point, and again one that directly relates to the core concerns of early utilitarianism, is that there was, during the 1960s, a clear reduction in the risks associated with criminal activity. Like a number of notable left liberals (see for example Lemert, 1972; Cohen, 2011), Murray is relatively unconcerned with the actual causes of crime. Instead, he makes the basic point that the perception that it was becoming easier to get away with crime, mainly because of lax sentencing and hamstrung policing, made it a more attractive option.

Murray returns to these core themes in his later works, which address more directly the establishment of an urban underclass. In 1990 he published *The Emerging British Underclass* after briefly visiting the country. Murray suggests that the key warning signs indicating the emergence of an urban underclass were already present throughout Britain: high crime, illegitimacy and unemployment. Again, social policies directed at the poor were the primary causes of these problems because they offered perverse incentives to remain poor and welfare-dependent. They encouraged the rise of female-headed single-parent households and allowed young men to abandon the responsibilities of fatherhood. There were fewer risks associated with criminal activity, and punishments were insufficient to act as an adequate disincentive. In particular parts of the city, the stigma associated with illegitimacy and welfare dependency had fallen away. In short, the desire of the state to help those in need had resulted in the generation of a class of people who were now disconnected from the labour market and mainstream culture and society. Britain could save itself only if it performed a rapid about-face, abandoning its outmoded attitude to welfare and recognising that clear incentives need to be in place that encourage employment, self-sufficiency and moral rectitude.

If all this was not enough to enrage the liberal left, Murray, in conjunction with Richard Herrnstein, then presented his analysis of education and intelligence in their 1996 book *The Bell Curve*. The book itself is huge and it contains lots of statistics that endeavour to support its decidedly shaky central thesis. Herrnstein and Murray essentially offer a social Darwinian model of intelligence and social hierarchy, which suggests that the poor are poor because they tend to be less intelligent than those higher up the class system. Implicit in their analysis is the claim that Black Americans, who are statistically more likely to be poor and form part of the 'underclass', are less intelligent than the white majority. For our Darwinian duo, intelligence results from a mixture of biological and environmental factors. The poor tend to underestimate the value of education and intelligence, resulting in poor intergenerational IQ scores. Among the more affluent, and in the more aspiring households of the deserving poor, education is valued and intelligence becomes intergenerational. Over time, a super-smart 'cognitive elite' develops that is capable of retaining its social and economic status. The members of the cognitive elite that hail from more modest backgrounds are intellectually equipped to fight their way up a meritocratic class system to take their places in the top strata of American society. For Herrnstein and Murray, the iron law of oligarchy still reigns supreme. The cream inevitably rises to the top, and the stupid are destined to occupy the very lowest strata of an essentially just social hierarchy built on the nurturance and application of intelligence rather than discrimination and exploitation.

We will not offer a detailed critique of Murray's work (instead, see Gould, 1996; MacDonald, 1997). Suffice it to say that it contains substantial theoretical and methodological problems, and his 'Bell Curve' theory has been proven to be entirely wrong. Murray's work has been picked apart by many social scientists on both sides of the Atlantic, and we do not intend to recapitulate the standard critique of his deliberately provocative opinion pieces. Instead, we want to address the basic liberal ontology from which he proceeds and investigate how widespread it is. He is a committed classical liberal who believes that humans possess a fundamental calculative ability that allows them to weigh up potential courses of action. For Murray, the urban underclass is responding logically with their inbuilt hedonistic calculus to behaviourist incentives placed before them. Why work in an unsatisfying job when one can get by perfectly well without working? Why get married when the state is willing to offer single mothers targeted welfare payments? Why bother to submit to the rule of law when there is clear evidence that it is possible, indeed probable, that crimes can be lucrative yet will go unpunished? In this way, Murray positions the subject ontologically as a virtual sociopath, entirely unconcerned with conventional morality and the benefits of civilised sociability. Until there is a clearly identifiable benefit to the self in committing to the rules of collective life, Murray's subject remains socially alienated and entirely self-interested. The poor respond to incentives and disincentives. For the modern state attempting to address the problem of embedded poverty, those things that promote order and independence need to be incentivised and disincentives need to follow those activities that threaten order and independence. There is little sense of social identity and long-term biographical planning; just a raw, asocial calculus that sees no further than immediate individual advantage. The perverse welfare incentives offered by the modern state ensure the non-working poor will remain poor and the working poor, as they appraise their economic options, are in constant danger of being drawn towards the immediate benefits of welfare dependency. The next generation are then born into poverty and raised with a clear appreciation of short-termism and the relative benefits of welfare dependency and crime over paid labour.

Murray is optimistic in the sense that he appears to believe these trends can be reversed if the nanny state were to allow the poor to experience the true pains of destitution, at which point they would quickly discover a willingness to work. Similarly, if the state were to stop offering welfare to single mothers, illegitimacy and the number of single parent households would decline. Women would seek out dependable long-term mates, and married men would then be encouraged to remain in work in order to guarantee the economic wellbeing of their families. However, Murray's later work displays a marked pessimism, as if the ship has already sailed and the poor of today can do nothing but beget offspring whose lazy, dependent ways destin them to poverty. Across the generations, the intelligent and diligent poor will naturally move up the social hierarchy and the stupid, lazy and dependent poor will congregate at the bottom. The answer to this bipolar society, in which the poor become progressively incapable of reattaching themselves to mainstream society, is the rise of a new socially segregated, carceral society (Murray, 2005). Murray now appears to believe that there can be no reintegration. Instead, Western states should accept the existence of the poor and manage their presence in civilised society, ensuring that they don't 'get underfoot'. The US experience now points the way forward for the British political establishment, who should adopt a zero-tolerance criminal justice policy and accept the rise of the prison population to somewhere in the region of 250,000 – the British prison population on 3 August 2012 was 86,745 (Ministry of Justice, 2012). For Murray, the downside is that taxpayers must fund the expansion of the criminal justice system if they hope to control the problems created by a growing underclass. As the US experience clearly shows, the benefit of this approach is that the most socially toxic members of the underclass will be criminalised, removed from the streets and prevented from polluting society.

The problems and omissions associated with the adoption of a liberal model of the human subject are now quite clear. The basic calculus that supposedly structures our social being is just too simplistic, yet it is the ground on which all classical-liberal derived ideology, including economics, is grounded. The assumption of a fully rational subjectivity that determines behaviour and self-identity through calculative decision-making divorces the individual from the objective social world around them and the realm of irrational drives inside them. This model of liberal subjectivity denies those social influences that shape our drives, desires, tastes, attitudes, goals and dispositions. Instead the subject is positioned as an atom in a social vacuum, concerned with the social only as a field for potential pains and pleasures. Despite the obvious problems associated with this very basic philosophical concept, it has been profoundly influential. It shaped the Enlightenment's philosophical outcomes and was the foundation of the classical economic models of Smith, Hume and Ricardo. It was then retained by the neoclassical economists of the nineteenth century and treated as a basic fact of human existence by the monetarist economists of the post-war twentieth century, so obvious that it was barely worth thinking about. This model of subjectivity is the basic ontological foundation of the current neoliberal period in which we live, pervading aspects of our lives from economic policy to the rehabilitation of offenders.

Turning our attention more directly to the topic of social exclusion, we should be immediately able to grasp that the complex dynamics that keep poor people poor cannot be reduced to a basic calculus of subjective decision-making. The fact that so many of our political leaders have led such sheltered lives – largely free from encounters with crime, poverty, and unemployment, let alone the embedded pathologies that can result from abusive relationships – appears to inform their fundamental presupposition that the socially excluded can reattach themselves to the mainstream simply by force of will. It is almost as if they imagine their unaffected selves in the position of the poorest, and then think of the steps they would take to relieve their circumstances. For the most part they fail to appreciate that the world may look very different to the stereotypically excluded young man with little formal education and few social connections. Their limited social experience also appears to ensure that they underestimate the objective impediments poor people face when attempting to find reasonable work or accessing the cultural forms that signal 'social inclusion'. We should also note that, in the sociological sense, the 'rational decisions' the individual makes reflect the huge complexities of socialisation, identity formation and ongoing engagement with everyday social and cultural life.

That said, we want to rethink this basic liberal ontological framework in the context of the profound historical changes that have resulted from the advent of neoliberal parliamentary capitalism. We have no intention of advocating the adoption of a basic liberal calculus in relation to the problems faced by marginalised social groups, but neither do we plan to adopt the basic social learning approaches of structural sociology. Instead, we want to return to Descartes, the architect of the rational subject, who pre-dates the early English liberals. Then, following Žižek (1997, 2007, 2009c), we will reposition Descartes' cogito in relation to the advent of liberal postmodernism and the precipitous decline of the symbolic efficiency (see glossary) that results from its cynical dismissal of truth claims. In the next chapter we describe clearly what we mean by this and try to connect our theoretical claims to the objective reality of social inequality and marginality in neoliberal societies.

4

Re-positioning Social Exclusion

In the following four chapters we will attempt to position social exclusion firmly in the contemporary intervallic period, in which the old order of parliamentary capitalism appears mortally wounded but a new truth project is yet to fully emerge (see Badiou, 2012a). Before the global economic crisis of 2008, history appeared to have ground to a halt. The social order created by liberal democracy and capitalism appeared to have defeated its ideological opponents and secured its position as the 'least worst' of all possible systems of political and socioeconomic organisation (see Badiou, 2002; Žižek, 2002). For a short time after the crash we appeared to occupy a strange historical interregnum of uncertainty that allowed us once again to consider the trajectory of our social and political world. Everyday people were again forced to come face to face with capitalism's boom and bust 'business cycle' and the significant human consequences of economic depressions. Throughout 2011 revolutions, riots, protests, marches and disturbances initially indicated a broad re-politicisation of what were, before the crash, the West's apparently apathetic and cynical post-political populations. Neoliberalism seemed to have been knocked off its lofty perch, becoming once again but one of many possible ways of organising an economy. The system's characteristics and outcomes were once again critically debated by politicians, academics and the politically-minded amongst working populations through the world. However, what was missing from this ostensible 'return' of real politics was a clear and popular oppositional narrative that endorsed an alternative model of socioeconomic organisation. Many protest groups could easily identify the fundamental flaws of global neoliberalism, but they failed in the task of identifying an inclusive, sustainable and more ethical alternative. They were *against* the worst excesses of global neoliberalism, but were not fundamentally *for* something that could be easily named and identified.

In some intellectual circles, especially Continental philosophy, the idea of communism came storming back on to the scene. One of its most influential advocates is the French philosopher Alain Badiou. For him (2010a, 2010b), communism is an eternal idea. It can mean different things in different epochs, but it always *insists* and returns in order to have its basic maxim reconsidered. That maxim, for Badiou (ibid., 2012c), Rancière (2010a) and many others (see Žižek, 2009b; Žižek and Douzinas, 2010; Bosteels, 2011; Dean, 2012), is simply the drive to create really existing egalitarianism, a fundamental equality that would re-moralise and restructure Western societies currently characterised by deep social divisions, inequalities and injustices. Outside of these very restricted intellectual circles, life was getting harder for many and a lot harder for some. However, even during a period when the fundamental problems of capitalism became starkly apparent, communism seemed to be incapable of attracting popular support. It seemed irredeemably tarnished by the horrors of Stalin's gulags, Mao's Cultural Revolution and Pol Pot's killing fields. Despite the fact that liberal democracy has also produced bouts of violent militarism and repression (see Zinn, 2010; Losurdo, 2011; Seymour, 2012) – including the genocide of native peoples, the forced starvation of millions in Africa and the Indian sub-continent, the democratic election of Hitler, Truman's sanctioning of the use of atomic bombs at Hiroshima and Nagasaki and myriad post-war 'interventions' – the people always appeared willing to give liberalism another chance. The horrors that have been carried out by democratically elected governments tend to be understood as contingent, reflective of the failures of particular administrations, the pathologies of key individuals or provocation by non-democratic 'alien' cultures. Liberal democracy allowed the people to dispose of these flawed individuals and administrations, reluctantly deal with the 'others' and start again; the horrors perpetrated by particular democratically-elected administrations seemed unrelated to the structure and core values of liberal democracy itself.

In liberalism's ideological universe the opposite holds true for communism. Public opinion seems persuaded that the very idea itself contains within it the unavoidable drive towards mass extermination and the exploitation and brutalisation of minorities. This rather crude distinction between two modes of political and economic organisation informs the exhaustion of history in the later years of the twentieth century (see Žižek, 2001). Throughout that century communism had been capitalism's main ideological opponent. By the end of it, only capitalism remained acceptable to the major constituencies of Western populations. Even with capitalism slumped on the ropes, communism appeared incapable of re-engaging its opponent to take advantage of its weakened condition. It conjured up black and white images in the popular imagination of Soviet-style repression, austerity, drudgery, crushing poverty and bland cultural homogeneity. Alternatively, capitalism, even during its bad times, was painted in *Technicolor* hues that suggested vitality, diversity, creativity, freedom and choice. Would the people willingly turn away from the shallow pleasures of consumerism and commit to the task of building a new order with equality at its heart? Even as the deep social harms caused by the 2008 crash began to reveal themselves, the answer appeared to be a resounding 'no'.

As quickly as it had arisen, the real politics of protest and dissent returned to the background. There was no clear political ideology for people to rally around, no clear narrative of progressive change that people could believe in. Dissatisfaction with the existing order seemed abundant, but it could not be channelled in a way that might lead to progressive social change and a world beyond parliamentary capitalism and the predictable social destruction caused by the 'business cycle'. This fundamental ideological absence seemed to allow capitalism to continue by default. Few ordinary worker-consumers really believed that capitalism represented the Good, but most would grudgingly accept that it remained the least worst of those political and economic systems that were immediately conceivable. The cultural consequences of this basic lack of a constructive political and ideological engagement are quite considerable, and we will discuss them at greater length later in the book. For the moment, we simply need to note that this strange ahistorical inertia allowed the pragmatic administrators of neoliberal parliamentary capitalism to continue onwards, buoyed by electoral victories that handed them a democratic mandate to govern. Securely in office, and after the clear failure of global neoliberalism and abstract financial markets, they turned their attention to the holy texts of neoclassical economics in search of a means of jump-starting the stalled global neoliberal juggernaut. In this move, which has caused deep unease in some groups on the broad left, the failure of neoliberalism – most clearly expressed in the 2008 crash and its continuing aftermath – may not inspire greater market regulation.

As we write these words, the opposite appears more likely. The ideologues of the neoliberal right have waged an unwavering and pervasive campaign to blame intrusive and spendthrift governments adhering to the Keynesian principle of deficit spending for the continuing economic debacle (see for example Sirico, 2012). For them, the market collapse should not be interpreted as the failure of free market economics. Rather, the model of the free market proposed by Smith and adapted by Friedman and Hayek had not been applied correctly by overly tentative administrations through the 1990s and the early years of the twenty-first century (Harcourt, 2010). The market model is not to blame; rather, individuals within it misbehaved, and they should be identified and punished. Indeed, governments should have done more to weed out wrongdoing during the boom times of neoliberal expansion. Governments had also continued to spend too much money on expansive welfare systems. They had spent wildly beyond their means, and as a result huge structural deficits plague America and many European states. In a move that echoes former White House Chief of Staff Rahm Emanuel's famous dictum, 'never let a good crisis go to waste', the key strategy of the neoliberal right appears to be to cut taxes and regulation as a means of getting flat-lining economies back to growth. The end point, for the neoliberal right, is a purer market system that is no longer hamstrung by interventionist government, even in a constrained 'third way' form. This, they are sure, will inspire entrepreneurship and investment, encourage consumers to throw themselves into a new era of credit-fuelled spending and return Western economies back to the levels of economic growth that benefit all citizens. Of course, many of those on the liberal and social democratic left are deeply anxious that the 'answer' to a global crisis of neoliberalism might be a purer and yet more aggressive variant of neoliberalism.

The contemporary intervallic period continues to be determined by the logic of the old neoliberal order; we are still incapable of thinking beyond the logic of markets and economic growth, and it is still impossible to think about any political system that is not dependent upon electoral democracy. Despite this, cynicism, scepticism and fatalism are abundant. We have little faith in neoliberal capitalism or the parliamentary system that accompanies it, but we also have little faith in any of the alternatives currently on offer, or in our ability to actively intervene in history to make a positive change. The contemporary neoliberal order therefore rules by default. Its popular image as the 'least worst' political and economic system allows it to continue, at least until oppositional political movements can construct a clear narrative of something better that everyday people can believe in. Despite all of this, neoliberalism's glossy image has been sullied by recent events and in a very practical sense it seems that it will be some time before we see a return to the levels of economic growth and prosperity for which neoliberalism, entirely unjustifiably (Harvey, 2007), is famed. Political opposition remains, but has yet to coalesce into a genuine ideological alternative that can inspire ordinary people. Can neoliberalism continue to secure its dominance by default? Is it possible for neoliberalism to win back popular support? If the drive of most of the political opponents of neoliberalism is to rehabilitate what currently exists (see Winlow and Hall, 2012b), might we see a return to the social democratic capitalism of the post-war period? At the moment it seems like the most probable outcome is that capitalism will continue, but it is also likely that capitalism will respond in some way to today's rather inarticulate popular dissatisfaction.

What next?

Historically, capitalism has proven itself to be remarkably mutable. Indeed, the history of capitalism in the West is often understood in relation to an ongoing process of perpetual but often imperceptible change. The industrial revolution of the late eighteenth and early nineteenth centuries established centres of mass production, but also brought with it child labour, disease and naked exploitation. A second industrial revolution brought us functional steam engines and the ability to mass produce steel. Then we saw the arrival of early mass consumerism and the mass production of plastics and cars; the growth of the global market and the movement of centres of production to developing countries; the rise of the global mass media and its associated lifestyle consumerism; and the relatively recent development of 'new media' and associated postmodern developments in the way humans 'add value' to basic materials and products (see Gorz, 2010b, 2010c). All of these changes, and a good deal more besides, affected our societies and modes of living, and shaped our cultures, tastes and political preferences. In the popular imagination markets are inextricably bound to the experience of change, while other forms of economic organisation can often appear static, and only change when forced to by circumstance (see Sahlins, 2003; Heilbroner and Milberg, 2011). Capitalism's apparent dynamism sets it apart from the command economies of communist countries and the traditional economies of earlier societies. It is only in market economies that the logic of 'economics' can develop.

Of course, not all changes that have taken place within capitalist economies are related to technological developments, or the exhaustion of old markets and the establishment of new ones. Capitalism has also been forced to change by social and political responses to its asocial profit motive and the recurrent 'boom and bust' of the business cycle. We should see these changes in relation to the complexities of historical processes, as counternarratives have arisen and sought to challenge the established orthodoxies of capitalist market development. While its underlying logic has remained pretty much intact (see Marx, 2008[1867]; Smith, 2008[1776]; Arrighi, 2009), historically capitalism has passed through a number of quite distinct phases. But we should make no mistake: capitalism has changed not on ethical grounds but when it has been expedient for it to do so in order to maintain or increase its fundamental drive, profitability (see Mattick, 2011). We should understand capitalism as a blind, abstract economic system, governed by financial calculations of investment and profitability, and free from any genuine grounding in morality or social needs. It is wrong to attempt to 'humanise' capitalism by projecting human characteristics on to its organisation of markets and capital flows. Rather, the best that can be hoped for is that capital's raw power can be adequately regulated by ethical forces in civil society. Market ideologues pursue the idea that the morality of those individuals involved in markets should work to ensure that harmful activities are avoided (Friedman, 1993, 2002), but this tends to marginalise the fact that capitalism itself possesses a reality that exists beyond our immediate experience of economic processes. As history shows quite clearly, those who work within capitalist organisations do not imbue capitalism with ethical qualities. Rather the reverse is true: ethical individuals can find themselves drawn into ruthless activities that would, outside of the work setting, be entirely unthinkable (Bakan, 2005). In this way, capitalist enterprises can cause quite incredible harms (see Slapper and Tombs, 1999;

Burdis and Tombs, 2012; Tombs and Whyte, 2012) despite the fact that those working in these organisations believe themselves to be fundamentally moral individuals. Rather than suggest that all of those who work at a senior level in corporations and sanction harmful activities are essentially immoral, it makes more sense to identify the corporation itself as an entity entirely unconnected to conventional morality. It may become involved in good deeds and charitable endeavours, but even here, it does so in order to gain an advantage in the marketplace. This is not to say that immoral individuals do not exist as agents of reproduction in the corporate and political world, or indeed that their immorality can often engender success before it leaks across the boundary into criminality (see Hall, 2012a), only that punishing them would not 'moralise' the system itself.

We should extend this logic to the transformation of capitalism throughout the twentieth century. Capitalism does not change as a result of its own moral or ethical self-analysis; *it changes only so that it may continue.* In Europe, the raw brutality and amoral exploitation that accompanied early capitalism were tempered by the rise of oppositional political discourses, the most notable of which was the working-class 'solidarity project' that made significant progress at the end of the nineteenth century and during the first three decades of the twentieth century (Garland, 2001; Reiner, 2007; Hall, 2012a). At the dawn of the twentieth century the British political representatives of capital introduced piecemeal reform and the first suggestions of state welfare, but the First World War and the great global crash of the 1920s and 1930s made social injustice more striking and the threat of radical social change was, for a time, very real (Hobsbawm, 1989, 1995).

The 'welfare capitalism' of the post-1945 epoch followed, and represented a new phase in capitalism's development in Europe. This new, more restrained capitalism was structured in relation to a historic class compromise between the interests of labour and the interests of capital: the working classes received an expansive welfare system and significant improvements to their lifestyles. The gap between rich and poor narrowed significantly and the working classes formed institutions that could successfully represent their interests against those of capital. Throughout the post-war period generations of working-class men and women were able to conceive of a positive and secure future for their children and the possibility of upward social mobility and relative financial security. On the other side, in an era where Soviet communism had not been entirely discredited and still posed an ideological threat, capital avoided a more radical intervention that might have threatened its continuity in Britain and elsewhere. The aggressive asocial accumulation of early industrial capitalism had given way to a welfarist, social democratic variant. The raw destructive power of the profit motive was now restrained by significant government regulation and politically-informed worker militancy. It is possible to see a similar pattern in the development of American capitalism during this same period. Despite seeming like a direct affront to the interests of capital, Roosevelt's New Deal might have effectively *saved* capitalism, inasmuch as it attempted to address the significant human costs of the great depression and placate the political radicalism that appeared to be developing among the poor and the industrial working class. As we have seen, the New Deal did improve the lives of the poorest, but it also allowed capitalism itself to continue, a process that accelerated as US preparation for the Second World War boosted demand in the economy. Political radicalism declined as prosperity rose, and a growing number of people were once again relatively sanguine about their lives in a capitalist system administered by a newly interventionist government now willing to provide a basic foundation of socioeconomic security upon which the vast majority could build a satisfying life. Without the New Deal, the history of the 'American Century' (Evans, 1998) would have been very different indeed.

Of course, compromise usually means that neither party is left entirely content. Those who believed capitalism itself to be fundamentally unjust faced the continuation of a class-ridden social system replete with structural inequality and injustice. In Britain, the destructive power of the profit motive was still restrained by the dam that had been constructed by the social democratic state. However, if systems of containment are not maintained, this destructive power is always capable of returning to further disrupt social life. Of course, the agents of neoliberalism viewed these state regulations with considerable displeasure; checks and balances prevented capital from extending its influence over the whole planet to extract resources from every available environment and squeeze the last drop of surplus value from waged labour. Neither contestant had landed a knock-out blow, but both could reasonably claim to have hurt the opponent. A rematch seemed likely.

Social protest against entrenched power grew during the 1960s and 1970s, and reached a high-point in the Paris uprising in 1968 (Ross, 2004; Seidman, 2004). This was not simply an uprising of the organised working classes against the interests of capital, as was often the case before 1939. Crucially, workers, trade unionists, students and intellectuals all took to the streets, and it is this amalgamation of quite distinct social groups under the banner of progressive politics which is noticeably absent from today's post-political protests (Winlow and Hall, 2012b). While American imperialism appears to have been a key issue for many of those involved, the basic narrative that drew disparate groups together involved a fight against socioeconomic predestination and inequality. Despite ongoing attempts to cloak the events of 1968 in the more socially acceptable garb of ethical and cultural opposition, they were in fact a *political* intervention, a genuine historical event in the Badiouian sense (Hallward, 2003; Badiou, 2011). Those involved clearly sought to transform the political and economic field, not simply register their displeasure about the direction of government policy.

As a result of these upheavals, and the growth of new forms of political opposition around the world (see for example, Borabaugh, 1992; Follain, 1999; Baumann, 2001; Zinn, 2005; Aust, 2008; Rudd, 2010; Orsini, 2011), capital found itself in crisis. If capitalism was to retain its place as the dominant global socioeconomic system, it must once again change with the times. But what else could capital concede to its political opponents? Opposition to its rule was no longer restricted to the industrial working class, and it was unlikely that the further expansion of the welfare state would stem the continuous flow of criticism. Its primary strategy appears to have been a concerted attempt to alter commonly held attitudes to its rule. If a significant number of people were disgusted by capitalism's inequalities and harms, it would have to become *something else* if it were to keep rolling forward (Žižek, 2008a).

The altered capitalist socioeconomic and cultural order that followed the upheavals of the late 1960s is a clear indication of the system's inherent dynamism, adaptability and logic of continuity at all costs. Boltanski and Chiapello (2007) analysed some of the major changes that occurred as a result of the radical interventions that were made during this tumultuous time. First, capital appeared to abandon its austere, patriarchal and steeply hierarchical image to present itself as a champion of social justice and improvement. The stuffy pinstriped image of 1950s capitalism evolved into the ostensibly open and 'democratic' hippy capitalism of the latter decades of the twentieth century (Frank, 1998; Heath and Potter, 2006). Post-1968 capitalism was represented by Richard Branson or Bill Gates rather than Henry Ford or John D. Rockefeller. 'Countercultural capitalism' took on the image of dynamic creativity and invention and appropriated many of the left's most valuable tropes: fairness, equality, justice and freedom were all captured by the neoliberal political discourse.

This new form of capitalism mocked the modernist state's ponderous bureaucracies and restrictive legal frameworks. Instead, it presented its new business activities as a battle fought on behalf of the creative individual against the stuffy old order. Its new image rammed home the message that it wasn't all about money but freeing up individuals as designers and producers of lifestyles to respond to the challenges of building something of value, expressing themselves creatively and providing consumers with products that could improve their lives. Once individual freedom, prosperity and lifestyle enhancement were assured, the new breed of savvy capitalists could then turn their attention to the plight of the poor and the destitute, but, unlike the patriarchal industrial philanthropists of earlier eras, their help would transcend mere financial support. They would apply their boundless creativity to solve the problem of reintegrating excluded populations into the sexy business of minimally restricted global commerce. Post-1968 capitalism would welcome all into its new meritocratic and socially permeable order. It didn't matter where you were from; it was about where you were at. The suitably revamped ideals of the American Dream appeared rapidly to traverse the globe. Now anyone with an idea and a work ethic could fight their way to the very top. Sure, inequality existed, but hard work could overcome any barrier placed before it. And no longer did you have to be a duplicitous, asocial, avaricious bastard in order to make it to the top (although behind the scenes these characteristics can certainly help – see Babiak and Hare, 2007). Rather, the new cultural capitalists wanted to put people first. Marxism, socialism and the other old leftist discourses of the twentieth century were declared dead. Capitalism itself would be the tool that would constantly improve the quality of life and empower all individuals to transform themselves into whatever they wanted to be.

In a remarkable about-face, capitalism had positioned itself as the answer to the problems of under-development and poverty rather than their cause (see Žižek, 2008a; Fisher, 2009). The way to solve entrenched harms and inequalities, in the developing world and elsewhere, was no longer to simply throw money at the problem; after all, life is not all about money! State administrations were corrupt and could no longer be trusted, and sclerotic bureaucratic agencies appeared incapable of successfully pursuing the strategies that could improve the lives of the poorest and integrate them into the global framework of the twenty-first century market economy. For post-1968 capitalists and their new 'third way' representatives in government, the answer seemed obvious: the best way to truly alleviate suffering and include the excluded was to introduce the market to poor areas. This would then encourage development and employment by means of creative and ambitious entrepreneurship (see Sirico, 2012). Hope was the biggest gift the state and various philanthropic individuals could give the poor. People needed to be shown what could be achieved with a little bit of ambition, application and resolve; all those with elementary educational skills could compete and become rich and successful. The market would give people the opportunity to become self-reliant and to develop the skills necessary to improve their lifestyles and those of their communities. The fundamental socioeconomic logic of capitalism, that some are rich *because* some are poor, was hidden behind a spectacle staged to hammer home the message that the best way for everyone to improve their lot was to apply unrestricted individual creativity to the task of making an ever larger pie.

Capitalism itself was no longer represented as the locus of power. The economic crisis of the 1970s appeared to suggest that the expansive welfare states and careful Keynesian economic management of the social democratic era were at an end. Rapid globalisation demanded the end of protectionism, capital controls, deficit spending and state involvement in the economy. In order to grow, states must liberalise their economies, encourage entrepreneurship, reduce taxes on wealth and throw themselves into the interminable battle to attract economic investment (see Friedman, 1993) by increasing productivity, lowering taxes and allowing the market to set wages. As Baroness

Thatcher famously observed in one of her oft-repeated catchphrases, *there is no alternative* to the liberalisation of the economy. Neoliberalism rose and spread across the globe and, despite the fact that it was prone to regular destructive convulsions (Harvey, 2007), the neoliberal 'Washington Consensus' was installed in key global economic institutions such as the World Bank, The World Trade Organisation and the International Monetary Fund. The answer to problems of state funding would, from the 1980s onwards, always involve cuts in spending, the privatisation of state services and the further liberalisation of the economy (see Chang, 2002, 2008; Peet, 2009). From its outset, neoliberalism failed to replicate the economic growth of the social democratic post-war period, but somehow it still managed to convince an electorally significant majority of Western populations that it was the only economic system likely to lead to the expansion of national economies and significant improvements to the lifestyles of everyday people (Harvey, 2007). Over time, neoliberalism shed its initially obvious ideological character. It became so ubiquitous, and its logic so entrenched in government, the media and the academy that it became *common sense*, the *doxa* that, in the absence of a plausible alternative, most took for granted.

However, 'the absence of a plausible alternative' is the key phrase. The ideas of the ruling class no longer needed to rule, or even to manufacture consent, in the traditional positive Marxist and Gramscian senses. We had entered the era of negative ideology, the end point of Adorno's (1981) negative dialectics, in which all ethical positivities are destroyed to leave nothing but the system's pure energy, and consent, no matter how begrudged, had become the default *doxic* position. The rise of neoliberalism was founded upon the disorganisation of political opposition and the systematic marginalisation of intellectuals willing to articulate an alternative economic model to a mainstream audience. In our daily newspapers or on our television sets, anyone advocating significant changes to the neoliberal tax regime or greater state involvement in the formal economy risked popular derision and instant dismissal as a laughably unworldly utopian, and might even be characterised as a potential terrorist threatening fundamental Western values (see Zaitchik, 2010). On the one hand people were told that anything was possible – holidays in space, cloned sheep, enhanced intellects by means of smart drugs – but any suggestion that the state should consider tax rises for the rich was impossible, an assault on freedom and a hindrance to wealth-creation. As much as they might like to encourage the rich to contribute more, politicians from all major parties were forced to accept the dominant logic; any attempt to raise taxes for the rich would reduce economic growth, investment and net tax receipts, and would therefore ultimately end up further disadvantaging the disadvantaged. Neoliberal hegemony from the 1980s onwards ensured that capitalism as an economic system secured unrivalled supremacy in the realm of ideas. After the collapse of the Berlin wall and the end of Soviet communism it seemed as if capitalism had triumphed over its only genuine opposition. The majority of left-wing radicals gave up calling for the end of capitalism; now, the most that they asked for was that the state attempt to curb some of capitalism's worst excesses.

Thus capitalism's ultimate victory over its ideological foes ensured that its logic became so ubiquitous that it was no longer considered 'ideological'. Capitalism had simply become 'the economy'. According to its expansive pool of pragmatists and committed propagandists, capitalism had patently proven itself to be the economic system best able to give the people what they want (see Friedman, 2000). By the end of the twentieth century, this became so obvious that it no longer required further thought; the liberal mind that prided itself on its 'openness' was closed on the matter of the economic system. Even in academia, the putative hothouse of free intellectual endeavour, critical discussion of capitalism virtually disappeared (Winlow, 2012a). Instead of debating the fundamental underpinnings and outcomes of the capitalist economy, our news media became obsessed with 'the markets', a reified postmodern abstraction that appeared to take on a life of its own. Our morning news broadcasts were accompanied by details of the latest fluctuations in world markets, which 'thought', 'responded', 'got worried' and 'liked' as if they were your Uncle George. Similarly, reports on consumer spending seemed to imagine that the audience was sitting at home praying that more money would flow into the coffers of High Street shops, believing this would positively impact upon their own economic position in some way. Even as we write, in 2012, in the middle of a serious double-dip recession, Britain's Chancellor of the Exchequer, George Osborne, structures his economic policy in relation to what he believes 'the markets' want to see. For him, the fact that Britain has retained its AAA credit rating is taken to be irrefutable evidence that his government's aggressive austerity cuts are the best of all available options for addressing the structural deficit. However, because 'the markets' are, as we have said, a reified abstraction, they do not think with one mind and they do not act in accordance with scientific laws. Indeed, they are often entirely irrational, and prone to the 'animal spirits' observed by Keynes (2008[1936]) as he analysed the path to the Great Depression. Despite his carefully coiffured image as a pragmatist, Osborne's desire to satisfy 'the markets' reveals his fidelity to a specific ideological category.

The disappearance of 'capitalism' as an object of critical analysis before the crash in 2008 is a telling indication of the ideological uniformity that had taken root in politics and academia. Capitalism's transformation into 'the economy' depoliticised thinking in general. Traditional debates about material equality and exploitation were supplanted by new politically neutralised debates about tolerance, social mobility, social networks, and empowerment. Some degree of structural inequality – although no one ever put their finger on how much – appeared to be largely accepted as 'natural', a mere reflection of the organic differentials in talent and determination and the selfish and competitive tendencies of our species (see von Mises, 2007[1949]; Kaletsky, 2011). Governments could attempt to enable the 'talented' poor to improve their social status, but there was nothing that could be done about inequality itself; the possibility that there existed an inexorably less 'talented' poor was simply not discussed. Most politicians accepted that the market was simply geared towards creating the economic growth that would benefit the vast majority of socially included individuals. If problems did arise, these should not be considered as problems of capitalism *per se*. Rather, they were connected to unfortunate or lazy individuals who were either unable or wilfully reluctant to apply themselves to economic activity; the former should be helped to compete, the latter should simply be removed from society. Such issues were to be administered as cost-effectively as possible by the politicians and social managers who administer capitalism (see Friedman, 1993). All the liberal-left could muster by way of riposte were constant repetitive complaints about inevitable social inequality and the loss of welfare rights and logically impossible economic opportunities.

In liberal democracies, the next election should provide the people with the opportunity to change things. If they are dissatisfied with the performance of the economy, they can choose another political party to take the reins. Importantly, the ire of the poor has successfully been channelled away from the structural inequities of politico-economic relationships and towards corrupt, self-interested or weak politicians. The manifold problems of the new communicative capitalism (see Dean, 2009) have been moved from the economic sphere to the cultural and ethical spheres. Neoliberal propagandists proclaimed all the malignant injustices and excesses of capitalism's previous incarnations to have been successfully purged. Neoliberal capitalism was not the enemy of fairness, justice and equality; it was in fact the very tool that could put these things into practice.

Even today, too often those on the left imagine capitalism to be simply a system of economic exploitation orchestrated by a super-stratum of incredibly wealthy and powerful individuals attempting to defend their privileges and reproduce their evaluated social status. By extension, if it were possible to depose the membership of this super-elite, a new period of inclusivity and justice would return to the post-political West. Of course elites continue to be integral to the reproduction of contemporary global capitalism, but these days it seems more accurate to invert the nature of this relationship and suggest that, rather than an elite pulling the strings to which the world dances, it is capital itself that structures our economic and political life and shapes our shared cultures and identities. We can see a revealing illustration of this in the new liberalised left's reaction to the 2008 global economic crash. Vitriolic critique was aimed at Wall Street's 'Masters of the Universe' and the key individuals in government who decided to liberate financial capitalism from its regulatory framework (Žižek, 2009b; Ferguson, 2012). The banking industry's culture of greed and self-interest was also subject to popular critique, as was its absurd bonus system, which appeared extravagantly to reward failure, gross misconduct and systemic corruption. In the aftermath of the crash, as people faced rising unemployment and reductions in welfare, pensions and standards of living, this new, liberal-leftist critique of banking excess and political corruption appeared to carry the day. Even those on the neoliberal right were compelled to engage in a measure of attenuated 'banker bashing' in order to ensure they did not alienate the voting public too much.

However, while these attacks upon the fundamental failure and striking immorality of abstract finance capitalism and its agents pandered to popular sentiments, one cannot help but conclude that an opportunity was lost to build on the general public's initial rancour. Rather than identify key individuals who behaved inappropriately and demand that they be prosecuted and punished, it might have been more productive to identify the actual nature of capitalist expansionism and the interminable business cycles of the marketplace as the fundamental issue at stake (Žižek, 2008a, 2009b), and, more fundamentally, identify the levelling off of the 200-year-old high growth and profitability curves without which capitalist expansion cannot continue (Mattick, 2011). After all, bankers were doing only what we should have expected them to do (ibid.; see also Wolff, 2010). Why would we believe that they would fearlessly challenge the fundamental logic of their business operations and their work cultures, adopt pro-social attitudes and attenuate their wild risk-taking when they had so much to gain from them? Bankers are fully integrated into the liberal-capitalist market system and see themselves as socially productive in relation to the tax revenues generated by their industry. They believe they work very hard, that they are immensely 'talented' and therefore fully deserve their 'special liberty' (see Hall, 2012a) and their extravagant remuneration (see Toynbee and Walker, 2009; Burdis and Tombs, 2012). Even after the crash of 2008, we must assume that they are still convinced that at least some form and degree of speculative risk-taking is exactly what the crisis-ridden system needs to get the economy moving again. There is no doubt that the banking industry's generous bonus system worked in tandem with the socialisation of risks to ensure increasingly reckless gambling (Harvey, 2010), but this does not detract from the fact that the fundamental problem lies not with bankers but with the system of capitalism itself. The 2008 crash was precisely that: a tumultuous yet predictable global economic adjustment (see Gorz, 2010c; Roubini, 2011; Stiglitz, 2010) reflective of the inevitable flaws that accompany capitalism's total reliance on markets (Harvey, 2010; Wolff, 2010). If we are to criticise bankers and supine politicians, it should be for their roles as reproductive agents of the ideology and practices that sustain the system and suffocate oppositional politics, not simply as incompetent, unethical and self-interested functionaries of the system itself.

Recentralising the actuality of capitalism's economic logic in academic and popular-political discourse, rather than passing it off as an ethical or organisational problem, might have contributed in some way to the return of productive dialectical politics. If the broad left is to advance its position from this point, it must surely do more to problematise the basic foundations of our collective socioeconomic life and encourage everyday people to see their own hardships in relation to it. As things stand, it seems like the aggressive denunciation of the banking industry has merely fed into a blind, apolitical dissatisfaction and cynicism that appears incapable of animating a new and progressive politics.

Just as decrying the banking industry appears to be a political dead-end, so the liberal left's critique of capitalism's super-elite fails to identify the real adversary of social justice and economic inclusivity. We would suggest that, rather than the super-rich controlling capitalism, capitalism's logic and base drives intrude upon the lives of the super-rich and cultivate in the emotional depths of their being the ideologies that ensure capitalism's continuity (Johnston, 2008; Žižek, 2009a, 2009c; Burdis and Tombs, 2012; Hall 2012a; 2012b). The ideology of capitalism then 'speaks through' an unconsciously impassioned super-rich, animating them and constructing their world view, driving them forever forwards to new accomplishments and ventures, and previously unimaginable levels of affluence. It may look like powerful billionaires are controlling the world economy, but we should instead consider them to be mere beneficiaries that capitalism can discard at any time. The Richard Bransons of this world come and go, as do our political leaders. In pursuing their apparently instrumental political or economic agendas, they blindly contribute to the reproduction of contemporary liberal capitalism. For them, we submit, there is no fully conscious desire to dedicate themselves to the endless reproduction of capitalist realism. Rather, that endless reproduction is an *outcome* of their everyday social action and business activity. The ruling ideology secures its rule these days by structuring actual social behaviour and harnessing unconscious human energy. The old world strategies of ideological mystification and the manipulation of consciousness are now far less important (Žižek, 2009a, 2011). The new breed of dedicated business people may see themselves as separate from the logic of liberal capitalism, engaging with capitalism in an instrumental way while never submitting entirely to its ideological content. However, in their very instrumentality they unconsciously reproduce capitalism, contributing the libidinal energy it needs to move forwards. The same is true of many across the West who believe they see the truth of capitalism. They may believe capitalism to be a monstrous aberration, but their critique matters little if they continue to fulfil their ascribed role as worker-consumer. They may flee the archetypal high street institutions in search of ethical services and sustainable economic relationships, or to free themselves from the stultifying homogeneity of mass consumer culture. However, rather than threatening capitalist hegemony, this behaviour perversely reasserts the dominance of a capitalism that has successfully incorporated and commodified dissent. Capitalism no longer merely manufactures consent; it manufactures dissent of the type it needs to continue on its way.

Žižek (2008a) suggests we see these processes in stark relief when we address the rise of the postmodern capitalism's 'liberal communists'. For Žižek, these liberal communists present themselves as the champions of social justice and upward mobility. They want to help people trapped in difficult circumstances and they are willing to use their considerable resources to attempt to alleviate suffering and want. Their approach is often to bypass sluggish state systems in order to get help on the ground as quickly as possible. Their easy-going liberalism also allows them to consider giving away things for free. They aren't as selfish and money-hungry as the traditional stereotype suggests. Rather, they are in business as a means of expressing their creativity in a socially productive way. They like to set themselves challenges, but they always hope there is a pay-off for all of humanity. The 'freedom' of the internet, and of key service and networking sites, suggests a new capitalism of openness and enablement rather than one of exploitation and private gain. Indeed, many of the world's billionaires are committed philanthropists. Bill Gates has undertaken to give away a significant proportion of his wealth to worthy causes. What does this tell us about the contemporary relationship between capitalism and capitalists?

Žižek (2008a) argues that Bill Gates and others are effectively taking with one hand and giving with the other in order to ensure that the externalities of markets do not become so extreme that they inspire serious political dissent and intervention. In this way, Gates is held in thrall by the seductive ideologies of liberal capitalism to the extent that he abandons individualistic conceptions of wealth and personal accumulation in order to lubricate the gears of global capitalist markets, pumping billions of dollars back into the system. Gates and others are *determined* by the needs of liberal capitalism. It is not Gates who *determines* the reality of this economic system at all. In the standard manner, he collects the abundant rent that flows from his business activities, but he then allows the money to flow back to those most in need, inserting as many lucky beneficiaries as he can into the investment cycle as intermediaries. Indeed, Gates himself acknowledges the absurdity of an economic system that allows individuals to accumulate so much wealth that it becomes impossible to spend. But his vast wealth, and the wealth of others in a similar position, must never be considered an end-point, the termination of anxious competition and risk-taking and the start of a new life of indulgent repose. As we have long known, philanthropy usually fails to address the root causes of distress and want. Instead it alleviates immediate suffering, gives the philanthropist a warm glow, and allows the world to carry on roughly as it is.

Above all, capital must remain in motion. It must be constantly reinvested. Indeed, this drive to reinvest capital played a considerable role in the banking crisis of 2008. In America, from the 1980s onwards, neoliberalism placed downward pressure on wages and simultaneously increased productivity (see Chang, 2011; Wolff, 2010). A huge pool of surplus capital developed, seeking profitable investment opportunities. A vital new opportunity came with the rapid development of abstract financial mechanisms through the 1980s and1990s and the accompanying deregulation of the sector. So much surplus capital existed that new investment opportunities needed to be created. If capital cannot find a reasonable investment opportunity, it returns to its original state and becomes once again merely money, a process that threatens the continuity of the entire system. Indeed, one of the major problems we face in encouraging Western economies back to growth is the unwillingness of the super-rich to risk investing in what is a decidedly sclerotic economic situation in both the USA and the Eurozone.

We gain a further insight here if we draw together Lacan's various observations about the nature of capitalism. One of his most counterintuitive and interesting claims is that, in capitalism, we all occupy the position of the proletarian. Despite being ostensibly a society dedicated to solipsistic, self-indulgent pleasures, we are in fact condemned to suffer a basic lack of libidinal enjoyment. As we will discuss later, contemporary liberal capitalism issues a cultural injunction to enjoy (Hall et al., 2008; Žižek, 2009a, 2009c). We must invest heavily in the symbolism of consumer experiences and strive to attain them, despite being forever incapable of fully realising the condition of ultimate pleasure for which we are taught to yearn. We are compelled to seek enjoyment in an endless repetitive loop, and failure to be actively involved in the search for pleasure ensures the ignominy of cultural inconsequentiality and causes deep social anxiety. For Lacan (2008; see also Zupancic 2006; Žižek, 2006a), we are encouraged to form relationships with objects rather than with other subjects. These objects must hold out the promise of pleasure but always fail to deliver it. Lacan's work is directly relevant to our discussion of 'liberal communists' as his analysis of capitalism suggests that the constant drive to reinvest capital deprives the capitalist of enjoyment. The capitalist is trapped in a vicious circle, exploited by objects that hold the promise of weakened libidinal enjoyment. Do we not see this in the mediatised lives of successful business people? Surrounded by sports cars, yachts and the other symbols of consumer wealth, they become bored and unimpressed, and are forced back out to the market to discover yet more surplus value. They look at the objects that yesterday seemed so alluring and feel entirely apathetic towards them, and then begin the process of accumulation all over again in the hope that future objects might provide the libidinal satisfaction they seek. For Lacan, the rich capitalist is master of nothing. Like the proletarian, he too is exploited by the objects he is compelled to desire. He derives no greater satisfaction, no greater enjoyment, than the proletarian, despite possessing the capacity to fritter away money on every passing whim. The true issue at stake, for Lacan, is the nature of a social order that encourages the subject to connect to objects that appear to carry libidinal enjoyment. This appears to encourage the subject to disconnect from other subjects as it pursues its infatuation with the object. As Lacan repeatedly stresses, libidinal enjoyment does not create bonds between subjects. Rather libidinal enjoyment tends to separate subjects. Only love brings them together (see also Badiou, 2012b).

This approach suggests that we should attempt to develop a more complex understanding of the nature of contemporary consumer capitalism. Elsewhere we have claimed that capital itself should now be placed in the Lacanian realm of the obscene Real (see glossary) (Hall, 2012a; Winlow, 2012a; Winlow and Hall, 2012b). In these times of global economic collapse, is it not possible to see capital as the unspeakable *Thing* that dominates our lives? Surely it is now clear that capitalism has a reality that goes beyond the mere sum of human economic activity? And further, is it not time to move our attention away from the problems caused by capitalism, and instead identify *capitalism itself* as the fundamental problem we face? We see this most clearly with the rise to prominence of abstract finance capital. Capitalism itself is an abstraction with profoundly important transformative effects that shape the lives of the richest as well as the poorest. While it may appear that the rich possess a basic agency in relation to their social and economic engagement, and even attain the heady heights of 'special liberty' in the ability to play out their deepest desires in the worlds of consumer objects, hedonistic pleasures and political power (Hall, 2012a), we should consider the possibility that they too are shaped by liberal capitalism's dynamic and incisive ideology. In relation to social exclusion and advanced economic marginality, it is a mistake to see the super-rich as entirely the cause of the problems faced by the poorest. Instead, the fundamental issue at stake is a capitalist economy that insists on its own reproduction, that blindly follows its own interests, driving relentlessly forward entirely ignorant of the human costs of its activities. In the next chapter we try to connect capitalism's inhuman drive to simply persist to the dispiriting world of liberal democratic politics.

5

Politics at the End
of History

The implosion of neoliberal political economy in 2008 has significant implications for the social structure of contemporary Western societies. We should expect the problem of social exclusion to grow and evolve in the years to come, although how this growth will affect politics and the social order remains to be seen. We will of course try to identify a number of pertinent issues as the rest of the book unfolds. But why should we focus so directly on the current economic crisis in a book about social exclusion? There is of course a crucial if rather basic connection between the two in the form of net reductions in employment opportunities and a renewed political and economic drive to reduce wages and restrict the legal entitlements of low-wage earners. As we saw earlier, the pressure currently being placed upon tax revenues in a shrinking economy is already encouraging the political elite to return to standard classical liberal narratives of self-sufficiency and the rapid removal of indulgent welfare regimes. In the current ideological climate, our economic situation demands that employers are provided with increased freedoms to dispose of workers quickly and without fuss. Similarly, it now appears to make perfect sense to cut welfare benefits, the minimum wage and support for young people entering education so that the economy can be liberated and quickly return to growth. At the other end of the class system, of course, cutting taxes on wealth and income seems sensible, as do cuts in corporation tax and programmes of quantitative easing that have been proven to disproportionately benefit the super-rich (Elliot, 2012). However, there is also a more complex economic connection to be found in the continued transformation of our shared social life, a process that continues apace during these years of economic crisis. We will discuss this in more detail in the next chapter.

In the meantime, we must recognise the fundamental changes that have taken place on the political field. Despite understandable popular disillusionment, politics is the field in which we create our social and economic future, and it is of course the field on which we address inequality, justice and the various problems associated with social exclusion and advanced marginality. However, fundamental changes have taken place in the field of mainstream politics, changes that deprive us of the opportunity to take decisive collective action about our shared future. When young people observe that politics is bland and characterless, they are entirely correct. But this need not be a universal feature of politics itself. Politics has become like this because genuine alternatives to our current way of life have been removed from the field and are no longer considered pertinent to mainstream debate. As we discuss below, it appears that most politicians these days agree that we have essentially found a formula for organising a twenty-first century state that surpasses all others. And of course once politicians of all political parties agree on the basic foundations of our world, all that's left to discuss are relatively small and rather dull aspects of policy formation. So it makes sense that more and more people believe the entire spectacle of contemporary politics to be boring, irrelevant, cynical and corrupt. As many voters observe, no matter which party wins office, the basic coordinates of everyday life remain pretty much the same.

There is also a growing feeling that our politicians have ceased to represent the interests of ordinary working and non-working people. In Britain, our politicians appear to have little sense of what the world is like beyond the restricted cultural life of Westminster. They pass from elite universities to junior government positions before moving on to senior positions within their respective parties without ever experiencing the real world of work, the realities of our cities or the hardships of unemployment and welfare dependency. The point to keep in mind, as we explore the transformation of politics in the coming pages, is that the disillusionment and withdrawal from the political field that is so common in contemporary liberal democracies ensures the continuation of the world as it is, with all its inequalities and injustices continuing and deepening as everyday people lose the capacity to make positive interventions in the world.

In order to be considered legitimate and worthy of consideration, contemporary mainstream politicians must position themselves as anti-ideological pragmatists dedicated to the skilful manipulation of interest rates, budgets and all the machinery of government. Any remaining ideological mavericks are dismissed as obscene radicals or charlatans who, in their desire to transform the world, would threaten the security of liberal democratic populations. All politicians must accept that legitimate politics extends no further than the horizon of liberal capitalism. Their role is essentially to reproduce what currently exists, while at the same time attempting to ensure improved living standards for the majority. If they are to be successful they must convince a sufficient number of voters that they will do a slightly better job than their opponents. In Britain and the USA, the differences between the two major political parties are negligible. Therefore, to give the impression that something is actually happening, small issues must grow in importance for a polity that has already found its unstated ideological truth. In the absence of ambitious policy innovations and dedicated ideological engagement, the media must focus on the personalities of the main candidates in order to convince their audience that the cut and thrust of real politics is still operational. We will try to identify what this means for a politics that genuinely seeks to reintegrate marginal populations. In relation to this, the second key issue we want to identify in the field of politics is the historic and systematic hollowing out of political being.

Post-politics

The rise of neoliberal postmodernism in the 1980s had an important yet very subtle effect upon mainstream politics across the West. In one of the most notable political science texts of the 1990s Francis Fukuyama (1993) proclaimed 'the end of history'; for him, liberal capitalism's democratic system was the pinnacle of our historic political and sociocultural evolution. For Fukuyama, liberal capitalism had defeated its ideological foes and proven itself to be the economic system most capable of advancing the lifestyles of the majority. Similarly, liberal representative democracy had clearly established itself as the foremost system of political governance. After the implosion of the Soviet Bloc at the end of the 1980s no ideological opposition existed capable of challenging the supremacy of liberal democracy, and so there would be no dialectical engagement to push society to the next stage of its development. Instead, all historical change would occur *within* the dominant framework of liberal capitalism, supported by a liberal democratic system that held out the promise of ever-expanding legal entitlements. Fukuyama's thesis acknowledged that authoritarian governments might briefly topple liberal democracy, but the central rationality and clear supremacy of liberal democracy would always return. The thesis has, of course, attracted a huge amount of criticism. He is perhaps second only to Charles Murray on the overall list of contemporary intellectual figures liberal academics love to hate. However, irrespective of one's political affiliations, it is possible to detect in Fukuyama's thesis an air of defeatism and resignation, as if what currently exists, with all its inequalities and injustices, is as good as we can ever expect things to get. We might also reasonably conclude that his thesis is structured by a political triumphalism in keeping with his neoconservative sensibility, as if the long hard journey of America's becoming was now complete; its liberal political economy, supported by conservative social institutions, had successfully out-produced and out-competed its ideological opponents to take its hallowed place at the summit of social evolution.

It is Fukuyama's unequivocal insistence that liberal capitalism and liberal democracy represent the absolute limit of human political and socioeconomic accomplishment that inspired the opprobrium of most left-liberal academics. However, there is more to their dissatisfaction than meets the eye. Despite the tidal wave of criticism that crashed down on Fukuyama's thesis during the final years of the twentieth century, it was far more prescient than many commentators imagined. Firstly, it is certainly true that a post-political age did result from the extinction of ideological opposition to liberal capitalism, and we explore this post-political reality later. From the collapse of the Berlin wall to the global economic collapse of 2008, liberal capitalism and liberal democracy certainly did take on the appearance of a universal socio-political and economic end-point. Even the most strident critics of capitalism failed to construct a viable alternative. For most Western populations the benefits of open democratic elections appeared self-evident: despite huge inequalities and the problems of exclusion and marginality, democratic governance appeared to ensure a degree of fairness, equality and inclusivity and political power was held to account. Even now, four long years into an economic crisis of historic proportions, it is difficult to even imagine a genuine alternative to this system. Throughout the period between 1989 and 2008 there existed a general sense of dialectical standstill as the liberal democratic ideal spread across the globe accompanied by the insistent logic of capitalist economic globalisation. The Western superpowers positioned their liberal democratic system as a fundamental good and a basic human right, and generously undertook to bestow this gift upon some of those nations struggling under the yoke of oppressive totalitarian dictatorships in the developing world.

Fukuyama was also intelligent enough to borrow Nietzsche's 'last men' allegory to supplement his rather simplistic quasi-Hegelian analysis of the termination of dialectical historical movement. He appears to acknowledge that a post-political historical end-point is likely to result in a culture of depressive hedonia (see Fisher, 2009), cynicism and withdrawal. In many respects our current cultural and political life is akin to that experienced and endlessly reproduced by Nietzsche's 'last men of history', who feared change to the extent that they resolved to keep the world as it is, focusing their lives on shallow pleasures and greeting all idealism with unwavering cynicism. The liberal democratic system, with which Fukuyama was so enamoured, now appears to inspire growing distrust rather than commitment, engagement and blind faith. We see this most clearly in the build-up to Britain's general election in 2010. Numerous members of parliament were caught fiddling their expenses and otherwise profiting financially from their role as political representatives of the people. This revelation actually appeared to bring out into the open what many of the electorate had believed to be the case for many years. Thus they approached the election with cynical resignation, believing that both major political parties were polluted by the influence of elites and corrupted by the selfish desire for personal wealth. But how was one to register one's dissatisfaction with the corruption of the political class? One could choose to protest peacefully against political corruption, or vote to get rid of the current crop of political leaders at the next election. Of course, in the current post-political climate, both of these options reaffirm the dominance of liberal democracy itself. Political protests these days are taken not as an indication that something is going wrong and that a significant number of the population are dissatisfied with the nation's political leadership. Rather, they seem to indicate that a healthy and vibrant democracy is in place, one that welcomes political contestation and vigorous public debate about government policy. 'Look at the wonderful world liberalism has created!', our politicians proclaim. 'Political protests like this would never be tolerated in a non-democratic totalitarian regime!' Of course, when the demonstration is complete, nothing has changed. The political protest ends up continuing only for a short time as an online blog or a Twitter post, offering nothing more than a cathartic opportunity to vent one's spleen accompanied by the sad recognition that in all likelihood no one is listening, and no one really cares. It is also worth considering whether the peaceful protest now offers nothing more than an opportunity for the protestor to relinquish their subjective sense of duty to battle injustice. Once the protest is complete, and the world continues unchanged, the subject is allowed the comfort of having registered her dissatisfaction; whatever happens, it does so 'not in my name'.

Similarly, voting to register one's dissatisfaction with political governance these days appears to be a self-defeating exercise. Liberal democracy enforces a horizon that limits rather than encourages political engagement. How is one to register one's dissatisfaction with a hollowed-out democracy that, at election time, simply allows the electorate to swap one set of public schoolboys for another? How, for example, should a voter disgusted at the inequalities of neoliberalism and the greed of the political class express displeasure at the ballot box? In the British election of 2010, one might imagine widespread dissatisfaction with a Labour government that had liberalised the country's economy and significantly contributed to the economic turmoil of 2008. However, in their desire to punish the Labour party for a nightmarish final year in office, the voter is forced to consider voting for the neoliberal fundamentalist Conservative party. No matter which party the voter chooses, they will get more of the economic policies that have caused such widespread disruption and dissatisfaction. So, rather than vote for a political party that reflects their political views, voters are forced into a dispiriting pragmatism. Are they so disgusted by the Labour party that they are willing to vote Conservative, or are they so appalled at the prospect of a Conservative government that they are willing to countenance another Labour administration? A pronounced air of postmodern cynicism descends on the land. Liberal democracy's popular image of openness, choice and vigorous change disguises a fundamental *inability to change*, to transcend the current economic impasse caused by the near universal commitment to the continuation of neoliberalism.

We should also note that, despite their vocal critique of Fukuyama's thesis, many on the liberal left appeared to subconsciously agree with his core claims (see also Žižek, 2008b). For the liberal left, Fukuyama's analysis reflected his right-wing political affiliations. They were unwilling to accept that liberal democratic capitalism was the end-point of civil society's historic evolution. Capitalist globalisation appeared to cause a vast array of human and environmental harms (see for example Chomsky, 1998; Harvey, 2007; South, 2007; Peet, 2009; Sollund, 2012). How, then, was it possible to position the current political system as the best way to organise the economy? The liberal left's critique of Fukuyama is well-founded. Contemporary capitalism does indeed cause a broad range of very serious harms to individuals, societies and the natural environment (ibid.). Fukuyama's faith in democratic elections was also misplaced. Despite their image of inclusivity and collective political will, democratic elections have not led to greater political engagement or a greater sense of civic involvement. Indeed, despite relatively high electoral turn-out figures, there is a clear sense of political disillusionment and withdrawal, especially now that all mainstream political parties agree on economic policies that facilitate the global free market. Of course, in order to register their general dissatisfaction with the world as it is, people must engage with an uninspiring electoral process, and their involvement in that process is taken as evidence that a vibrant and inclusive democratic system exists that is capable of addressing the demands of the people. However, despite their often quite reasonable critique of Fukuyama's thesis, many left-liberal critics appear to agree with Fukuyama at a deeper level and join him in accepting the horizon of liberal capitalism and liberal democracy. They wanted to take issue with the organisation of markets and uneven geographic development, and they wanted to ensure that the views of all eligible voters were represented in election results, but basically they accepted the continuation of capitalism and parliamentary democracy and at no stage advocated the end of this mode of organisation and the shift to something else. This immediate integration of political opposition, even in the rarefied climes of academic debate, tells us something about the operation of contemporary capitalist realism and its ideological uniformity, and we will return to this theme later.

The liberal left essentially hope to humanise capitalism, and we see this in their critique of Fukuyama. They want to ensure that the poor are included in the liberal democratic process, and that environmental issues are taken seriously. These are noble aims, but we must also consider whether capital can truly be held to account in this way. If we are to retain democracy and humanise capitalism, will sufficient people really vote for tax rises, or for policies which appear to suggest withdrawal from the logic of the global free market? Would increasingly instrumental voters elect a government that hopes to attenuate consumer lifestyles and champions a new era in which everyday people must get by with less? Furthermore, what does it say of contemporary leftist politics if the most that we ask for these days is a slightly less beastly version of global capitalism? Is it possible that the radicals of the liberal left are not nearly as radical as they think themselves to be? Are they in fact acting as the officially approved democratic opposition who appear to hold the system to account but ultimately end up reinforcing the view that our future most involve the continuation of parliamentary capitalism?

Twentieth-century politics was energised by deep ideological commitment and passionate debate because, at that time, it was still possible to be a true *subject of belief*. Even during Britain's social democratic post-war consensus, mainstream politicians expressed deeply-held commitments to ideological visions of a better world. They often presented these views to the electorate, and during that time the majority of voters held clear party allegiances that were rooted in a sense of class belonging. Ideology informed political debate and structured policy proposals. Both politicians and voters possessed deeply-held convictions about social justice, fairness, equality and progress. These convictions spectacularly locked horns with one another in mainstream political debate and encouraged the electorate to invest further in the democratic system. While modern politics was far from perfect, its foundation in ideology encouraged genuine dialectical movement, hope and the political engagement of the masses.

The arrival of postmodernist culture and neoliberal political economy transformed the fundamental basis of social cohesion and encouraged the subject to abandon belief. Instead of believing in religion, politics or ideology, the postmodern subject is encouraged to understand all of these things as dangerous, totalising modern myths that prevented post-war populations from seeing the fundamental truth of their lives, and which produced catastrophic brutality in political struggles. Instead of submitting to belief, postmodernism encouraged the subject to be immediately dismissive of truth claims. In academic life, postmodernism was expressed most clearly by Lyotard (1984), who proclaimed a new age of 'incredulity to metanarratives'. The growing complexity of the postmodern world encouraged a sense of constant flux, so much so that the grand explanatory systems offered by modern theorists appeared overly restrictive and ill-suited to a world of perpetual change. Postmodernism attempted to clear the intellectual ground of traditional ideologies to create space for a new assortment of postmodern ideological injunctions rooted in cultural heterogeneity, non-hierarchical systems of knowledge and an unequivocal dismissal of any fixed sense of truth.

Rather than submitting to the rule of restrictive ideologies, the postmodern subject should instead be a coldly instrumental and dispassionate *subject of rationality*. For postmodernists, Catholicism, for instance, is an ideology that contains no more 'truth' than any of the infinite number of belief systems that have existed throughout human history. One should reflexively withdraw from these belief systems in order to grasp the only true reality; that the metanarratives of modernism were merely system-ised accounts of the world that could not be proven, and should therefore not be believed. The postmodern subject should believe in nothing that could not be confirmed by their immediate experience of the real world. Of course, postmodernism did not extinguish belief as such. Rather, belief itself was disavowed but retained in the subconscious. Postmodernism instead appeared to change *the way* we believe. For example, religious belief these days tends to be structured in relation to the needs of the subject, so sub-jects rationally engage with their chosen 'belief' and seek to make it 'work for them'. Following the central logic of postmodernism, the believer is choosing to believe in falsehood. Their faith therefore becomes a matter of subjective choice. It is no longer reflective of deep, all-encompassing and embodied truth. Followers of contemporary religious faiths tend to instrumentalise their belief rather than submitting to religious dogma. They develop a personal relationship with their god, and appraise that relation-ship for its utility. In this way, religious belief often takes the form of a subjective 'spirituality' borne of a *desire to believe* in a higher power that exists beyond our often difficult and dispiriting experience of the everyday material world. As Žižek (2012) has suggested, those who proclaim them-selves to be 'religious' are in fact the true atheists of our time. Contempo-rary postmodern society continues to believe in the sense that we remain fundamentally committed to rationality. The belief in rationality is the one thing that the archetypal postmodern subject must not submit to critical examination. Similarly, commitment to cynicism and scepticism, and our inability to consciously believe, creates a sense of lack and subjective loss that inspires a desire to find something that will demand that we ditch our cynicism and once again submit to *faith*. Our dismissal of truth results in a deep subjective desire to have a genuine truth revealed to us. We will explore this claim in more detail in Chapter 9.

What does this mean for politics? First, postmodernism pushes us into a new post-ideological era in which we are immediately dismissive of grand political narratives. We now appear to believe modernist political ideologies to have been pure mystification and manipulation. Thus postmodern poli-tics has no need for vigorous ideological debate. Instead, political beliefs are held at a distance. Contemporary liberal democracy believes itself to have surgically removed all the malignant excesses and passions that animated subjectivity and politics in the twentieth century. On the surface of things, it has become a smooth system of apolitical governance administered by a new elite technocratic parliamentary administration that utilises expert know-ledge to ensure economic growth, the maintenance of legal freedoms, health and wellbeing and the defence of the population against internal and exter-nal threats to our 'way of life'. Of course, this move to sanitise politics and cleanse it of passionate ideological debate also removes the basic ingredi-ents that make political debate productive, real and in any way worthwhile.

Dismissing ideological commitment means that we deprive politics of the energy that drives dialectical movement and progress.

How did this transformation take place? By the 1990s, in the USA and the Eurozone, most mainstream parties accepted that neoliberalism offered the best available means of improving the living standards of the voting populations. As political parties agreed on this issue, strident political debate on the general direction of economic policy became obsolete. The vigorous cut and thrust of party politicking remained to feed the public spectacle as the political class attempted to curry favour with an increasingly instrumental electorate, but this tended to magnify relatively minor issues. As the differences between major parties narrowed, the media inevitably focused more and more on personalities, sound-bites and deliberately manufactured political squabbling and scandal. This in turn informed party strategy and reinforced the growing sense of artificiality that descended upon the new media-focused mainstream politics. A new breed of postmodern political leader rose to prominence and secured key party positions because they could perform well on nightly news broadcasts, and, in the USA, because they might encourage significant campaign contributions from oligarchs and corporate elites. This new breed of politician appeared to have no fully conscious political commitments beyond a desire to secure political office (see for example Badiou, 2009; Seymour, 2010). They must appeal to the party's grass roots, to floating voters, and to disillusioned members of their opponent's party base, and they must do all of this at the same time, without alienating anyone, and without attracting negative political commentary in the media. These competing demands compelled the main political candidates to commit to pragmatism. Candidates must restrict public expressions of their beliefs as much as possible; this process, in a way deeply indicative of the times, appeared to hollow out and devalue the symbolism associated with key political ideals. So, if a politician were to be asked what they believe in, they would do best to restrict their answers to those things that the entire audience might agree with, no matter which political colours they sail under.

The mid-range of politics was discarded. Politicians could discuss tiny concrete aspects of policy, or they could discuss the broadest and vaguest political abstractions. However, they must avoid any discussion of what those political abstractions meant in practical terms, or how they might mobilise their convictions with new policy developments. For example, all politicians were encouraged to express a belief in freedom, justice, fairness, democracy and equality of opportunity. The outcome, of course, is that these phrases could be endlessly manipulated and reconfigured, to the extent that even the most earnest commitment to them was rendered meaningless. This desire not to alienate potential voters was encouraged by the integration of new specialists into the democratic realm of parliamentary politics. Any political candidate hoping to win office these days must listen closely to the sagacious advice of media experts and spin doctors, who calculate the potential outcomes of every media appearance and strategically leak information to the press with a view to ensuring positive media coverage, while at the same time depriving competitors of the same.

In their desire not to offend potential voters, this new breed of political candidate comes to rely on feedback from focus groups when attempting to develop policy. The goal is to discover what it is that a majority of voters want, and how they are likely to respond to specific policy suggestions. The candidate then fills his political manifesto with policies structured in the hope of attracting popular support. While this may seem like a progressive expansion of the democratic ideal into the usually restricted arena of policy formation, in fact the growing reliance on focus groups is a clear indication of the hollowing out of democracy. Rather than key parliamentary candidates leading on the issues of the day, they follow. And what do they follow? They make a utilitarian calculation that attempts to discern the will of the majority in terms of the Benthamite 'greatest happiness'. For them, there is no fundamental commitment to truth, no political goal upon which they are unwilling to compromise. If the people appear to want lower taxes and less immigration, then that becomes the calculative politician's truth; those are the policies that should be adopted if they hope to triumph in the desperate battle for political office. In this climate, the future's fundamental truths – for instance that we might need to downsize lifestyles to avert ecological and social disaster – cannot be mooted in the political or cultural mainstream.

Parliamentary democracy, even when it was animated by ideological commitment, always contained this fundamental problem. It is a political system that deprives the subject of their determining character and reduces them to an abstraction to be measured alongside other abstractions. In this sense, the enlightened and politically-informed voter driven by a desire for social justice and progress is no more important to the democratic system than the racist voter, or the voter who votes for the candidate they believe to have the most charming smile. In democracy, the particularities of the voter are entirely unimportant. They become no more and no less than 'one', to be tallied against all of the other 'ones' that choose to participate in the election. Of course, the very basic equality of this system is its primary attraction for Western liberal electorates. Liberal democracy is determinedly anti-elitist, despite the fact that this commitment to populism now appears polluted by corporate interests and the political agendas of the super-rich. Election results appear to confirm the basic will of the people and are therefore judged to possess a powerful purity that ensures democracy's moral superiority over its competitors. Of course, there are no guarantees that the electorate have based their decisions on even a basic knowledge and understanding of key issues, or that those individual decisions are in any way connected to a moral or ethical good. What becomes problematic is the amalgamation of the decisions of abstract individuals into final election results. After a major election in America, the media tell us 'the American people have spoken! They have decided that the nation should be led by a new Republican president!' Of course, this too is reliant upon a fundamental abstraction. The American people do not speak with one voice. Indeed, it's likely that the vast majority of potential voters did not in fact vote for the candidate who has won the election. In Britain, this becomes more complicated with the election of a coalition government, as was the case in 2010. In fact not one single voter voted for a coalition government. Yet still we are told, 'the people have spoken; this coalition government is the will of the people'.

In British politics throughout the 1990s the image of 'Mondeo Man' became important to the constructions of political policy for both the Labour and Conservative parties. The Mondeo was a popular type of car, apparently favoured by low-level, middle income, home-owning, non-manual workers who were likely to display no firm allegiance to either of the main political parties. This image of the 'Mondeo Man' appears to have been constructed by professional pollsters and demographers, and 'Mondeo Man' was judged to be important as he represented a key political constituency that could sway election results. The party that could construct the policies that would win him over would, apparently, carry the day. However, the pollsters responsible for 'Mondeo Man' actually went much further than this. Their careful demographic analysis allowed them to determine the newspapers that 'Mondeo Man' would read, what qualifications he had managed to attain, and what were his favourite leisure pursuits. They could then, using a combination of statistical analysis and educated guesswork, construct a family around him, and from there, an entire life. Of course, 'Mondeo Man' did not exist. In fact, such was the abstraction of the pollsters' analysis that *no one* fitted the model they had created for an apparently archetypal British male voter. The more sophisticated their analysis of 'Mondeo Man' became, the more abstracted it was from the actual reality of the voting public. So, for example, the number of thirty-something Mondeo drivers who were home-owners, who earned a middle income, who held no great political affiliations, worked in non-manual jobs, who were married with a child under the age of ten, read *The Sun* newspaper every day, and who liked to holiday in Spain was, in reality, almost non-existent.

Yet still the main political parties structured policy in relation to this abstraction, which appeared to communicate a truth about the electorate despite the fact that it did not closely represent the reality of male voters during the 1990s. This should suggest to us that the supposed pragmatism of mainstream post-political parties is not all that it seems to be. In striving to identify what it is that voting populations really want, post-ideological politicians ultimately end up constructing policy in relation to an unconscious ideological abstraction. The abstract 'thing' that they hope to satisfy is the ideology of liberal capitalism at the end of history. Similarly, the dismissal of ideological commitment from contemporary parliamentary democracy is not as straightforward as we might imagine. Rather than eliminate ideology, the pragmatism and cynicism of the contemporary post-political period acts to reassert the dominance of the ruling ideology. As we have already suggested, the ideology of contemporary liberal capitalism becomes so ubiquitous that it is no longer understood as an ideology. Instead, it becomes mere common sense. With the advent of the contemporary post-political scene, we might also go one step further and suggest that anti-ideological political pragmatism in fact acts as its opposite; it is a fundamentally *ideological* operation that re-enforces the horizon of post-political capitalist realism.

Be afraid...

The cynicism and pragmatism of post-ideological politicians spoke to disaffected voting populations who believed that the very best that can be hoped for in political terms is a democratic administration that will improve the individual's lifestyle somewhat, and defend the people against the manifold terrors and threats that appear to typify postmodern cultural life. All utopian images of the future melted down into subjective visions of personal safety and enrichment. Voters no longer displayed clear class affiliations or firm, durable allegiances to the major political parties. A residue of party identification lingered, but this became far less important than it once was. Instead, voters were forced to follow political leaders into a new post-political era of cynical pragmatism. Idealism became anathema, a hangover from an earlier and more politically naïve time. Importantly, the new political consensus built upon a cross-party acceptance of neoliberal economics had brought with it an acceptance of individualism and a deep distrust of narratives of progressive change built upon political universality.

Post-political pragmatism might have eclipsed all the grand political narratives that are external to the project of parliamentary capitalism, but it still retained a suggestion of optimism and progress. On the liberal left, much of this optimism related to the apparent diversity of the postmodern era and the cultural logic of liberal multiculturalism, despite the increased willingness of mainstream politicians to play upon the anxieties of voters by making immigration a key issue at election time. The apparent diversity of liberal multiculturalism usefully covered up the growing homogeneity reflected in other registers of neoliberal postmodern culture. Throughout the 'happy 90s' (Žižek, 2005, 2008a), it seemed that Western liberal democracies welcomed all races, nationalities and religions. A cultural injunction to tolerate otherness was issued that appeared progressive and in keeping with the onward march of postmodern liberalism's expansive freedoms. However, this tolerance of otherness suggests a grudging acceptance of the competitive other rather than a historic move to genuinely embrace diversity.

The injunction to tolerate was also deeply indicative of a fragmented and increasingly anxious social order that sought to create and maintain a social distance between subjects who were forced to engage every day in a socioeconomic struggle against each other in a shrinking economy (Hall et al., 2008). For us, the hidden ideological supplement that accompanied the mantra of toleration was a drive to keep the other at a safe distance. The competitive individuals of postmodernism did not want the sanctity of their immediate subjective experience and fragile security sullied or threatened by the over-proximity of the other. The mantra of toleration therefore dressed up the desire to maintain a marked distinction between the self and the other in positive political garb. The other would be tolerated as long as they did not get too close for comfort (see Chapters 8 and 9), and liberal democracy could maintain its progressive image of openness and inclusivity as long as it did not press the issue of the real socioeconomic obligations that might make demands on the individual's lifestyle. In Britain, much of the new crime and social order legislation produced by Tony Blair's New Labour administrations was essentially geared towards maintaining and policing the gap between the subject and its other. They hoped to ensure that the uncouth tendencies of the barely tolerated other did not impact upon the sanctity of the post-political subject (see for example Squires, 2008; Burley, 2009).

We should also note that diverse cultural groups would be tolerated only when they agreed to become more tolerant of the cultural diversity of Western liberal democracies. Newly-arrived immigrant groups, magnanimously granted access to the West's progressive order and civility, must accept liberalism, the rule of law and freedom of speech as markers of Western civilisation itself. In this way, *genuine* otherness was, from the outset, disallowed. Only surface otherness would be tolerated. Liberal democracies would certainly not accept public sacrifice, female circumcision, forced marriages or public stonings. Nor would it accept any form of religious hatred, or any aggressive bias against minorities. Liberalism had faith that radically different cultures and religions could be brought together and live happily in peaceful co-existence, even joining together to make new communities of genuine diversity, deep acceptance and mutual support. Otherness was therefore attenuated and increasingly planted in the apolitical sphere of 'culture', reduced to the surface signifiers of music, fashion, festivals and non-problematic aspects of traditional worship. Diversity may have existed in post-political societies, but it was a functional diversity that masked a structuring universality at the economic level. You could worship your own god or gratify your own erotic desires – indeed religious, ethnic and sexual diversity contributed to the dynamism of the economy – but you must accept the ultimate horizon of democracy and liberal capitalism.

Cultural anxiety

Many social theorists have recognised that our entry into a postmodern era brought with it a growing sense of anxiety. Postmodernism's assault upon the certainties of the modern world engendered a vague yet potent sense of insecurity and unpredictability. The recession of modernist certainties and the rise of irony and contingency at first glance seemed to free individuals from the more rigid structures that defined social life in the mid-twentieth century (see Bauman, 2000). Traditional forms of collective identity were marginalised as the postmodern subject was compelled to busy itself with creative identity-construction. This new subject could throw off the shackles of modernist idolatry and be free to make individualistic, informed choices about its life.

However, if the modern world had an advantage it was that its values, forms, structures and identities were relatively stable and comprehensible to individuals. In many respects identity and life course were mapped out at birth. There was sufficient flexibility for a degree of creative agency and social mobility, but generally speaking most of those born into the working class would live their entire lives within it. The same was true for the middle and upper classes. Social structures are now increasingly fluid and amorphous, a transformation predicated on fundamental changes in the capitalist economy, yet they have most emphatically not dissolved into classless equality. Most importantly, the decline of traditional industrial work in the West has contributed enormously to the general destabilisation of the social structure and to the rise of economic exclusion.

Many sociologists do acknowledge that the collapse of class and gender structures has been overstated. These are relevant criticisms, but they tend to omit a crucial factor; the nature of subjectivity (see glossary) itself has changed (see Johnston, 2008; Hall, 2012a; see also Chapter 9). Our perception of the objective world around us, and our position in it, is no longer as it was during the modernist era. The responsibility for the construction of our identities and biographies now weighs almost entirely on the individual. In the realm of collective belief far less can be relied upon. The postmodern subject is a pan-sceptic, avowedly reluctant to believe in anything. Despite our humdrum everyday experience, there exists a nagging sense of doubt, as if at any moment the rug could be pulled from under us to propel our lives in a radically different direction. This is not simply the price of winning a great historical struggle for freedom and self-determination, but again predicated upon changes in the capitalist economy. Work is now, in the West, largely contingent, unreliable and subject to unpredictable fluctuations. Increasing proportions of Western workforces are now employed on short-term contracts, and must live with the constant worry that their contract will not be renewed. Today's world of work certainly does not display the same degree of continuity and dependability as it did in the modern era. We get a sense of this with Standing's (2011) analysis of the rise of a new and precarious labour market, but missing from this very useful body of theory and research is a deeper recognition that *all work* is increasingly precarious, as are all biographical projects in a world in which the future appears as a multi-layered paradox; at once prescribed and predictable in the sense that capitalism now seems unassailable and will frame the rest of our lives, but also deeply unpredictable and likely to collapse at any moment. In this sense, we appear committed to the perpetuity of parliamentary capitalism, but we also seem to accept, perhaps in the unconscious and rarely represented domain of our psyches, that it simply *cannot* continue. Post-political electorates and politicians may mock idealism and utopianism, but their own faith in the system's eternity is itself profoundly idealistic and utopian. The awkward truth that current culture and politics refuses to confront is that unless change is accepted and enacted by conscious and willing subjects, it will be forced upon us in circumstances not of our choosing. For instance, we secretly know that our environment is finite and that constant economic growth and material enrichment of our lifestyles is impossible. We know that neoliberalism is prone to increasingly destructive downturns and yet more economic turmoil lies further down the road. But, for the moment at least, this knowledge is repressed (see glossary) into our unconscious and we lack the conviction to implement changes that might propel us into a new era. Today's atmosphere of strained silence about what *we really know* and what *really matters* is a product of our postmodern historical and political inertia.

To understand this, we need to make a clear distinction between anxiety and fear. Anxiety is an imprecise sense of danger. Fear is quite different; it is triggered by a clear, objective and communicable cause. In the contemporary period the 'politics of fear' is made possible as a secondary symptom only by the underlying 'politics of anxiety'; we appear to be increasingly anxious about something that cannot yet be objectified. We are not yet sure what is causing our emotional disturbance, but we seem assured that there certainly is *something* dangerous out there that threatens us and our way of life. Fear is often positioned as being a more disruptive and harmful emotional state, but in fact the opposite is true; fear can be ideologically manipulated only in the gap provided by 'objectless anxiety' (Hall, 2012a). If we were to become able to identify precisely what is really troubling us, we would then be capable of transcending ideology's manipulated and often prejudicial objects and taking the steps necessary to meet the challenge (ibid.). It is not 'fear' but the lack of any fixed sense of certainty in relation to objective threats and what we can do about them that is most disconcerting and politically dangerous.

If contemporary liberal democratic politics is bland and uninteresting, populated by politicians who possess no genuine political commitments beyond the desire to constantly recreate what already exists, why does politics still resonate in popular culture? Žižek (2008a) has made the point that politics is animated by fear and obesity. Rather than the naïve utopianism of modern politics, it is the specific fears constructed by politics and mass media that find expression in postmodern political discourse. We should be able to see this quite clearly: fears of ecological catastrophe, of the implosion of the Eurozone, of immigrants, of crime, of the criminal poor, of terrorism, of radicalised Islamism, and so on. Here, in this decentred and fragmented realm, plausible fears can co-exist alongside pure prejudice. However, this spectrum of fears can be constructed in the realm of perception only because a climate of generic anxiety has also been constructed by removing the true object of fear, which of course is the chronic instability of a system reaching its historical limits. Thus postmodern political commitment is fragmented and focused on a multitude of specific *causes and symptoms* rather than the system itself and its expansive ideological framework. Sections of the electorate can appear to discard cynicism and become quite animated by particular issues that are thrown up from the general ebb and flow of post-political dialogue. They can demand change in a quite determined manner, but the change that they demand appears to relate only to *particular causes* that relate to *particular effects* and *particular fears*.

What we are seeing here is the rise of a postmodern biopolitics (see glossary); that is, a politics concerned primarily with the safety of political subjects, a system designed to save them from multiple threats. Of course, biopolitics is a necessary outcome of the general trend towards post-politics we outlined earlier in this chapter. Once politics has renounced ideology and progressive change, the main role of government is to ensure the safety of its subjects, to protect them from the risks and problems that crop up in a world destined to continue on as it is. This also has a strangely ahistorical aspect to it. If we reduce biopolitics to its absolute essence, the role of government becomes simply to preserve life; that is, to preserve a life free from its usual civilised associations, free from any political commitment to improve the fundamental conditions of life on behalf of current and future generations.

Since the 1990s it has become possible to identify an important aspect of neoliberalism-in-practice: despite an apparent distaste for 'big government', neoliberal administrations, in America and Britain in particular, have expanded their military and security spending significantly (see Harvey, 2007; Chang, 2011). They have also, especially since 9/11, introduced new legislation that has withdrawn previously sacrosanct legal entitlements. We see this most clearly with Bush's Patriot Act of 2001. The electorate appears to have become so generally anxious and fearful of whatever threat that can be constructed (see Mythen and Walklate, 2008), that they embrace rather than challenge legislation that removes or suspends basic civil liberties.

Agamben (2005) has suggested that, with contemporary post-politics, we see an increased tendency for Western governments to deprive the population of established legal entitlements, and also to deprive individuals of the rights of citizenship. Agamben begins with an analysis of political sovereignty. Where does sovereign power reside in modern states? It resides in the ability to declare a *state of exception*. A state of exception is simply a situation that appears to necessitate the suspension of the nation's usual legal framework. On the surface of things, crises appear to arise that demand determined unilateral state action that goes beyond the usual legal mandate of government. Thus, with post-politics, we see a return of debates relating to the ethics of torture (see for example Žižek, 2002, 2008b; Levinson, 2006). Those things that were once judged entirely unethical and were unreservedly disallowed return as a pragmatic response to an extreme, identifiable threat that is depicted as having no connection to the crisis of the system itself. Agamben's crucial point is that the suspension of the established legal order is increasingly used to extend state power over the population. So, the prevailing fear that has resulted from the Islamic terrorist threat acts to enable the state to suspend the rule of law and impose its will upon the people (see for discussion Mythen et al., 2007; Mythen and Walklate, 2008), and to deal with other aspects of a systemic crisis that has itself been erased from popular consciousness. Thus social exclusion is conscripted to the ranks of all other 'single issues' to be depicted by politics, mass media and the social management apparatus as a *specific social problem* that is of great concern but able to be dealt with by specific policy solutions; it is not a product of an objective, systemic crisis.

A sense of politics

In the previous sections we have briefly sketched out a number of key changes in the field of politics. However, to really get a sense of the state of politics at the end of history we must also take a look at how everyday people relate to contemporary politics. We have discussed a growing sense of cynicism and withdrawal, but, related to this, we can also discern a general absence of political subjectivity. During the industrial modern period across the West, everyday people were allowed, indeed encouraged, to understand the connection between politics and their everyday social experience. In comparison with today, working populations appear to have been much more politicised and politically concerned about the realities of social class and economic and political power (see for example Rose, 2010). People joined labour unions, and understood and appreciated the political utility of these institutions both for themselves and for their communities. Unlike the contemporary world of institutionalised individualism, people were encouraged to accept collective forms of identity and to see their own subjective hopes and needs in relation to those around them. In the industrial modern period there did not exist to the same extent the fundamental drive to differentiate the self from one's community, or to triumph in a perpetual competition to achieve social status.

In contrast, the culture of contemporary consumer capitalism is built upon deliberately cultivated insecurity and envy (Hall et al., 2008; Žižek, 2011). These proto-symbolic drives – aspects of the continual process of identification – activate libidinal energy to animate consumer markets, pushing the consumer back out to the shopping centre in a constant elliptical movement that holds out the promise of pleasure and reassurance. The consumer subconsciously hopes that the image reflected back from the social mirror will be one that confirms her cultural relevance, but the consumer also clings to the hope her informed consumer choices might lead to a position of social distinction confirmed by the envy of others. The desire to be something different, something better, is not a hard-wired characteristic of our species. Even if we look just a short time back into our history, back to the old world of industrial modernism, we can see that this drive to constantly reconfigure the self in the hope of achieving a greater degree of cultural recognition – usually associated with the vanity of ruling elites across history – simply did not exist on anything like the same scale in popular culture as it does today. In Britain's industrial working class, for example, people seemed far happier in their own skin than they do today. Even though they faced material hardships and actual physical dangers, contentment appears to have been much more available in their world than it is in ours. This is not to say that Britain's industrial working class were generally satisfied and lethargic – they certainly were not. Rather, our claim is that the industrial worker sought to improve his material circumstances as part of a politicised collective. Rather than seeking to triumph over those who shared her community, the worker sought to improve her material circumstances alongside her peers.

We do not want to offer a rose-tinted view of the past, but it was certainly possible for the industrial working class to act in accordance with a shared sense of collective identity and wellbeing. This sense of collective identity, and of community and solidarity, always possessed a political potentiality. In an important sense, the decline of these things, and the rise and naturalisation of possessive individualism, remove from contemporary culture the political substance that might allow us to move beyond capitalist realism to a new and inclusive historical epoch that is built upon equality and inclusivity; an epoch that is not characterised by staggering inequalities and a fraught battle for cultural significance.

What we see, in the wake of the global financial crisis, is a broad and deep dissatisfaction with the organisation of contemporary political economy. A significant number of people across Western societies know the world to be deeply unjust. However, in the absence of a genuine politics of transcendence, the ethical individual can do nothing other than feel deeply aggrieved at the reality of the world, and cynical about the possibility of progressive change. Such dissatisfaction cannot yet be discharged onto objects, alternatives and routes away from our current impasse because there are no compelling ideologies to rally around, and no genuine sense of community, solidarity or class struggle to engage with. Rather than directing our dissatis-faction outwards and into the political sphere with a view to reanimating dialectical movement, we appear to interiorise and subjectivise our dissatis-faction, turning it into apolitical resignation, cynicism and withdrawal. The institutionalisation of individualism means that we tend to understand the problems of the world in relation to our own wellbeing, and refuse to commit to shared political projects. The hard work and sacrifices needed to genuinely enact change in the world are too much for the post-political citizen to bear. No matter how bad their situation becomes, the socially excluded will receive little empathy or help from the post-political citizen. For the moment at least, there exists no compelling, practical vision of how a better world might be organised. Here it is useful to remind ourselves of Žižek's (2006a) suggestion that often the true ethical response to crisis is to *do nothing*. Rather than act immediately and without adequate critical thinking and planning, it is the job of the critical intellectual to withdraw from this foreground of crisis and begin the difficult task of *rethinking* the entire basis of the crisis itself, and of course the forms it produces. In the next chapter we return to a more direct discussion of social exclusion. We will expand on some of the themes raised in this chapter to offer what we hope is a constructive critique of the contemporary social exclusion discourse, which will identify one or two new avenues for analysis.

6

A Reserve Army of Labour?

In the following two chapters we want to investigate more closely the common claim that the poorest are *excluded* from the formal economy and separated from its determining logic. In global and local economies that appear to be changing rapidly in line with new technological advances and in response to the neoliberal financial system's recent crash, how should we understand the economic position of the West's poorest populations?

For a number of commentators, the shift of most mass industrial labour to low-wage economies in the East cuts off the West's poor from traditional forms of productive labour. The cultural and political consequences of this change have been enormous (Martin and Rowthorn, 1986; Winlow, 2001; Wacquant, 2001, 2009; Webster et al. 2004; Hall et al., 2005). The relatively stable cultures of the traditional industrial working class have all but disappeared, along with forms of solidarity and anti-utilitarianism that enabled the post-war working classes to develop powerful institutions to defend and advance their collective interests. The evaporation of working class collectivism and the growing dominance of identity politics in the left's political institutions ensured defeat as neoliberalism began its ascent during the mid-1970s and 80s. Labour unions appeared to be a spent force, leftist and social democratic political parties had accepted the inevitability of the market economy, and the former working class was fragmented, depoliticised and fully incorporated into classical liberalism's cult of self-interest.

Deindustrialisation in the West and rapid industrial growth in the East caused a net reduction in the number of Western workers, who became surplus to requirements. This major global shift in the locus of production caused not just a transformation in the normative conditions of employment – from stable and exploitative to unstable and extremely exploitative – but also a shift in the normative conditions of *unemployment* – from periodic joblessness to permanent exclusion. In this unprecedented situation, pragmatic leftist political bargaining has shifted from the demand for more pay and benefits to the polite request for capital to exploit a greater proportion of the ex-working classes in the downgraded, deskilled forms of employment that remain.

The rise of new forms of 'affective labour' in the retail, service and leisure sectors of the economy are no compensation for the loss of stable industrial jobs (see Byrne, 1989, 1999). The 'growth in employment' in these sectors is a move towards part-time and short-term contracts, often mediated by commercial employment agencies. The majority of these jobs are low-paid, insecure and non-unionised, and often require unsociable shifts at short notice (see Southwood, 2011; Lloyd, 2012). In some cases, actual pay levels are so low that there is little economic benefit in taking the jobs in the first place. The experience of many occupants of economically excluded locales who want to work is a constant circular movement from welfare into the worst forms of work and back again (see for example Shildrick et al., 2010). Old-school social democrats believe a net growth in jobs to be the crucial factor in addressing the problem of 'social exclusion'. However, the only net growth neoliberalism can offer is in those forms of work that provide very low economic and cultural rewards. In conjunction with a genuine decline in available work, the replacement is increasingly downgraded and insecure.

This suggests that we must move analytically and politically beyond the standard liberal-leftist call for 'more jobs'. We must square up to the reality of a global capitalist economy that has little use for the labour of unskilled Western workers beyond facilitating consumer markets. The jobs available for the contemporary poor are precisely those jobs they do not need. The call for 'more jobs' has lost the traditional caveat that they must provide workers with a reasonable standard of living and host work cultures that encourage both self-respect and mutual recognition. Can we even imagine a future capitalism capable of producing full employment in the West, let alone creating full employment in reasonably remunerative and satisfying forms of work? If we can, which forms of political activity might encourage this fundamental reorientation? If we can't, what hope is there for genuine social inclusion?

It has also been suggested that the Western poor are excluded from the formal economy because they are unable to access the lifestyles that carry status in consumer culture. Here we must move beyond Bauman's (1998a, 2007a) claim that the contemporary poor should be understood as 'flawed consumers', cut adrift from mainstream symbolic life. Certainly, Bauman is right that consumerism is crucial to post-industrial economies and, in the absence of many traditional influences, the symbols of consumer goods and lifestyles function as tools for the construction of social identity. This is especially true in those countries most committed to neoliberal political economy. Social relationships are mediated by these symbols, and, as Bauman claims, the inability of the poor to actively engage in the central symbolic and economic logic of our times guarantees redundancy and exclusion. Their lack of relevant skills and their inability to adapt to the new economic reality ensures that they remain unable to access the apparently diverse and exciting world of lifestyle consumerism as a signifier of social inclusion and cultural relevance. In sum, their economic redundancy means that they become surplus to requirements: they create nothing, contribute nothing, their skills are redundant and they do not have the wherewithal to engage in the forms of ornamental consumerism that are so central to the way we live now. However, there is more to this.

In one of the most widely-read books on social exclusion yet published, Byrne (1999) challenges Bauman's claim about the economic redundancy of the contemporary poor by suggesting that the socially excluded continue to fulfil a crucial role for post-industrial capitalism. For Byrne, this group act as a 'reserve army of labour' in the traditional Marxist sense, systematising insecurity in the workforce and undermining their collective bargaining position. This counterclaim merits some discussion here. In the pages that follow we will investigate the work of Bauman and Byrne in more detail before attempting to develop new lines of inquiry that reflect our continued historical stasis, the ongoing problems of the global neoliberal economy and the transformed nature of postmodern social life. In particular, we will claim that the 'socially excluded' continue to be seduced by the symbolism of contemporary capitalism's libidinal economy, and remain subject to its ideological injunctions. It is certainly true that they have fewer opportunities for work and acquisition of contemporary consumer culture's social symbols. However, their role is far more active and reproductive than a 'reserve army of labour' (Byrne, 1999) or 'flawed consumers' (Bauman, 2004). They act as a *reserve army of consumers*, constantly providing the negative symbolism against which the economically included can demonstrate their social distinction from the poor. Our research has shown that this reserve army of consumers do not simply accept their position of exclusion or acknowledge the socioeconomic structure from which they are excluded; a significant proportion wait with what can only be described as the delusional belief that they will be the lucky ones who will one day obtain the symbols of status that can radically transform the way they are seen and valued by the others who surround them (Hall et al., 2008; see also Smart, 2010).

Global economic competition and the shift of production to selected non-Western economies have severed the traditional relationship between Western labourers and their 'reserves'. In Britain and the USA, the archetypal Western neoliberal states, productive industry now contributes less and less to GDP. Job competition is no longer simply an internal matter for national governments and domestic employers; it has become global in its reach. Workers in the West's remaining production centres operate under the constant threat of imminent closures and the relocation of entire industries to low-wage economies. They have done so since neoliberalism came to define the economic policies of successive governments from the 1980s onwards. Trade union membership and influence have declined significantly, wages in this sector are down in real terms, and there now exists a culture of precariousness and a general sense that jobs can be immediately

extinguished despite low wages, high productivity and sustained profitability. The source of job anxiety and its accompanying social status anxiety can
no longer be located entirely in a pool of reserve labour occupying the city's
low income areas. Rather, workplace anxiety feeds into a general, nebulous
and unfathomable anxiety that cannot be adequately objictified, an anxiety
that has become endemic throughout huge swathes of neoliberal economies
(see Hall, 2012a). Insecurity and precariousness in the workplace and the
broader society are in fact the 'new normal', not just in the manufacturing
sector. The gap between low-wage factory workers and high-wage professionals remains huge, but the undercurrent of instability, absence and vague
yet corrosive anxiety appears to affect all.

In the same way that neoliberalism represents a regression to earlier forms
of capital accumulation (see Badiou, 2002; Harvey, 2007), so contemporary
precariousness is the marked effect of a regression to earlier unstable and
hyper-exploitative forms of employment. What this suggests is that entirely
asocial modes of capital accumulation represent the internal truth of capitalism itself. Capitalism and its drive to extract the absolute maximum amount
of surplus value from labour can be contained by government regulation,
but should that regulation be withdrawn, it appears that capitalism will
rapidly return to its most destructive, avaricious and anti-social form. As we
go on we should keep this point in mind: neoliberalism is not a nastier, more
aggressive historical form of capitalism but a contemporary manifestation
of the reality at the core of capitalist enterprise. Capitalism has not just got
nastier; its regulatory cushion has been melted down by the intense heat of
the global economic competition to which politics has surrendered.

The growth of job insecurity reflects the modus operandi of neoliberal
managerialism and political capitulation to the basic abstract principles
of neoclassical economics, which are little more than macro-accountancy
(see Shutt, 2010; Varoufakis, 2011). Neoliberalism portrays itself as doggedly efficient: sniffing out waste, cutting costs, formulating new strategies
in order to increase market share, profits, rents and share values. But in
truth there is nothing particularly 'efficient' about neoliberal managerialism (see for example De Angelis, 2007; Chang, 2011). The expectation that
costs can be cut, and cut again *ad infinitum*, often appears to work against
the long-term interests and continued market viability of many businesses.
Rather than 'efficiency' in the proper sense, neoliberal governance represents merely an efficient means of reallocating resources from the majority
to the super-rich under the camouflage of a supposedly free and open political economy (Rasmus, 2010; Shutt, 2010). Short-term increases in share
values and profitability continue to dominate neoliberal market strategy,
despite this having been identified as the core problem in the casino capitalism that was largely responsible for the economic meltdown of 2008 (Keen,
2011). The impetus is therefore towards the appearance of profitability to
attract investment rather than the long-term development and expansion of

companies and corporations, and towards immediate trading profits rather than long-term profitability in the field of socially useful production. It is also worth acknowledging that investment capital also operates in accordance with this economic short-termism. Investing in a FTSE 100 corporation is increasingly left to conservative investors, especially pension funds, who are in it for the long haul. In the 1990s before the dot-com bust, the really exciting opportunities appeared to be in internet start-ups and speculative venture capitalism. As abstract finance capitalism grew and became more complex, the action shifted to highly innovative and complicated investment vehicles such as credit default swaps, equity, currency and interest rate derivatives, and of course the mortgage-backed securities and collateralised debt obligations that have featured in so many accounts of the US sub-prime housing market collapse (see Stiglitz, 2012).

This is the field upon which some saw a new breed of capitalist emerging, an executive class of highly paid employees who were rapacious, ruthless, aggressively self-confident and comfortable with risk-taking (see Frank, 2008). The industrial world of long-term capital investment in production had in the West given way to aggressive, risky profit-seeking and short-termism, which, aided by expansive market deregulation, appeared to have freed capitalism from its repetitive boom and bust cycle. Of course, as we can now see, just as neoliberalism's strutting self-confidence was reaching its peak, a cavernous vortex was opening up underneath its feet that would drag the entire global economy to the brink of collapse.

Of course, Wall Street's 'Masters of the Universe' cared little about the messy business of actual productive work, and they were almost entirely separated from the social effects of deindustrialisation (see Toynbee and Walker, 2009). But their global world view found many vocal propagandists in the media, in academic economics and in government. These ideologues argued that if workers were to remain employed in a competitive global marketplace they should be willing to accept job insecurity and reduced levels of pay. They supplemented this with the suggestion that employers should offer no more than the absolute minimum needed to employ labour. Of course, what is being suggested is that, in a general 'race to the bottom', workers work for the absolute minimum so that their employers can achieve higher profits and consumers – ironically, workers and ex-workers themselves – can buy cheap goods and indulge in status-enhancing 'affordable luxury'. According to neoliberal logic, this boosts the entire national economy and benefits all. The government is then able to tax corporate profits and high-income executives and entrepreneurs, using the revenue to provide vital public services. (Here it's worth noting that, in 2011, the British Chancellor of the Exchequer, George Osborne, announced plans to reduce corporate tax to 21 per cent by 2014. Throughout the 1970s this figure was 42 per cent. Personal top-rate income tax was around 90 per cent during the fifties and sixties. In 2011, Osborne cut this figure to 45 per cent:

see www.hmrc.gov.uk.) Of course, neoliberal logic tells us that taxes should not rise too high or this will dissuade investment and innovation, resulting in economic stagnation and rising unemployment. In the realm of neoliberal economics, the only way to improve the lifestyles of the poor is to free the rich from unnecessary regulation and burdensome tax. This will ensure that the poor can at least find low-paid employment. However, here lies one of neoliberalism's elementary contradictions; one minute we are told that the poor are dependent on the unburdened entrepreneurial drive of the rich and the next that it is up to the poor themselves to improve their lot. At the Randian core of neoliberalism is the perverse ethos that in reality it is the poor who exploit the rich and not the other way round; therefore it cannot be fair to expect the wealth-producing elite to pay for the poor. Besides, the decadence of the super-rich is entirely functional as it provides a large market for luxury goods and a vital symbolic impetus for the poor to improve their own status; we are told by neoliberal ideologues that the 'politics of envy' is a bad thing, yet the system's crucial sociocultural symbolism is ultimately dependent upon this potent psychosocial driving force (Žižek, 2011; Hall, 2012a). The poor need to be made aware that a better world exists for those willing to work hard, accumulate skills and take entrepreneurial risks; it is only fair that those individuals who refuse to make an effort to do this, or refuse to serve faithfully those who do, should be 'excluded'.

There is now a surfeit of evidence to suggest that money does not 'trickle down' through the class system, enriching and including all, just as there is a huge amount of evidence to suggest that corporations and high-net-worth individuals contribute relatively little in terms of tax (see for example Frank, 2008; Galbraith, 2008). Indeed, an entire industry has arisen to help these individuals and businesses avoid tax (Shaxson, 2012). The glaringly obvious result is that the richest 1 per cent of the population have seen both their income and net-worth increase rapidly, even during the ongoing global recession (ibid.; Harvey, 2007; Dorling, 2011). Similarly, we have seen the income of the poor either stagnate or decline, and the gap between rich and poor become higher than it has been for many decades (ibid.; see also www.poverty.org.uk). In the USA, Galbraith (2012) claims that such extremes of socioeconomic inequality have not been seen since the economic crash of 1929.

The broad social harms that result from this huge and growing social inequality are well known (see Wilkinson and Pickett, 2009; Dorling, 2011), but still neoliberalism, dominating over a pliant mass media and political system, retains the image of progress, productivity and prosperity. Even those who disbelieve the message are bereft of concrete ideas for an alternative socioeconomic system (Winlow and Hall, 2012b). If the economic system encounters problems, it is the poor rather than the rich who should contribute more (Frank, 2012). If, as David Cameron says, 'we're all in it together', the contribution of low-wage workers should be to work harder for less, while at the same time accepting that previous legal entitlements secured during Bauman's (2000) social democratic 'golden age' are no longer tenable. Demands for higher pay and the defence of employment benefits hamper the nation's economic recovery, we are told, ensuring that our industries remain uncompetitive on the global stage. Similarly, the talented super-elite are being held back by ponderous, lazy and dull-witted welfare recipients (see for example MacAskill, 2012, or Ayn Rand's turbo-capitalist manifesto, *Atlas Shrugged*). Be pragmatic, we are told: if the economy is to recover, the wages and benefits of low-paid workers must be cut, and state welfare systems must be scaled back or abandoned entirely. In straitened economic times, and with a considerable structural deficit, these are indulgences we can no longer afford. Everyone benefits when the economy grows, and we must all make sacrifices if we are get our economy moving again. If Britain can accept these changes, the boundless talent and entrepreneurial zeal of the super-rich will propel us back to growth and, in so doing, improve the lives of all.

For neoliberal ideologues, although some inequality is natural, timeless and fair, gross inequality is temporary, inevitable and functional to markets as they 'correct' themselves. It is natural and inevitable because the desire to achieve high status and distinguish ourselves from our peers is written into our genetic make-up, and it is functional because it encourages others to fight to achieve their own distinction, which in turn elicits from individuals – as they innovate, produce, trade and consume – the human effort that sustains and accelerates the circulation of capital. Here we encounter yet another aspect of the ruling ideology that has made the journey from the realm of ideas to the status of self-evident truth. Today, only dangerous radicals or ridiculous utopians suggest otherwise. Even the established left believe that, although unregulated capitalism produces harms, injustices and inequalities, we should attempt to curb its worst excesses while taking advantage of its legendary efficiency and productivity in order to give a growing percentage of the population the consumer items and experiences that constitute a good life. In contemporary Western democracies the political scene is now so bereft of genuine alternative thought that, even amid global economic turmoil and growing signs of dangerously unaligned mass frustration and anger, the choices offered to Western electorates usually extend no further than hard-core neoliberalism and its softer 'third way' variant. Again, we are faced with the cynical logic of post-political capitalist realism: all alternatives to liberal capitalism involve totalitarianism, barbarism and the denial of the citizens' rights to the free acquisition and trade of property and virtually limitless consumption.

According to Harvey (2007), this is what neoliberalism is actually about: a class war waged by the rich against the poor; a fundamental reallocation of income and resources from the poorest to the richest. In Britain we see the ideological structure that facilitates this reallocation every day on our news broadcasts. Michael Fallon, a Conservative Party MP and a business spokesman for the current coalition government, recently spoke of the need to view senior business leaders as we do the nation's Olympic champions, fighting heroically in the business sector to create wealth and jobs for Britain (see Hennessy, 2012). For Fallon and his colleagues, 'the politics of envy' continues to hold the country back. Fallon wants the nation to 'get behind' and 'salute' its wealth-creating business champions and, to that end, he has announced that he will fight aggressively for a new policy that will get rid of outmoded employment regulations and free businesses to fire employees at will. For all of those who doubt that ideology is still operative in a post-modern world, this, we suggest, is but one brief example of the operation of the ruling ideology in its new and more direct mode, built as it is on a platform of pragmatism and economic self-interest: 'it is in your interests to allow the rich to get richer and the poor to get poorer. Both deserve their allocated social position, and the national economy needs the risk-taking investments of the entrepreneurial super-elite to provide everyone else with employment and the cash to fund basic public services'. What Fallon and those he represents want is for insecure workers to accept their status as expendable units of production, and to accept that the titans of industry, in their relentless desire to accumulate, are the only hope workers have of remaining economically viable, and indeed the only hope we all have for a viable economic future. Be pragmatic: accept the reallocation of money and resources to the rich as an inevitable process. At least there exists the possibility that low-grade, insecure work might result from their desire to find new revenue streams.

In recent years the rise of executive 'bonus culture' has complicated this picture. Increasingly the appearance of profit and future profit has become more important than the real economic viability of commercial enterprises. The drive to secure cash and share bonuses has clearly led some senior executives to artificially inflate profitability predictions in an effort to boost the share prices that, in a short-term investment culture, signify success (see Elkind and McLean, 2004). Predictably enough, there is also evidence to suggest that the allure of bonus payments encourages workers in the financial services industry to mislead customers and investors (Bachelor, 2012). With the rise of abstract finance capitalism, the 'real money' is made in the fluctuations of currency markets, in the trading of assets and shares prior to the release of profitability figures, and of course in credit default swaps, collateralised debt obligations and brazen short-selling. The real, objective world of production, commodities, value and sales, in which ordinary workers earn a living, is almost entirely disconnected from this new economic reality (Mattick, 2011). As we have already claimed, the staggering levels of remuneration creamed off by bankers, corporate executives and rich investors should not be separated from the operation of contemporary capitalism in general. Rather, the availability of such enormous pay packages is an indication of the dominance of contemporary capitalism's new 'immaterial reality' lodged in the abstract realm of financial markets.

In 2009, just one year after the most catastrophic financial collapse in living memory, over £6 billion was paid in bonuses to city bankers in London. This may have been down on the £10.2 billion paid in 2007 (figures from www.bbc.co.uk), but still, one can only marvel – especially after the harsh lessons of the 1930s – at the palpable lack of political restraint placed upon this occupational group. The ideology that justifies such extravagant bonuses appears to be accepted by government: any attempt to reduce pay or increase taxes for this banking super-elite will result in them taking their unique talents to a competitor state. When we say 'good riddance' we are admonished and told that we don't really mean it. As an occupational group they may have failed monumentally, but to move forward we still need individuals with such rare and refined skills. But what else does the continuation of this obscene culture of excessive remuneration tell us about the current conjuncture? Of course, when considered alongside the decline of average wages in real terms (Harvey, 2010; Wolff, 2010), we begin to see quite clearly what the reallocation of resources from the poorest to the richest actually means. More importantly in the medium term, however – by which we mean the probability of further serious convulsions over the next few decades precipitated by an irrecoverable global slowdown in growth (Shutt, 2010; Heinberg, 2011) – we can also see that capitalism continues to possess an inherent tendency to catastrophic self-destruction. It seems that if these bonuses are not held in check by politicians aware of the popular hatred of the elite's bonus culture, they will continue to grow and grow until the global economic system as it is cannot keep up and 'social' relations become strained to breaking point. In a parallel process, the sycophantic praise heaped upon the banking elite encourages them to believe that they are superhuman and incapable of mistakes. And of course risk means nothing special to those who are incapable of making mistakes. Unavoidably, the gambles grow larger and financial market trading accelerates again – witness today's 'high-frequency trading', a practice that renders the 'ownership' of assets virtually meaningless – the money itself becomes irrelevant, save for a means of quantifying achievement, and the people whose livelihoods are dependent on the industries that underlie these financial markets become entirely inconsequential. In other words, political functionaries and their underfunded welfare institutions must be seen to look after people whose existence cannot even be recognised by the economic system's 'logic'. The excessive character of the libidinal financial economy threatens the stability of contemporary liberal capitalism's entire system of processual economic dynamics and political governance.

And who precisely are these bankers who secure such extravagant pay packages? They do not fit easily with the traditional image of a 'bourgeoisie'. Essentially they constitute a new class of technocratic trading executives who are judged by relatively ignorant shareholders to possess such rare and valuable skills that only the most extravagant pay packages can attract and retain them. We can proclaim the death of the old bourgeoisie or the birth of the new bourgeoisie, it makes little difference to anyone but the pedantic sociological filing clerk playing around with this year's edition of the Weberian stratification colouring book (see for example Scott, 1996); this new class now has the reins of the global financial system. Of course, they drive forward the financial markets and dominate our economic life, but they increasingly sit alongside democratically elected politicians keen to ground political campaigns in their entrepreneurial success. The traditional capitalist investment class appear to be much less directly involved, especially as ownership is now far more dispersed than it once was. Focused on securing an adequate return on their investments, they submit to requests from the board for ever more extravagant pay packages. Millions, indeed hundreds of millions, are needed in basic salaries, stock options and bonus payments to secure the services of this new technocratic overclass, no matter how incompetent they might be.

For example, Richard Fuld, the former CEO of Lehman Brothers, the bank whose collapse precipitated the global financial crisis, is rumoured to have earned half a *billion* US dollars between 2000 and 2007 (Sterngold, 2010). In Britain, Bob Diamond, the former CEO of Barclays Bank, is believed to be worth around £100 million. He commanded an annual bonus payment of £6,500,000 before his recent resignation, which appears to have been prompted by an investigation by financial regulators. The investigation revealed that Barclays employees had rigged the Libor inter-bank lending rate. Barclays were eventually fined £290 million (Treanor, 2012). The appointment of this elite, and their position as *employee* rather than traditional capitalist investor, clearly indicates the increasing immateriality of postmodern capital and the reconfiguration of its social relations. Despite being employees, we should continue to view this group as a new, dominant and exploitative class capable of attracting what Milner (2011) has called a 'surplus-wage'. The huge sums of cash involved are a clear indication that the appropriation of surplus-value continues apace. However, this process is now partially disguised in the wage form. What is it precisely that justifies such extravagant pay? What is it that these managers do that their immediate underlings could not? Why do members of this elite, who have so obviously failed, continue to attract such high wages and excessive bonuses (see for example Treanor, 2011)? Critically investigating these questions allows us to better understand the ideological edifice that supports today's capitalism.

If this new salaried managerial bourgeoisie are increasingly defining the reality of contemporary global capitalism, what happened to the old class of middle managers who facilitated the smooth functioning of modern capitalism during the industrial period? They increasingly constitute what has become known as 'the squeezed middle': those middle-income earners who are not welfare dependent but also fall some way short of the financial security of the new economic elites. The fully integrated and ideologically bound 'organisation man' (Whyte, 1957) of the 1950s and 1960s appeared to embody a period of quasi-egalitarian capitalist expansion, a corporate world of stability, suburban cultural uniformity and rising consumerism. This modern industrial class has no obvious postmodern equivalent. Many of the middle managers of today appear to be increasingly insecure and reflexive. They are fully incorporated into the ideology of liberal capitalism by the very fact that they refuse to believe in it with much enthusiasm as an actual socioeconomic system on which the lives of others depend, which provides a window into the obscene Real of cynical and nihilistic pragmatism at capitalism's core. They appear less integral to the reproduction of an increasingly immaterial postmodern capitalism, and often appear reduced to the role of institutional functionary, a briefcase-carrying 'labour aristocrat' in capitalism's new 'social factory' (Terranova, 2004).

While the super-elite of highly remunerated executive managers are deemed 'irreplaceable', the old group of middle managers are now eminently expendable. In a world of mass Further and Higher Education and rapidly evolving markets, the middle-manager's status appears reduced and their employment far less secure. They too must ensure that their skills remain updated and relevant as they attempt to defend against the next generation of energetic and enthusiastic graduates eager to replace them. For those at the top of such institutions, the strategy now appears to be that middle managers should also be exposed to job insecurity and labour market competition in order to extract higher productivity and ensure ultra-compliance to lower wages. Here we see a percolated postmodern variant of Marx's 'reserve army of labour'; it is now the middle managers of private and public sector organisations who are perennially anxious about their continued employment and status, and the 'reserve army' also includes the mass of graduates churned out annually by our university system rather than just the archetypal socially excluded 'lumpen proletarian'.

If the socially excluded populations of the West's post-industrial cities also constitute a 'reserve army of labour', which groups of potential workers are rendered insecure and expendable by their existence and social position? The jobs available to this potential workforce exist at the very bottom of the service economy and what remains of the West's productive enterprises. In these sectors, there is no stable, organised workforce seeking to retain jobs. Rather, in a process of endless selection and circulation, temporary workforces emerge from a broad pool of unemployed and underemployed populations to be exploited for the required period before again being pushed back to their allocated position among the redundant. Others will quit these jobs because the gradual accumulation of indignities that shape the work experience in these sectors becomes too much to bear. Some will return to be exploited and humiliated again, others will search in hope for a better paid and more rewarding job, and others still will accept worklessness, at least until they are forced back into exploitative work by increasingly aggressive government employment agencies. If the reserve army of middle managers displays cynical and instrumental tendencies, the reserve army of unskilled service workers displays no enthusiasm whatsoever for the work on offer.

Neoliberalism's post-middle class

As they attempt to address structural deficits and significant budgetary constraints, post-crash neoliberal governments proceed on the basis that it is counterproductive to tax the rich. Yet it seems obvious that tax revenues need to rise and spending needs to fall if any progress is to be made. The result is that the reduced-status middle managers discussed above are taking the brunt of post-crash tax rises, while those at the bottom take the brunt of government austerity cuts. In the same way as sociologists increasingly talk of a 'post-working class' – fragmented to such an extent that it is no longer reasonable to talk of them as a cohesive class in the traditional modernist sense – we might talk of this group of middle managers as a 'post-middle class', occupying a vague position somewhere in the middle of a class hierarchy whose boundaries appear fluid and open but whose internal structures are replete with hurdles, obstacles and powerful currents and slipstreams that might propel individuals upwards or drag them downwards to the very bottom. The class hierarchy has changed so much as a result of capitalism's recent dynamic shift, but in ways that have perpetuated social exclusion amongst the 'underclass' and extended its potential to the middle class, in general diffusing the powerful constraints that work against upward mobility throughout all sub-elite strata.

The class system appears fluid and open only in the sense that liberal capitalism *truly accepts* all identity groups into its upper managerial echelons. It cares not if new arrivals at the top are women, from lower-class backgrounds, talk with an accent, have black or brown skin or incline towards any form of non-heterosexuality. Of course, residual structural impediments can prevent the ascent of these groups, but if they do make it to the hallowed gates of the super-strata by applying unusual effort and determination, they will not be denied access. In fact they will be welcomed for their additional use-value as ideological pin-ups to demonstrate liberal-capitalism's intrinsic fairness. What matters for the continuity of liberal capitalism is the willingness of new inductees to fully identify with and internalise its ideology as an unconscious belief and to work tirelessly to lubricate the circulation of capital. In the same way, liberal capitalism no longer has any loyalty to the elites of the old world. Their refined speech, social comportment, elite education, old school connections – as well as their good old-fashioned nepotism – act as obvious brakes upon downward mobility, but if these brakes fail, then capitalism will not ensure a soft landing. A failed marriage, a redundancy or a bankruptcy might accelerate downward mobility, but the real pressure falls on the young educated children of the middle class in their socially appointed role of replicating the economic and cultural position of their parents. Again, this group can draw upon significant advantages, but nothing is guaranteed. The general degradation of employment opportunities in consumer-driven Western economies affects the ex-middle classes too, and we are already seeing the children of middle-class parents accepting jobs that would have been scorned by their families just a few decades ago. The social advantages of their birth will not provide total protection. If they are to succeed, they must make the sacrifices that accompany full commitment to the market. Either that or they can join others on the increasingly difficult path into the lower-status bureaucratic professions that continue to pay a surplus wage.

Like the post-working class, the 'squeezed middle' are fragmented, individualised, anxious and, for the moment at least, politically neutralised. In a period of huge labour market instability, anxiety and rising unemployment, the traditional image of the 'middle class' can be nothing other than an empty signifier. The contemporary middle class possesses no obvious cultural substance or clear economic function. If, during the modern period, we could talk of middle-class culture in relation to conservatism and deferred gratification, can we still deploy such a framework today? The socially reproductive conservatism and soft social liberalism displayed by previous incarnations of this middle group appears to have been disrupted by the prevalence of advanced insecurity and anxiety. The safety net of a 'good education' can no longer be relied upon. The routes to upward social mobility have changed, and now demand aggressive individualism and a commitment to economic liberalism, innovation and risk-taking. Similarly, the deferred gratification of the traditional middle classes has been dragged off course by a new cultural injunction to enjoy (Žižek, 2008b, 2009b). This new injunction demands that even the conservative middle classes dedicate their lives to seeking out pleasure and personal indulgence, and judge their lives in relation to the accumulation of hedonistic and commodified 'experiences'. Žižek's (ibid.) core point is not that this new injunction has compelled us to discard old, repressive structures that restricted our social experience and condemned us to a doleful, ascetic life of unfulfilled desire. Rather, the putatively permissive injunction actually denies access to true happiness because we cannot truly enjoy that which we are ordered to enjoy. Modernism might have appeared rather mundane and monotonous (see Bauman, 2000) – a culture of limited consumer opportunities, restrictive social attitudes towards sex, and so on – but at least it enabled the subject to experience genuine pleasure and excitement in the act of transgression (see also Hayward, 2004; O'Neill and Seal, 2012). A consumerised world in which we are ordered to seek our own enjoyment offers no such opportunity (see also Winlow and Hall, 2012a).

We might suppose that we are again seeing a further diffusion of the process of proletarianisation first experienced by low-status non-manual workers during the 1970s and 1980s (Lea, 2002). While many of this salaried and consumerised 'squeezed middle' remain some way from the social position occupied by the genuinely marginalised and poor, it certainly seems reasonable to suggest that they too – especially the lower echelons – might constitute part of the precariat. In contemporary Britain, for example, pay awards since 2008 have in most cases fallen well below the level of inflation, and public sector pensions in particular have come under sustained attack. This old middle-income group is indeed on the whole becoming poorer and less capable of engaging in the conspicuous consumption that is the key marker of social inclusion. What we see within this group is growing insecurity about status and social position, and their ability to maintain their consumer lifestyles. In Britain, we can also see that the tenor of the public conversation about the deficit and public sector employment has evolved quickly into an aggressive conflict between private sector workers – who are relatively poorly paid, have poor pensions and face the constant threat of redundancy – and public sector workers, who at least have reasonable pension arrangements and a greater degree of job security. This of course represents a classic race to the bottom, a process of taking away from one's adversary rather than attempting to improve one's own conditions. Insecure private sector workers believe that it is unfair that public sector workers continue to have reasonable pensions and job security and so side with the interests of capital. They demand the removal of these privileges and the relegation of public sector workers to the same state of constant insecurity the private sector occupy, a classic case of Rousseauian *amour propre* as justice is seen to be done and pleasure taken at the downfall of the other.

This removal of social entitlements that were once judged markers of civilisation and progress is done under the banner of 'justice for taxpayers'. Why should the exploited precariat of the private sector foot the bill for extravagant public sector pensions? This is but one of many discourses of *negative solidarity* that suggest a fundamental transformation has taken place to the constitution of our shared social life. The 'interests of taxpayers', a phrase so often used to justify government austerity programmes, do not exist in any real sense; for example, it makes little sense to identify common economic interests between the low wage earner and the extravagantly paid banker. The abstraction of the 'taxpayer' from a variegated concrete reality possesses a radical negativity cloaked in the language of unity and common purpose. In reality the phrase is a product of the ideology of parliamentary capitalism. It involves the taking away of benefits from even the most deserving social groups. Of course, this abstraction fails to even consider that 'the taxpayer' on a lower income may also benefit from those things that are purchased collectively and provided free or at low cost for all. If followed to its fullest extent the logic of this political abstraction leads inevitably to a situation in which the contemporary public sector appears condemned to disappear. The concept of the 'interests of the taxpayer' is a manifestation of the deeper right-wing ideology of classical liberalism and libertarianism, which sees tax as theft and state expenditure as profligate – and also immoral, as Republican Presidential candidate Mitt Romney recently declared in a TV interview – and desires only reductions in tax and the end of excessive state interference. In the name of 'justice for ordinary taxpayers' we move towards a society that appears increasingly orientated towards nihilistic atomisation and pragmatic economic self-interest, and in which there remains no space for the traditional substance of civility and sociability.

As for those radicals who believe a return to history is imminent, one only has to look at the current public antipathy towards public sector unions – which would threaten Britain's economic recovery and inconvenience private sector worker-consumers with strikes – to see the extent of parliamentary liberal-capitalism's continued ideological triumph. We see a similar process taking place in the USA in the form of opposition to Obama's healthcare reforms: ordinary people opposed to the very processes and institutions that might improve their lives and those of their community (see also Frank, 2005, 2006). It's worth noting that some British public sector workers appear to be increasingly radical. But why this group and not the insecure private sector workers who have a tougher time of it? Public sector labour unions are once again returning to strikes, stoppages, working-to-rule and even the threat of a general strike, suggesting a greatly needed *repoliticisation* of a particular stratum of the expendable workforce. It's clear that this militancy is closely related to the threats posed to workplace entitlements, jobs and pay levels by the government's austerity agenda, and the rapid downward mobility that is already in train. What is striking is that many of these workers seem to be aware that the skills they possess would not guarantee a return to work in the private sector, and even for those lucky enough to find new employment, it's unlikely that they would be employed at a similar level of pay with roughly equivalent benefits. There is a palpable sense that the last vestiges of the social democratic welfare state are disintegrating, and that the services it provided and the stable and socially productive forms of work it offered are about to be disrupted and radically transformed by the raw competitive forces of the market. This new militancy represents an entirely legitimate fear of falling to the very bottom. The reawakening of the trade union movement and the increased activism of public sector workers are developments that reflect a growing social fear about falling, about losing something of great utility in demonstrating one's being-in-the-world. However, they are quite distinct from traditional socialist forms of worker representation that sought to advance the interests of those *already at the bottom*. The new militants are afraid of sinking into the bottom layer, not inspired by the dream of its abolition by means of political action.

What should we conclude from this? We should perhaps begin by noting that it is the 'squeezed middle' who appear more likely to articulate a reasonably coherent political response to the continuation of parliamentary capitalism. It is easier for politics to return to the educated ex-middle classes, many of whom have now passed through Britain's university system, than it is to politicise the increasingly nihilistic, consumerised and incorporated 'socially excluded' populations who are already bearing the full weight of social regression, fragmentation and brutalisation. While frustrations and dissatisfactions accumulate in abundance at the bottom, it is the 'squeezed middle' who appear most able to articulate a political alternative to neoliberalism, even in an attenuated social-liberal form. What we are suggesting is that the old modernist conflict between the working classes and the middle classes demands reconsideration. There are clear shared interests that exist across traditional class demarcations, even if the growing politicisation of the 'squeezed middle' is structured in relation to an anxiety about becoming part of the very group with whom they should be constructing new narratives of community and solidarity. Whether a new universal politics can emerge to bring together the interests of the 'socially excluded' and the deeply insecure 'squeezed middle' remains to be seen.

7

A Reserve Army
of Consumers?

In the decades that followed the Second World War, modern capitalist enterprises often recognised the utility of a relatively content workforce that felt valued and integral to the business. Paying a little more and offering permanent work positions ensured a greater degree of effort, commitment and docility. What we can now see quite clearly is that, during the modern era, job security and rising living standards for workers translated into greater productivity, which in turn produced profit, attracted investment and sustained economic growth (Hutton, 1995; Harvey, 2007, 2010). This sense of continuity and dependability may appear quite dour in comparison to the apparently seductive qualities of contemporary neoliberal risk-taking and entrepreneurship, but it provided an important reproductive role that stabilised communities and identities, allowing a degree of the psychic repose and security that fostered altruism, reciprocity and civic-mindedness (Hall et al., 2008). When we are faced with claims of neoliberalism's remarkable efficiency, we must immediately note that it has in fact been unable to match the long-term economic successes of the modern era (see Harvey, 2007; Wolff, 2010; Galbraith, 2012), which grew the real productive economy up to 32 times since the introduction of the steam engine (Heinberg, 2011). Since the burst of increased productivity caused by further automation and the introduction of the PC into the workforce in the early 1980s, it has become less productive, and severe economic contractions have been much more regular and a good deal more harmful (Harvey, 2010).

So, can we continue to claim that the real threat to industrial jobs is materialised in a socially excluded 'reserve army of labour'? The now long-established mobility of finance enables businesses and corporations to move quickly, setting up shop in other countries if it is financially expedient to do so. But we should not understand this situation solely in relation to the competition offered to the Western industrial workforce by workers in low-wage economies around the world. Rather, the life-world of the West's remaining industrial workforce is threatened and made constantly insecure by the incessant drive to increase profits by inflating prices and reducing costs. If we are to retain what is valuable in Marx, rather than, as Byrne (1999) does, attempting to apply Marx's unmodified original ideas to the establishment and growth of apparently surplus populations throughout the West, might it not be more fruitful to ask: what would Marx have made of the present reality of global capitalism? What would he have had to say about immaterial labour, casino capitalism and the net reduction in reasonably rewarding employment opportunities across the West?

One obvious aspect of continuity in Marx's thought might be the economic and political *connections and commonalities* that exist between members of a new global proletariat. Despite the surface competition that appears to pitch low-wage workers in different nations against each other in the fight to secure paid labour, globalisation also opens up a deterritorialised space in which new relationships between exploited social groups across the world might be forged. They may speak different languages and worship different gods, but their shared relationship with the means of production and consumption bonds them together as a non-traditional, globalised exploited class. In this way, the American ghetto poor have more in common with ghetto inhabitants of São Paulo, Beijing and Mexico City than they do with the rich Americans who inhabit the gated enclaves just a short geographical distance away from their own neighbourhoods. It is the recognition of their collective interests and the disavowal of capitalist competition that might allow them, in the Marxist sense, to become a genuine global political *class for itself*.

But does Byrne's (1999) claim that the socially excluded continue to function as a 'reserve army of labour' hold water? Of course, the leisure and service sectors now make up large swathes of Western neoliberal labour markets. As Byrne (1989) has noted, these jobs have certainly not compensated for the loss of industrial labour. They are usually non-unionised, low paid, short-term, insecure and part-time. We should also note that few of these jobs enable workers to construct and maintain an image of themselves as socially valuable (Winlow and Hall, 2006, 2009a; Southwood, 2011; Lloyd, 2012); in fact, many of these McJobs (Ritzer, 1997) communicate the exact opposite: the low-level, low-paid service worker is seen as disreputable, exploitable and untrustworthy, the *homo sacer* of the post-political order, waiting tables, flipping burgers and sweeping rubbish. These are fundamentally insecure and alienating jobs. The people who have these jobs do not want to retain them beyond the obvious and pressing need to earn enough money to pay for their immediate living expenses (Winlow and Hall, 2009a). Most of the positive symbolism associated with traditional work has already been stripped away. They do not cling to and seek to defend an image of themselves as fast food workers, call centre operatives, cleaners, supermarket shelf stackers or factory box-packers.

The 'competition for jobs' that was supposed to herald new efficiencies, compelling workers to acquire the new skills that would drive forward

British business on the world stage, is in fact more akin to job competition in Victorian England: competition for jobs that workers in fact *do not want*, competition not for status and social advancement but simply in order to survive, or to facilitate a lifestyle (Southwood, 2011; Lloyd, 2012). A liberalised capitalist labour market no longer needs a 'reserve army' of workers in order to make workers feel insecure. Insecurity already courses through the lifeworld of the precariat, engulfing it from innumerable directions. For some, job tenure is reduced to a matter of hours (Southwood, 2011). Workers know that their jobs will come to an end in the not-too-distant future, and in many cases, they have no great desire to retain jobs that pay very low wages and symbolise little more than the impoverishment, humiliation and degradation of the classic 'skivvy' (Winlow and Hall, 2009a; Lloyd, 2012). In Britain, we should also note that a significant body of empirical research suggests that a circular conveyor belt carries many of those on benefits into the worst jobs and then back to benefits again; the so-called 'reserve army' and the underemployed 'precariat' constantly morph back and forth into each other's form. The gap between leaving work and signing on to claim benefits allows many of these people periodically to disappear from the public record, being neither in employment nor on state benefits, somehow fending for themselves. The established ideological trope of the ambitious but poorly-skilled worker who climbs to the top through internal systems of advancement is largely a myth.

What we are seeing is the normalisation of workplace insecurity. Workers do not redouble their labours in order to appear indispensable to their immediate line manager; often their immediate line manager is also subject to the same insecurities and recognises that few will stick with a job that is entirely devoid of positive symbolism (Toynbee, 2003; Southwood, 2011). The substance has already been removed to leave only mechanised exploitation, a short-termism of counted seconds, forced smiles and phoney sincerity.

If Marx's idea of a 'reserve army of labour' is no longer of much use to our understanding of the reality of post-industrial labour markets, might a 'reserve army of consumers' furnish us with some further insight? We will not dwell on this point beyond the claim that the ubiquity of consumerist fantasies is deeply indicative of the dominance of contemporary liberal ideology. Consumerism is a libidinal fantasy common to all but those who actively negate it (Stiegler, 2011), not simply the preserve of the newly squeezed and increasingly insecure middle classes, or the relatively small group of individuals who have the money necessary to structure their lives around the acquisition of new products. Our previous ethnographic research in low-income areas throughout the north-east of England (Winlow, 2001; Winlow and Hall, 2006; Hall et al., 2008) suggests very clearly that even those who do not possess the resources to indulge legally in hedonistic consumption with any degree of regularity continue to imagine and mentally calibrate their social value in relation to it. They too are aware of the power of stylised individualism, of designer labels and of hedonistic adventures in the leisure playgrounds of the city's non-places. Following incessant TV advertising and the general current of Western culture, they imagine a life in which they are magically able to indulge their most vivid consumer dreams. The ubiquity and potency of these dreams almost inevitably leads to the subject living a life in their shadow, believing themselves somehow not to be living life *as it is supposed to be lived*, while at the same time always hoping against hope that things will change for them and that they will be catapulted to the elite's lofty stratum, able to indulge consumer fantasies and elicit the envy of others. In the acidic culture of *amour propre* that pervades contemporary Western liberal democracies, inciting envy in others is the clearest indication that one has both social value and a primary socioeconomic function; a structural value *within* the system and a functional value *to* the system.

Contrary to the perennially optimistic left-liberal academics who currently constitute the Grand Order of Pangloss, we do not believe that run-down housing estates are bursting with organic oppositional politics, radical otherness and the seeds of new communal life. Nor do we believe the right-realist myth of inferior cultural otherness. Some of the occupants might possess a range of behavioural norms that are distinct from – and in some cases rather irksome to – the cultural mainstream but, at the deeper level of values and drives, they are entirely normal members of late-capitalist consumer culture. They want what the majority want. Generally speaking, they don't spend their time debating post-capitalist economic organisation or constructing their own organic forms of corporate-free culture. They want big screen TVs, flash cars, new clothes, foreign holidays and, rather than forge new solidarities, to elevate themselves above those around them (Hall et al., 2008; Treadwell et al., 2012). The 'reserve army of consumers' therefore act as a window on the almost total triumph of liberal-capitalist hegemonic ideology and culture. They are 'flawed consumers' only in the most narrow and practical sense. They might not have the cash to engage in regular bouts of consumer spending, but the powerful desire to do so remains very much in place (Smart, 2010; Stiegler, 2011; Treadwell et al., 2012). In our own research, we have often witnessed the poor spending money first on symbolic consumer items before turning their attention to more mundane and vital acts of consumption. Rather than paying a bill or buying food, our respondents often bought expensive brands of clothes, shoes, electronic gadgets, cigarettes or alcohol (see Hall et al., 2008). Of course this is certainly not true of the poor in their entirety, but it is nonetheless true, and this blunt fact – that consumer-orientated desire triumphs over need – should be a telling indication of consumerism's intoxicating symbolic power. The compulsion to seek out, experience and display conspicuous enjoyment and indulgence as markers of social relevance compels many relatively poor individuals to forego basic items (see also Nightingale, 1993; LeBlanc, 2009).

Indeed, it must give the liberal-capitalist elite great comfort to peer down through the layers of the allegedly fluid class system to see that even the poorest are fully incorporated into capitalism's competitive and individualistic consumer culture. The poor's dissatisfaction, nihilism and occasional self-destructive behaviours relate specifically to their inability to achieve a degree of security and recognition in capitalism's sociosymbolic structure. Dissatisfaction, however, is entirely unrelated to awareness of capitalism's precipitous hierarchies and structural inequalities or distaste felt towards them. The claim that oppositional politics and alternative cultures exist to any great extent among the poor in socially excluded neighbourhoods is little more than wishful thinking from a liberal-left establishment that abandoned serious opposition itself in the 1980s. Too often, this is a middle-class ideological projection that covers up the far more troubling reality of mass ideological incorporation and rising but apolitical and objectless discontent (Hall, 2012a; Treadwell et al., 2012; Winlow and Hall 2012b). These problems are compounded by the dominant ideology's emphasis on apolitical individualism and the almost total absence of political narratives that might encourage new solidarity projects that seek to pursue the cause of social justice.

Despite the ideological incorporation of the West's poorest populations, we should not assume that the poor are content to live life fully in accordance with capitalism's deep structural inequality, ideologically reproduced as the product of a natural meritocracy and the 'price of freedom'. The general mood suggests that they are deeply aggrieved by their inability to access legally those things that they are told constitute a good life and confer social status. However, their discontent cannot yet be directed at their true enemy. They are vaguely 'pissed-off' but continue to believe that the acquisition of more of consumer culture's symbolic objects can address their torment. This is a disoriented anger that struggles to find realistic symbolic representation, and can, in acts of impotent rage, harm those things that continue to be of real value (see Winlow, 2012b).

Of course, we are not at all suggesting that the contemporary poor are incapable of being happy. Rather, we are attempting to capture their deeper and enduring emotional unease, a pervasive sense of absence, an inkling that something is missing compounded by a sense of disjuncture from the world and the inability to find emotional tranquillity and enduring satisfaction. Indeed, Cornel West (1993; 2004) has suggested that the cultural life of the ghetto is now structured firmly around a core of nihilism, an outcome that reflects 'the lived experience of coping with a life of horrifying meaninglessness, hopelessness and (most important) lovelessness' (1993: 22–3). These emotional states are not peculiar to the socially excluded. That is precisely our point. What distinguishes the dissatisfied poor from the dissatisfied rich relates to their distinct socioeconomic positions and the ways in which their immediate social experiences colour their different modes of dissatisfaction and give shape to their immediate subjective responses and attempted solutions.

This crucial and ubiquitous sense of *dislocation* should be understood in relation to the rise of liberal-postmodernism and its assault upon collective identities and all fixed truths, faiths and commitments (see Chapter 9). This dislocation affirms and reproduces commitment to subjective isolation and the view that connections and obligations to others are hindrances to subjective interests in an incessant, competitive and joyless game played to maintain the circulation of capital and the development of new markets. The profound sense of loss and absence is a product of the subtraction from the social world of faith, community, stability and solidarity, and installs in its place a post-social milieu of instrumentalism, atomisation, cynicism, envy and withdrawal. While the really existing social life of the modern era was in fact built upon an illusion, it was a *vital illusion* that sustained faith and encouraged the symbolic efficiency that allowed us to engage faithfully with the cultures and communities we inhabit.

The sense of absence in economically excluded neighbourhoods is palpable and extreme. What appears to be the growing resentment of younger inhabitants should not be regarded as a permanent characteristic of twenty-first century marginality. The raw anger that develops in relation to the inability to access consumerism's surrogate social world could once again drive forward history in a radically different direction. The growth and concentration of a shared sense of suffering and dissatisfaction has throughout history driven progressive politics, and it can do so again. However, these same sentiments have often been perverted and knocked off course to descend into regressive nationalism. There are already signs throughout Europe of strange, postmodern nationalisms developing as post-political populations experience a profound sense of social anxiety and loss. As we have already suggested, these populations are anxious about something they can't quite put into words: the loss of something – a way of life, an identity, a sense of security, commitment to a truth – that was once of great value. We should consider carefully the possibility that liberalism's great fear of working-class collectivism might in fact inspire a return to the very thing it hates most: an aggressive postmodern-nationalist hybrid that seizes upon this pervasive sense of anxiety and loss before redirecting the righteous indignation of the poor towards ethnic or religious minorities.

Immaterial exploitation?

If we are truly to grasp the economic position of the West's poorest, we must briefly acknowledge that contemporary capitalism is increasingly reliant upon immaterial labour (see for example Lazzarato, 1996; Hardt and Negri, 2000; Virno et al., 2004; Virno, 2007; Berardi, 2009). As we have suggested above, the old world of the factory is, for most Western workforces, entirely forgotten. Instead, we see the growth of what autonomous Marxists (ibid.) have called 'affective labour', a phrase that principally refers to forms of post-industrial service provision involving an emotional and relational investment. Lloyd (2012), for example, outlines the multiple stresses placed upon call centre workers in the deindustrialised north-east of England. They experience their work as deprived of virtually all positive content and they struggle to manage the burden of subduing and satisfying angry and aggressive customers while at the same time selling additional services and 'smiling down the phone'. Affective labour is what remains when traditional forms of industrial labour disappear and the forms of intellectual labour that constitute the rarefied 'knowledge economy' fail to fill the gap.

Connected to the growing predominance of affective labour in deindustrialised Western societies, we see the growth in the use of computers in virtually all forms of work. Indeed, such is the dominance of information technology over our working lives that Hardt and Negri (2000: 290) talk of workers being forced to 'think like computers'. What we now see, as many authors attest (for example Bell, 1973; Castells, 2010a, 2010b), is a new form of cognitive capitalism driven forward by knowledge, information and the continued appropriation of surplus value from developing forms of cognitive labour.

These developments have altered the relation between capital and labour. In Western labour markets, the body's physical capacities are now less important. Rather, surplus value is secured by appropriating the immediate *intellectual* capacity of the worker, in most cases a process mediated by computerisation. Rather than appropriating the physical strength, skill and endurance of the modern factory labourer, postmodern capital circulates its commodities and expands its markets by securing the cognitive capacity of a largely office-based workforce, which now outnumbers those involved in physical production and distribution. Rows upon rows of downgraded office workers, staring at computer screens, are now engaged in demanding and draining but essentially immaterial forms of labour, producing what Lazzarato (1996: 131) describes as 'the informational and cultural content of the commodity'. The production of the informational content is still understood as labour by workers, whereas producing the cultural content demands activities and relations that cannot be understood as labour in the traditional sense. Here, the interests of capital commandeer the personality and subjectivity of the worker and utilise them as a source of informational capital. Lazzarato's work highlights ways in which the contemporary form of capitalism spills over traditional demarcations into the subjective life of the worker, appropriating forms of knowledge and experience gathered by workers in all dimensions of their lifeworld, from leisure to personal relationships and fantasies, as the building bricks of cultural content.

Berardi (2009) suggests that contemporary capitalism can now generate profit simply by appropriating and commodifying everyday forms of communication. The line between labour time and non-labour time is now so porous as to render inapplicable all traditional ways of distinguishing between them. But the production of value continues apace, diffusing beyond the formal world of work into the intimacies of our personal and private spaces. We see this most clearly in the huge growth of networked media devices that cultivate a constant 'plugged-in' mediatisation of social experience in which we are encouraged to 'live', constantly producing demand-side value as our opinions, sentiments and desires are laid bare for advertisers and commodity producers. We cannot understand media platforms such as Facebook and Twitter as essentially free services that facilitate communication. We must recognise the vital role of users in the generation of value. If Facebook is believed to be one of the most important cultural developments of recent years, accessed by an estimated 750 million users worldwide, and worth 104 billion dollars (Cellan-Jones, 2012), how precisely does its value accrue? Here the autonomous Marxists draw upon the concept of the 'general intellect' and use it to address *the intellect in general*. For them, it is precisely this intellect in general that is being appropriated by the interests of twenty-first century capital.

We mention the growth of immaterial and affective labour for a number of reasons. First, we must recognise that exploitation is no longer contained entirely in the employer/employee relationship and the drudgeries of the working day. The production of economic value has dispersed much more broadly through our post-political, media-dominated society as the traditional boundaries containing work relationships have been breached by postmodern capital and its attendant consumer culture. While much of mainstream social theory addressing the growth and influence of the internet has focused on the liberating effects of information and knowledge and the purported 'political' potential of new forms of e-community (Lash, 2010), if we look more closely we can see new forms of labour and economic exploitation emerging that reflect capital's indefatigable ability to adapt to changes in social, political and technological reality. While immaterial labour may not strike us as an especially important issue compared to the material and financial pressures faced by the poor, it is precisely this form of labour that is establishing itself as hegemonic and, therefore, a vital locus of competitive individualism and the processes of inclusion and exclusion.

Of course, traditional exploitative relations of production continue to exist, especially in the East and in the global South. They also continue to exist in the interstices of consumerised Western economies in a downgraded, insecure and deeply exploitative form; even those with stellar technological skills are becoming progressively less indispensable. However, the infiltration of capital into every intimate dimension of human life means that new forms of productive labour that are *not fully understood as such* now play a crucial role – often without wages – in maintaining global capitalism's profitable circulation of commodities. The ability of the market to evolve is truly something to behold, and capitalism's ability constantly to adapt and renew itself in spectral forms that are less dependent on traditional productive labour compels us to rethink Byrne's (1999) claim that socially excluded Western populations continue to function simply as a 'reserve army of labour'.

We also need to understand that the growth of media-centred immaterial labour indicates the fundamental absence at the heart of contemporary social life. We will expand on this theme in the next chapter, but at this stage we can briefly identify one or two key issues. Earlier in this chapter we mentioned Žižek's (2008b, 2009b, 2009c) analysis of a new cultural injunction to enjoy. He is suggesting that the ceaseless search for personal satisfaction has become central to the organisation of Western culture. A good life is a life in which we have tasted extreme indulgence, a life in which we have denied ourselves nothing and exposed ourselves constantly to the thrill of the new; a life of sexual adventure, global travel and committed consumerism, in which we forge our own path and blithely ignore decaying conservative accounts of frugality, commitment, obligation and work. For Žižek, this cultural injunction reflects a historic transformation in the nature of our super-ego, the part of our psyche that attempts to socialise by means of repression and sublimation (see glossary) the id's raw libidinal drives and the early ego's narcissistic desires. The super-ego is a complex internal mechanism that issues a range of aggressively ethical demands that often cannot be met, but it also acts to regulate and direct our social behaviour. During the modern period, for example, the healthy super-ego demanded the repression of the subject's narcissism and encouraged the subject to be mindful of the rules and protocols of its culture. The super-ego acts as the ethical guide for the calculative ego as it forces us to think about the consequences of our actions and the likely reaction of our culture to those things we say and do. For Žižek, the contemporary super-ego now issues a demand that the subject must commit to enjoyment. Rather than instructing us to pull back from excessively libidinal and egotistical activity, the super-ego demands that we forge ahead up to and sometimes beyond the legal boundary, never missing an opportunity to experience extreme subjective pleasure as *jouissance*. In the postmodern world, we submit to the rules of our community not by attenuating or redirecting self-interested libidinal drives but precisely by committing to personal indulgence and gorging ourselves on stupid, solipsistic pleasures.

We see the results of this super-ego injunction all around us all of the time. It structures the accumulation of consumer debt, it is complicit in the increased disposability of personal relationships, and it is expressed directly in media outputs that encourage us to fill our lives with the supposed liberating experiences of committed hedonism. Travel more. Have more sex. Buy new clothes. Take drugs. Get drunk. Start a new life. Become your own boss. Do something different. Be something different. Ensure that you live a life less ordinary. As we have already suggested, populations defined as 'socially excluded' are also subject to this injunction. They too wish to comply with this dominant super-ego injunction, but have fewer material opportunities to actively engage in *consumer* forms of hedonistic indulgence. However, the cultural injunction insists, and they continue to be pulled towards hedonistic consumption. In many cases, if money comes into their lives, it is first spent on the consumer items and experiences that are usually out of reach. This can often appear to confirm conservative accounts of the profligacy of the poor, but the indulgent consumerism of those least able to afford it is a much more complex process than these accounts suggest. Rather than demonstrating a cultural otherness, the committed consumerism of the poor instead suggests a radical sameness, an unadulterated uniformity indicative of the ubiquity and incorporative power of consumerism's seductive symbolism.

More pertinent to our discussion of immaterial labour are the forms of self-exclusion from the social that are seen among mainstream young people. Žižek's key point in relation to the super-ego injunction to enjoy is that it ultimately leads to a prevailing sense of lack, an enduring sense of absence, the constant feeling, as insistent as it is vague, that something is missing. The injunction to enjoy compels us to seek out enjoyment, but the mere fact that we have been ordered to enjoy removes any possibility of subjective pleasure and fulfilment. The interminable search for enjoyment is therefore an essentially joyless task. We play the game of pleasure-seeking, and commit ourselves to activities that appear to suggest a surface level of pleasure and indulgence while at the same time taking no real satisfaction from these activities. We *sub*consciously recognise that the injunction to enjoy sends us on a fool's errand, searching endlessly for something that was never there to be found. But still we search, becoming despondent and disgruntled, surrounded by the consumer items we once believed would lead to us to elusive contentment but now bore us. Isn't the common refrain of 'disaffected' young people, 'I'm bored'? However, this has little to do with Max Weber's obsolete notion of 'disaffection'; in fact the problem is *too much contrived and rerouted affection* for a seductive spectacle that melts away as soon as we try to grasp it. Surrounded by gadgets, games and new forms of media, detached from grounded, obligatory social experience, a growing proportion of young people succumb to an endless cycle of stimulated libidinal affectivity, disappointment and lethargy, positioned somehow external to the social, looking back at it in quiet disappointment, with smirking irony or routinised postmodern cynicism. A retreat from the drudgeries of work, the pressures of college and the dispiriting experience of pleasure-seeking can be found in new mediated forms of virtual sociability. These media experiences do not lead to pleasure, but at least they retain the appearance of 'socialising' and 'leisure'. If little else, they are *not work*, or *not college*. They exhort only minor pressures and demand nothing other than a mild form of shallow, disengaged attention. In exchange, they provide the useful function of filling in time and space that might otherwise require social re-engagement, commitment, sacrifice or effort.

This analysis of immaterial leisure reveals to us an additional economic dynamic that draws libidinal energy by means of the super-ego injunction to enjoy, connecting it not to any transcendental, political or communal ideal but to consumer culture's order of symbolic objects, the circulation of commodities and the production of market value with 'immaterial labour'. The order to 'live life without a safety net' and to accumulate rare and indulgent experiences animates consumer markets and contributes to the continual redevelopment of consumer capitalism. The fundamental desire we all have to be something else, to achieve more, to gather social recognition – and increasingly to elicit the envy of others as a palpable indication of our social distinction and cultural relevance – ensnares us in what Bernard Stiegler (2011) calls consumer capitalism's 'libidinal (dis)economy'.

Students are an obvious example of this new mode of entrapment. Students in British universities often spend many hours each day connected to social media platforms such Facebook and Twitter. Here they engage in the low-level immaterial labour that is appropriated by capitalism and used to generate profit. The content they upload and the words they type are not understood as labour, and they see no connection between their mediated activity and the generation of value and profit. For them, Facebook is a useful means of keeping in touch with the world; an opportunity to express an opinion, to comment on a photo, or to engage with a distant friend and possibly experience a brief moment of humour or pleasure. But the cultural drive towards these forms of leisure, socialising and consumption constantly fails to yield the expected social experience, and, further, it involves a self-exclusion from the social *in the name of the social itself* and *in the name of social progress*. That is, the subject effectively removes itself from the immediacy of real social experience in order to engage in a commercialised virtual social experience that demands and appropriates a degree of immaterial labour.

Many of our students spend hours at a time connected to Facebook. They usually do this at the expense of everything else. They do it because these media experiences are understood as 'not work'. They appear redolent of the social characteristics of leisure, and may also offer a shallow and fleeting pleasure, or perhaps an easy indulgence positioned in opposition to the harshness of the real world, the indignities of work and the pressures of building an identity and a biography. They do it because it provides a degree of comfort, a place of retreat. In extreme cases, this retreat can be such that real social relations atrophy as they pursue a virtual project, managing and elaborating their social material profiles in the hope of a future social benefit, while at the same time making an unconscious contribution to the further development of postmodern capital. In common rooms and other public spaces across the country, social space is mediated by cyberspace. People sit close to each other, but gaze into mobile devices, often accompanied by their own musical soundtrack, entirely disconnected from their surroundings, in the social, but not fully of it. The political – a true 'body politic' – no longer exists in the realm of the social.

Liberal optimists will of course characterise this brief digression into the world of postmodern immaterial labour as an unnecessarily bleak interlude that ignores the vibrancy and diversity of progressive media cultures in which young people can develop their own communities, identities and values. They will suggest that the huge growth of personal, hand-held media devices offers new forms of liberation, communication and a powerful political potentiality. This may or may not be true, but our goal is not to suggest that social media and mobile devices are corrupting young people or contaminating our culture. We are not Luddite technophobes, we have no desire whatsoever to remove these devices from our world, and we have no faith that doing so would cure even a modicum of the world's ills. Our point is really quite simple. First of all, we want to address the place of capital accumulation within new social media, and challenge the dominant accounts that see only beneficial knowledge, information and new sociality flowing from these media. But more importantly, and as a precursor to our more comprehensive analysis in the next chapter, we simply want to suggest that the traditional social world is being rapidly transformed. The growth of virtual social space necessarily impacts upon our engagement with actual social space. It suggests change, evolution, perhaps even rupture, in the constitution of the social, and as such warrants a brief examination in this book. In the chapters that follow we will try to draw the issue of *self-exclusion from the social* into the mainstream social exclusion discourse.

Self-exclusion from the social is not simply a matter of media, technology and the growing complexity of virtual worlds occupied by fantasy cyberselves. In recent years we have also seen other powerful indicators of a radical disjuncture in 'the social'. One of these is the apparent desire of the rich to retreat into private enclaves free from the malignancies of the real world. They want to encounter only those judged safe, subservient or 'like them' – and even then only in sufferance – and to restrict their social experience to appointed outlets or institutions that also offer safety from any encounter with the Real. This suggests a growing desire to *evacuate the social* to occupy a strange post-social and entirely artificial securitised world comprised of sanitised, protected and approved nodes and arteries that cut lines of travel and repose across what was once social space. The movement of the relatively rich from office to gated community, from gated community to private school, from school to retail space, from retail space to country club, from country club to airport, and so on, indicates quite starkly the 'problem of the social' in the present. Acts of individualistic self-exclusion should also encourage social exclusion researchers and theorists to extend their analyses beyond unemployment, underemployment and good old-fashioned discrimination.

Conclusion

In this chapter and the chapter that preceded it we have sought to *rethink* two of the key theoretical claims that structure the social scientific analysis of 'social exclusion'. Byrne has claimed that the socially excluded continue to acts as a 'reserve army of labour'. This, we suggest, needs to be reconsidered in relation to the shifting dynamics of a global capitalism that does not need a 'socially excluded' reserve army to inspire anxiety among its workforce. Anxiety already exists in abundance. We should also be aware that the jobs available to populations categorised as 'socially excluded' exist at the very bottom of labour market. These sectors are dominated by transient workers, and they are often so exploitative and humiliating that many workers do not invest in them to any great degree. In the diverse panoply of pressures and stresses workers in this sector face daily, the insecurities of job competition do not appear to figure particularly highly. Poor work is often available for those willing to take it, but the hours available for work and the money paid for that work are often so low that it is barely worth giving up welfare benefits and submitting oneself to neoliberalism's dauntingly complex bureaucratic processes. If we add to this the various indignities that often accompany these terrible jobs, then the harnessed social division and competition at the centre of the traditional 'reserve army' thesis needs to be modified and recontextualised if it is to represent the current conjuncture.

That is not to say that this thesis needs to be entirely abandoned. In this chapter we claimed that there continues to be a slight indication of a 'reserve army' dynamic in downgraded forms of middle-class labour. Many working in these sectors appear painfully aware that they are increasingly expendable and that genuine competition exists in the form of recent graduates ambitious to fight their way into those forms of reasonably remunerative labour that continue to exist in post-crash Western economies. We also claimed that this growing awareness appears to be fuelling new, non-traditional forms of protest. In Britain, the growing radicalism of public sector unions represents the anxieties particular socially included populations have of falling to the very bottom. Crucially, we must not mistakenly assume that the suggestions of the factional radicalisation exhibited by anxious but employed and included populations also suggest a radicalisation of those already at the bottom. We also looked at the importance of consumerism to the economies of Western liberal democracies, and we suggested how the divergent theses of Byrne and Bauman might be brought together to speak to the real economic position of the contemporary 'socially excluded'. We must recognise that the very poorest continue to be fully incorporated into contemporary capitalism's ideological project. They may not have the money regularly to engage in bouts of expressive consumerism, but they are, for the most part at least, deeply connected to the act of consumption as a means of achieving social recognition and displaying cultural relevance. They await the next opportunity to become expressive consumers, and should therefore not be considered permanently excluded from the social as a result of their inability to consume. We have also sought to identify one or two ways in which new forms of economic exploitation are coming to the fore. Our goal here has again been to look critically at the reality of capital and what it means for marginalised populations. The contemporary Western poor may not work regularly or consume regularly, but this does not mean that they are entirely divorced from the logic of markets and the new dematerialised 'social' forms appearing within them.

8

Occupying Non-places

How does the incorporation of the economically excluded compare with the incorporation of those who have maintained a precarious hold on late capitalism's unpredictable economy? We often assume that 'the mainstream' is the site of safety and a rich social life, a Promised Land that beckons the excluded, and, should they succeed in their struggle to enter it, solves their problems. However, there are critical philosophers and artists – too often ignored by today's proudly anti-intellectual vanilla sociologists – who warn us that mainstream culture offers no such comfort. In many classics of leftist cinema, mainstream culture is depicted as bland and homogenised, deprived of all positive social substance. In most of these films social relations are steeply hierarchical, and the lifestyles of those who occupy the cultural mainstream are dependent upon an exploited class which is denied full membership. For instance, John Carpenter's too often overlooked *They Live!* and George Romero's *Land of the Dead* both contain a clearly identifiable structural critique of ideology. To see it all we need to do is strip away the immediate storyline (in *They Live!* aliens have taken over the planet, and in *Land of the Dead* humans have retreated into a large shopping centre surrounded by zombies). In both films the nature of the excluded class's enslavement is eventually revealed to them and they respond by battling heroically against their oppression.

Both films are keen to elicit from the audience an acknowledgement that mainstream consumer culture is ultimately hollow and exploitative, and our attachment to it ensures that our ties to the 'real world' are severed as we lose sight of those things that should be absolutely central to civilised social life. With regard to social exclusion, what is interesting in both of these films is the depiction of excluded space as the site in which an open and progressive civility develops. An enlightened potential vanguard underwhelmed by consumerism's fetishistic objects of desire mingles with those excluded from the consumer sphere by divisive social relations in an attempt to develop affective and mutually supportive relationships. The cultures of the excluded space display a diversity and vitality that the audience are encouraged to interpret positively, especially when placed alongside the sterility of the consumer space. The material deprivation of those who occupy the excluded space is compensated by a genuinely organic and egalitarian community life. In both films, and other overtly leftist films such as Alfonso Cuarón's *Children of Men*, oppositional politics grows organically in excluded space; people actually speak of politics, power and the necessity of change. In *They Live!* and *Land of the Dead*, the act of exclusion opens up a space of authenticity and the possibility of a regenerative cultural flourishing. Exclusion cuts the ideological ties that bind the subject to the oppressive social order and opens up the possibility of organised resistance to it.

The narrative structure of these films, and many others like them, displays an obvious similarity to the accounts of exclusion offered by the Hegelian 'beautiful souls' of the liberal left. However, as we suggested in Chapter 2, the romance that 'the excluded' are capable of creating their own organic cultures free from the corrupting influence of the conformist mainstream is essentially a falsehood. It is an ideological projection of 'confirmation bias', what the supposedly objective social scientist would like to see in excluded social space. Of course many amongst the excluded always possess Gorky's inner spark of humanity, but whether that can be consolidated into a reproductive culture or a political movement is another question; our past research has confirmed that in today's excluded space there is no immediate and articulate cultural or political critique of the existing order. In these pages we have argued at length that there is, rather, a preponderance of anger and dissatisfaction that lacks articulate cultural expression and cannot coalesce into an organised political opposition. In this chapter we will argue that the old modernist community ideal – that during the middle third of the twentieth century came close to *really existing* in some working-class neighbourhoods across the West – has reached its historical end-point, and that contemporary marginalised neighbourhoods are now haunted by a forgotten history of affective communal identity, obligations and politics, a spectre of what might have been had history taken a different path.

The collapse of modernist communalism is not simply an issue for the poor. All genuine community life – genuine in the sense that most members are devoted to each other's material and emotional wellbeing – seems to have vanished from everyday social experience. As we will see, *all public space* in the West appears to be dominated by the logic of neoliberal governance and the vicissitudes of commercial investment and market logic (see Graham, 2011), and the positive substance of modern social space has been replaced by an ideologically moderated climate of foreboding, insecurity and absence. This regrettable transformation reflects the decline of symbolic efficiency (see glossary) and the other historic changes we touched upon in the last chapter. We should also note that what we see in socially excluded space is not at all a genuine 'otherness', a dangerously disconnected space with its own structuring norms and values. It is certainly true that these spaces can be more dangerous and some of the inhabitants may exhibit aspects of behaviour that are marginally different from those displayed in fully integrated neighbourhoods. But at the crucial level of values, there is no profound difference between 'them' and 'us' (see Hall et al., 2008). Just as it is false to contrast crime-free, positive and mutually supportive mainstream social space with a dangerous and crime-ridden excluded space floating at its outskirts, it is wrong to champion the authenticity and progressive civility of the ghetto and criticise the moral degeneracy of the mainstream. Mainstream culture and fully integrated social spaces display lower rates of reported crime, but they also tend to be riven by sublimated forms of aggression, enmity, self-interest and corruption. Until the ruthless and spiritually deadening commercial meritocracy of the neoliberal era can be disturbed by the return of history, it seems that these cultural characteristics will continue to be displayed across the entirety of Anglo-American societies – from the sink estates of northern England to the boardrooms of Wall Street.

The mainstream may appear pacified and stable, but barbarism and aggressively cultivated thymotic passions (see glossary) are integral to the contemporary neoliberal project. It is this drive to differentiate ourselves from our peers – to reduce the other in order to elevate the self, secure the self's interests in a broad range of social encounters and display the symbols of triumph by conspicuous consumption – that fuels the onward march of consumer markets and typifies the asocial, disaffected and happily-stupid base populism that characterises Anglo-American culture (Presdee, 2000; Hall et al., 2008; Naylor, 2011). We might reasonably speculate that the high crime rates and other social problems exhibited in marginalised neighbourhoods reflect the gradual disintegration of those forms of social insulation and pacification that clearly existed during the modern period to hold potentially destructive thymotic passions in check and harness them to the economy as libidinal drivers (see Hall, 2012a). The self-interest, defensiveness and often quite aggressive competition that structures contemporary Western culture appears, in places of social excision, to be seeping through the gaps that are opening up in modernity's rapidly decaying cultural defence systems and external control systems to pollute public space in an era that can be reasonably described as *post-social*.

Bored to death in the city

Of all the changes that have transformed our experience of urban life in recent years, perhaps the most deceptive has been the 'commercial redevelopment' of city-centre space. Under the banner of 'progress', 'investment' and 'prosperity' (who could be against such things?), we have seen authentic indicators of our history and cultural life disappear. In their place have risen bland and homogenised shopping precincts operated by corporations, policed by security guards and populated by disengaged consumers trudging between big-name high street retailers. Inevitably, it becomes difficult to differentiate one city centre experience from another. H&M, Marks and Spencer, Sports Direct, Argos, Starbucks, Costa, The Body Shop – nothing remains in these commercialised spaces to connect them to history and locality unless it has been hopelessly reproduced, deracinated from its original context, commodified and resold to consumers seeking at least a memento of authentic culture.

Markers of history are reduced to mere exhibits, novelties that seem to mock the symbolism of the past as they contribute to the city's brand image. As such, they encourage no thoughtful aesthetic critique, no studied introspection, no rumination about the ticking clock of history or a reality long forgotten. Furthermore, our consumer space is now so littered with crass reproductions that authenticity appears to matter not at all. If the essence of a place reflects the desire of history to reach beyond the constraints of chronological time in order to maintain its grip upon the present, to demand recognition of what once was, to constantly cast its shadow over contemporary experience, then we must recognise that a growing proportion of our shared social space is profoundly ahistorical. Commercial spaces in particular are effectively, to use Marc Augé's (2008) term, *nonplaces*. Much city centre space is now beyond the reach of history's long shadow. Instead, it sits uncomfortably under the artificial sunshine of the city shopping arcade, surveilled by privately operated CCTV cameras and security operatives keen to ensure that consumers enjoy a peaceful and unobstructed shopping experience.

The establishment of privately-owned retail environments in our city centres, known as Business Improvement Districts (BIDS), has two obvious surface benefits. Firstly, these places are clean and well-lit, and occasionally roofed and heated, and this is often seen as a significant advantage over the draughty and dishevelled public spaces of the post-industrial city. Secondly, they are safe. The operators of these shopping environments pride themselves on ensuring that consumers are not inconvenienced or discouraged by unsightly litter or the threat of unwanted encounters with threatening and potentially criminal urban populations (see Minton, 2012: 40–59). We might immediately assume that cleanliness and safety are not at all problematic, and that these things represent useful additions to our experience of urban space. However, underneath these benefits lies a fundamental commitment to ensuring the frictionless accumulation of capital unhindered by the economically excluded. Only those likely to spend money will be granted access and welcomed into these consumer environments that have colonised what used to be the city's central public spaces. Those who display the external characteristics judged likely to disrupt the consumer experience are immediately identified by the CCTV cameras and ejected by private security guards. As Minton (ibid.) notes, these spaces are totally devoid of anything that might signal a really existing social space: no diverse multitude, no impromptu musical performances, no novelty, no imagination, no political campaigning, no symbols of a shared past or future: only the perpetual present occupied by those with money to spend, and those who accept the unwritten rules of post-social engagement.

The established market tactic seems to be to stick to a winning economic formula and endlessly reproduce it through British cities. The logic of market forces ensures that smaller traders tend to be squeezed out, and this compounds the sense of dull uniformity that characterises the British city centre shopping experience. These spaces may contain a flourish here and there, a display of some sort – perhaps the authorities will license someone to play the role of a busker in the hope of providing shoppers with an innocuous distraction from the fundamental artificiality of these environments – but these things immediately seem forced and deprived of their power to please or inspire. Outside these oases of calm, a growing proportion of retail space stands empty (Fletcher, 2012). The warmth and light of the BID contrasts sharply with the boarded up shop fronts, the empty office buildings and the sense of drabness and waste that prevails in many of Britain's post-crash city centres.

The presence of anyone not intent upon spending money is discouraged; only people who are at least open to the idea of spending money will be granted admittance and welcomed into the post-social atmosphere of the city centre shopping arcade. Those who have no money to spend are simply not part of the plan for this dominant type of urban space. They represent a threat to the cleanliness and safety crucial to the BIDs image, an unseemly stain to be removed, an unpalatable reminder of the outlands beyond, the poor zones about which no-one – the category 'no-one' includes governmental functionaries and many of today's liberal-postmodernist sociologists – really wants to know. The security industry maintains the smooth asocial experience of a peaceful, unobstructed consumer space constituted by a seamless contiguity of branded outlets, a crime-free carnival of consumption available to all willing to spend money. It is located *in* the city, but also at the same time both *separated from it* and *deeply indicative of it*. It is a space through which many individuals pass, but not a social space in any meaningful sense of the word. In these non-places the public interest appears to have collapsed into commercial interest; pure, uninterrupted buying and selling that is the *whole* rather than an *aspect* of the urban landscape. No matter what happens we must ensure 'business as usual'. The financial wellbeing of global corporations is in the best interests of all. As George W. Bush famously suggested after the 9/11 attacks, the patriotic individual can best help her country by going shopping.

However, the transformation of the city centre from a place with character, history and cultural diversity to a total capitulation to consumer symbolism and the profit motive is not the end of the matter. We can also see, scattered around the city, and especially at its periphery, an assortment of business parks, industrial parks and other strange non-places. They share a pecu-liarly alienating and melancholic ambience that suggests the dominance of neoliberal business imperatives and its culture of base individualism. These spaces are usually defined by their box-like constructions that rarely reveal a clear purpose, often bordered by forbidding spiked fences, razor wire and CCTV cameras: *keep out*, they say to all. Costs and tax exposure are kept to an absolute minimum, which adds to the overall air of privatism and secrecy; pedestrians and passers-by can fuck off or else. Even the retail parks that continue to strangle the economic vitality of the central city are essen-tially characterless warehouses – giant rectangular boxes full of knickers, cosmetics and refrigerators – that rise out of nowhere and have no obvi-ous relationship with the immediate environment and its history or culture. These places are of course premised on car ownership. In some cases they are bordered by manicured lawns and hills, but these features are intended only to be looked at on the way to the car park rather than walked through and enjoyed.

What, these days, is more British than the retail park, the enterprise dis-trict, the out-of-town shopping centre? Martin's (2008) analysis of the non-places that border the M62 motorway, a road that runs east to west across the centre of England, suggests that the stultifying monotony of these non-places, animated only by commercial interests and the shopper's desire to find a bargain, is becoming a regrettable facet of everyday life for a growing proportion of the population. Some 20 per cent of the British population live along the M62 corridor, and somewhere in the region of 180,000 vehi-cles use the road every day. What we are seeing can no longer be reduced to a process of suburbanisation or exurbanisation, a movement away from the city, as the city itself no longer acts as the fulcrum of everyday life for a significant proportion of the working population. New housing is built strategically to appeal to individuals and families who need easy access to these commercial arterial routes that keep Britain's post-industrial economy moving. It is increasingly argued that the future prosperity of cities along the M62 might best be achieved through a suppression of their individual identities; instead these decaying post-industrial centres should accept that it would be best to merge into one discrete, linear 'Supercity' along the motor-way (ibid.). It seems to us reasonable to claim that we no longer simply visit non-places on occasion. A growing proportion of us now live, work and find our leisure there.

How did all this happen? The death of industry in the north of England changed entirely the complexion of the urban experience (see Hobbs et al., 2000, 2003; Hayward, 2004; Hadfield, 2006; Winlow, 2010). The new neo-liberal orthodoxy compelled local government to respond to this historic economic reconfiguration by shifting from *municipal socialism* to *municipal capitalism*, abandoning its established social democratic ethos and throw-ing itself into the tumult of the market. One aspect of this change was the drive to redevelop the inner city by once again making it relevant to post-industrial urban populations. The logic of the time determined that the only realistic way to do this was to rebrand the city centre as a commercial space, with great emphasis placed upon new consumer and leisure markets. It also determined that the best way to fund the transition, while minimising taxpayer costs, was to attract commercial partners willing to invest in the north's city centres, transforming them from foreboding post-industrial ghost towns into shiny new commercial centres reflective of the north's new dynamism, diversity and ascending entrepreneurial spirit.

This drive to regenerate and commercialise the post-industrial city was also, in part, a response to the rapid development of the types of commercial space outside of the city that we discussed above. The relaxation of planning laws encouraged the development of huge American-style malls and smaller out-of-town retail parks. This novel consumer experience was enhanced by abundant free car parking, allowing the customer the convenience of driving to the shopping destination of choice and loading giant bags of booty into the car, heading home without ever having to deal with the discomfort of rain or the awkward mix of shopping bags and public transport. The post-industrial city responded to this threat by incorporating the architectural and commercial logic of the out-of-town retail park into the very heart of the city centre. The drive to regenerate the city, and in the process create an atmosphere conducive for commercial enterprise, led local councils across Britain to a privatisation agenda, selling off parcels of city centre land to a variety of private entities, the majority of which were profit-driven global corporations. Minton (2012: 21) notes that the sale of publicly-owned land to private landlords is a 'major plank of government policy, with a government target of sales of £30 billion by 2010 and billions of sales already recorded'. What we are seeing here is of course a deeply regressive shift in political attitudes to public space. The last 30 years have shown quite clearly that the orthodox neoliberal position is to dispense with publicly-owned assets. Neoliberal ideology demands that our politicians accept that these assets can be used and developed more effectively by business entities. In many respects they are seen only as liabilities with the potential to incur costs, and it is therefore in the public interest to dispense with them as quickly as possible. The firmly established drive to regenerate the decaying industrial city in line with commercial imperatives reflects the broader neoliberal drive to remove from public ownership those very things that twentieth-century social democrats believed were integral to the development of modern civility, fairness and justice (see Jacobs, 2005; Judt, 2010, 2011). Now, significant portions of our city centres have been removed from public ownership and sold to private landowners capable of applying their own criteria relating to who is allowed to access these spaces and under what conditions. This is part of a global private land-grab, a new postmodern 'enclosure movement' now extended to the developing world (see Pearce, 2012).

What interests us most about the rise of post-social non-places is the ways in which they speak to a particular historical conjuncture. In urban sociology and associated fields there is little consideration of the subject who occupies and engages with non-places. How do we react to these spaces and what might that reaction say about the shifting dialectic between the individual and the social? How do we respond to crass commercialisation, to bland homogenisation, to the McDonaldisation of the city? We might believe we struggle under the weight of it all, that the stultifying bland-ness of commercialised space is a fetter upon our very humanity, and that we subjectively yearn to resist, break free and create for ourselves a more diverse and aesthetically pleasing space that is conducive to a vibrant and progressive culture that allows the subject the space to think and to grow. There is an element of truth in this account, in that non-places engender a sense of aversion and critique. Some of our colleagues in the academy often appear to disassociate themselves from such spaces and refuse to spend time and money there. Their tastes favour other more middle-class forms of com-mercial phoniness – the farmers' market, the artisan coffee emporium and the charity shop appear to be particularly popular amongst the liberal left.

However, simply assuming the existence of the indomitably resistant and creative individual in a faux-Hegelian romance of urban space produces little more than intellectual laziness and wishful thinking. We must recog-nise that only a minority are critical of these non-places, just as we must recognise that simply abstracting ourselves from the more vulgar aspects of consumer culture in no way disturbs that culture or threatens its domi-nance. This supposedly ethical process of distancing oneself from vulgar commercialism is a variant of self-exclusion from the social; like it or not, these non-places come closest to representing the actuality of contempo-rary British life. There is no more 'reality' or 'authenticity' to be found in the charity shop or the ethnic café than in a branch of Tesco or Starbucks. Capitalism is not threatened by our desire to buy fair trade coffee or locally sourced fruit and vegetables. In fact these new niche markets are exactly what contemporary capitalism needs to present itself as heterogeneous and democratic, the principal ideological strategy that ensures its acceptability, continuity and growth by maintaining the practical allegiance of those who still credit themselves as having values over and above it. We must accept that many people, indeed the majority of people, find an attractive utility in commercialised non-places, and this is not simply a matter of submission to the bland homogeneity of consumerism.

In some of the commercial spaces we have visited over the last few years, especially the older and shabbier ones in towns and cities that continue to suffer profoundly as a result of post-industrial economic restructuring, there is an almost palpable sense of drabness and despondency. Despite the clean-liness and the piped-in pop music, these are not spaces that exude a sense of happiness, fulfilment and cultural vitality. In some of the commercial non-places in Britain's most economically depressed regions, there isn't a great deal of shopping actually going on, but still people wander around window-shopping, or sit in one of the chain coffee bars nursing a latte for as long as it stays warm. Overall, these people do not resemble the models on the advertising billboards at the entrance: young, lean and cheerful with consumer desires well and truly consummated by an armful of designer shopping bags. In what follows we will attempt to think through the paradox that is missed by both celebratory and critical studies of urban centres; that which appears to exist between the prevailing atmosphere of oppressive homogeneity and the obvious desire of people to occupy such spaces, even when they are not shopping or using their services.

Hell is other people

For much of our post-Enlightenment history, 'public life' has been considered a fundamental aspect of progressive sociality. Engagement with it removed individuals from the introspective privatism of home and family and cast them among strangers and acquaintances with whom they might develop emotionally nourishing bonds of various kinds. Public life encouraged the individual to connect with others, to discover similarities and shared interests and of course to encounter and learn about difference in a civilised and mutually respectful way. Even fleeting interactions with strangers might be deemed enlightening or potentially satisfying. As Sennett (1977) notes, the late twentieth century has seen a gradual withering away of progressive social space. We are compelled to view the stranger as a threat rather than a source of social or intellectual sustenance. These days, we dash through public space in a way that has evolved to sidestep the kinds of encounters once regarded as the essence of urban civility. All who would strike up conversation, or force us to abandon our retreat into instrumental subjectivity and desire, immediately appear as mad, dangerous or out to trick us in some way. We utilise the tools of social distancing to keep the public as far away from us as possible. Don't talk to me; I'm reading my newspaper. I can't hear you; my iPod is playing. I'm obviously in a hurry with people to see and places to go to, don't stop me. Peter Sloterdijk (2011) talks of such retreats into subjectivity in terms of a contemporary desire to occupy microspheres of subjective space. We now move through social space cocooned in a bubble that functions to keep the threats and obligations of the social at bay. In our micro-spheres each individual operates as a veritable statelet – free to determine for ourselves the degree to which we engage with or retreat from others. We might expand this theme by suggesting that our occupation of immediate, subjective bubbles also grants us full sovereignty over our immediate environment. In this space everyday people experience a democratised, miniaturised and affordable variant of *special liberty*, the freedom forged by aristocratic and bourgeois elites over the centuries to, on a far grander scale, enact their dreams, desires and prejudices with minimal restraint, interruption and obligation to others (see Hall, 2012a).

The primitive urban land-grab that is occurring throughout Britain, and the gross commercialisation of our urban centres more generally, is but one aspect of the gradual removal of really existing social space. The rise of gated communities is another obvious manifestation that reflects our subjective response to the decline of symbolic efficiency (see Atkinson and Flint, 2004; Atkinson, 2006; Atkinson and Smith, 2012). On the surface of things, these places represent the desire of the postmodern subject to retreat from social space in order to occupy a position of safety, free from the imprecise threats that are believed to exist all around us. We are anxious – and, very often, in a hyper-competitive and unstable world, not without reason – but we hope that retreating behind high walls and locking gates will help us to address our potent and enduring sense of *objectless anxiety* (see Hall, 2012a; Winlow and Hall, 2012b), the feeling that some unknown force out there threatens to destroy the fragile sense of order and continuity we have managed to construct for ourselves. Of course, much of the literature relating to the rise of gated communities addresses the ways in which this enduring subjective anxiety is projected onto particular urban populations, but, as Atkinson and Smith (2012) note, there is no clear evidence that moving into a gated development in any way reduces it. Even though our immediate neighbourhood appears to be populated only by people 'like us', there still exists a nagging sense of doubt. And, of course, that doubt fuels an array of market 'solutions'. Move to a yet more secure gated community. Buy additional surveillance and security devices. Buy the services of a private security firm. Install a panic room.

If the gated community is created to address our subjective sense of objectless anxiety, it does not appear to be particularly successful. Research shows that people who live in gated communities are *at least* as anxious as those who continue to occupy open access areas of the city. Similarly, one's actual physical safety is not guaranteed by CCTV systems, locking gates and the presence of private security operatives on patrol. Others who occupy the defensible space of the gated community also threaten our safety, and of these threats our immediate family is the most significant (ibid.; see also Atkinson, 2012). What is missing from much of the literature, which still rests on tired concepts such as 'moral panics' and 'fear of the other' – the ideological strategies and effects rather than the underlying causes and conditions – is any concerted attempt to theorise the subjective sense of anxiety that is driving this retreat from the social. The standard liberal tropes of 'cultures of fear' and 'the age of anxiety' do not take us far enough if our goal is to explicate the subject's desire to flee from the affective ties of really existing social life. Here, two points occur to us.

Firstly, the desire to flee the social represents a powerful desire for *atonality* (Badiou, 2013), to occupy a space in which there exists no master signifier (see glossary). The collapse of symbolic efficiency means that we are denied access to the consistency and certainty that accompanied modern social identity and community life, a denial that increasingly exposes our raw subjectivity (see glossary) to the cold light of day. The creation of a stable identity went some way to addressing the fundamental sense of lack that lies at the heart of subjectivity, but now there is little that appears fixed and dependable. The substance of modern community life cannot be sustained in the face of postmodernism's cynicism and relativism, and we know that any biographical plans we formulate are likely to prove worse than useless in the face of constant socioeconomic instability and change. We know that something important is missing, but we cannot fill the empty space at the core of our being with the forms of identity, belief and commitment that once dominated modern social life. We now know these identities to be built upon a falsehood; we know that no god exists, and that there is no religion or political ideology that is free from corruption and self-interest. We are, effectively, denied the intellectual repose that accompanies true belief, and the 'oceanic' (Freud, 2002) sense of unconditional commitment and devotion. The deep, somatic commitment to morality that once prevented the subjective descent into raw utilitarian self-interest is replaced by a calculative, intellectualised moral relativism. This sense of incompleteness is fundamental to our subjective experience of the postmodern world. This profound sense of lack can be seen around us as a constant in everyday life: a sea of anxious people attempting to discover the unknown *Thing* that will make them complete and allow them to withdraw from social competition to occupy a space of quiet and assured security, whilst repressing conscious recognition that, in all likelihood, there is no final destination, no missing ingredient to be discovered. These days it seems that nothing can be fully relied upon, which reinforces the prevailing sentiment that some imprecise threat exists that will swoop down and irreparably damage all those things that are of value to us.

Secondly, we subconsciously hope that a dominant other will return to our social world to allow us once again to occupy a space of fixed certainties, but, simultaneously, we remain consciously cynical and dismissive of this possibility. Therefore we *actively solicit* the forms of post-social life we see in the shopping mall and in the gated community; no matter how fake it might be, anything is better than the nothingness our postmodern cynicism places before us. We subconsciously mourn the passing of lost community, despite knowing it to have been an empty façade. We laugh at the stupid behavioural protocols of our forebears, while yearning for the return of clear rules to structure our relations, identities and biographies. We want what we haven't got, and believe that our eventual ownership of the *Thing* will satisfy the irksome sense of lack that threatens to break out of its subjective space and intrude upon social reality. Perhaps there is one way to begin intellectually to break free from this overwhelming sentiment: as we continue to experience the aftershocks of the most damaging financial collapse in living memory, we must be brave enough finally and unsympathetically to dismiss the affirmative postmodern claim that the contemporary subject enjoys and courts indeterminacy, thriving on the capacity to forge its own identity by free, active decision-making. We must discard outdated theoretical frameworks and in their place construct an ultra-realist account of the world as it is. We will expand on this point in the next chapter.

The nature of post-social life inside the gated community is a stark indication of what is happening within Western urban spaces in general. The drive of those who occupy gated developments to cut themselves adrift from the social is displayed throughout our post-political landscape. It exists everywhere. The rich most clearly display the desire to exclude themselves from the social, but this is a tendency that has metastasised throughout the remnants of the modern social order. The rich simply have a greater material capacity to sever social ties immediately, effectively and securely, and to surround themselves with consumer toys as a fetishistic compensation for the lack of a genuine intersubjective encounter that is not disrupted by some aspect of utilitarian calculation. If those we term 'the socially excluded' were magically to become rich, would they want to remain in decaying neighbourhoods, close to the bosom of their really existing community? Would they use their wealth to drive a new project of imaginative architecture, more in keeping with the tastes of the multitude, or a new political party determined to achieve social justice, or would they also retreat from the social by taking up residency in the same high-status gated enclave in whose shadow they once lived, separated from the envious hordes by walls, gates and security guards?

Asocial atonality

However, the forms of post-social life that predominate behind the wall are of most interest to us. The fundamental artificiality of interpersonal experience inside the gated community, we claim, reflects a much broader drive towards asocial atonality – a privatised experience in which no social demands beyond overt compliance with the law are placed upon us. Here we can at least attempt to cut ourselves adrift from the remnants of the defunct modernist social order and its damned petty rules. Inside the gated community the vibrancy of a really existing community life, held together only by the shared meanings reproduced by conspicuous displays of consumer symbolism, is reduced to occasional shallow displays of neighbourliness. Social expectations relating to interaction continue to exist, but they are two-dimensional, structured only in relation to the weak rule of the *little other* (see glossary) (see Winlow and Hall, 2012a); their substance has been withdrawn, and they exist only as tedious instrumental obligations that allow us to negotiate unavoidable intersubjective encounters quickly, efficiently and with minimal trouble.

The occupants of the gated community know there is a degree of expectation relating to how one should engage with neighbours, but they are also condemned to experience these interactions as pointless and banal, a burden to be endured grudgingly. Liberalism has taught us only to tolerate the other rather than welcome her into our lives, thus we dutifully perform acts of tolerance, like anything else, with as much efficiency as we can muster. Of course, there exist clearly defined conversational parameters to structure those difficult interactions that occupants of the gated community would normally prefer to avoid. These encounters with neighbours are entirely devoid of all the positive social substance that existed in really existing community life. Instead they function politely to keep the other at a safe distance, away from the subject's unsullied uniqueness, both its beauty and its horror. If one is unlucky enough to encounter a neighbour in the elevator, one can complain about the weather, or discuss some shared aspect of service provision within the gated community. One might ask about the neighbour's family, even though it is immediately clear to all involved that the person who utters these words is not really concerned about the family's welfare, and would rather traverse the space between the elevator and their front door in serene solitude. Avoiding these interactions, we claim, is becoming a regular part of the daily experience of a growing proportion of urban denizens more generally. We would rather take the long route to work if the short route means an awkward, forced conversation with a neighbour or someone from our past. We pretend to be absorbed in our mobile devices, distracted by traffic or lost in a daydream simply to avoid giving anyone else the time of day. The *Big Issue* seller doesn't exist, and the homeless man in the doorway is a threat, but not simply to one's safety; we also fear that they might seek out an interaction that effectively bursts our bubble, returning us to the uncomfortable requirements of the real world.

One might reasonably claim that these asocial tendencies were always present in really existing communities presided over by Lacan's big Other (see glossary), but this is to miss the point. Of course every form contains its own nemesis at its own core; this is the fundamental logic of the dialectic. The history of Western individualism unfolds gradually (see Macfarlane, 1979; Hall, 2012a), even if it is clear that the historic changes associated with the rise of neoliberalism have radically accelerated the disintegration of community sentiment and inculcated self-interest even more centrally in Western culture. What we see in the growing popularity of gated communities and the strange palliative effect of commercial non-places is the latest aspect of this evolving process, and it involves not simply the onward march of unashamed individualism and self-interest; what we are seeing now is a historic retreat into the instrumental monadic subjectivity that can exist only in the disintegrative phase of the historical interregnum between social epochs.

It was once possible to display to the neighbour the full spectrum of one's social identity, to be in turn happy and morose, helpful and dismissive, friendly and rude. It seems to us reasonable to claim that during the modern period we began to care less about the judgement of others as the continuity of the community experience demanded at least a partial acceptance of the neighbour's otherness. The neighbour was at once an imponderable abyss, but also a potential source of emotional, economic, communal and – during the later phase of modernity dominated by the proletariat and a gathering sense amongst its members of their mutual interests – political support. Some neighbours were potentially lifelong friends, with whom one might periodically fall out and make up, a fully social presence with a complex personality that was far more likely to be immediately and unashamedly disclosed; precisely *not* the subject who must adopt a false happiness and fake sincerity while navigating the post-social space of the gated community. Similarly, we may have once asked about a neighbour's family despite being generally uninterested in their welfare. The key distinction between then and now is that it was then still possible for the neighbour to *believe* that you possessed some interest in the welfare of their family. Now, the neighbour is compelled to consciously accept that you do not care at all. Even if, by some strange twist of fate, the resident of the gated community does care, his solicitation will be judged as a mere conversational device used to lubricate awkward post-social encounters. If he makes mistakes about the family's names or ages, we are not disappointed but comforted because it confirms our presupposition that he doesn't actually care and that his petition for information is only an awkward attempt to 'be polite' while remaining socially detached. The neighbour must walk away from the encounter knowing that this encounter is simply a functional pretence that enabled both parties to maintain a degree of distance, which guarantees that one is not drawn into obligations that might demand the divulgence of something personal from the private subjective space. If an obligation continues to exist, it is that the other should be polite enough not to overstep the mark and intrude upon the privacy of the individual. After all, it would be vulgar and intrusive to ask about the neighbour's family and *actually mean it*. The other of the gated community is then always the unknowable other. We may encounter him from time to time, but we will never move beyond the rhetoric of politeness that enables us to keep our distance and doggedly defend the sanctity of our unique subjective being-in-the-world.

The same is true of post-social encounters in the shopping mall. A shop assistant, following clear instructions to be friendly, must cope with the stresses and pressures that accompany this kind of emotional labour (see Hochschild, 2003; Lloyd, 2013). An essential aspect of the job description is to put shoppers at ease in the hope they will spend money. Of course, shop workers want to maintain a degree of subjective distance from their work. They might be forced to ask about the shopper's day, but there is no pre-existing relationship that would make the interaction meaningful beyond its commercial function. Yet each working day they must be seen to practise this contrived friendliness. The result is that the phrases supposed to put shoppers at their ease are delivered in a practised monotone with a forced smile followed quickly by a blank stare. Of course, if the shop assistant does not fully commit to the task of asking about a shopper's well-being, the effect can in fact be counterproductive. Post-1968 capitalism has wised up to this. Increasingly managers encourage their staff to be natural and authentic. This is understood first as a rejection of the formalism of modern capitalism. Post-1968 capitalism believes itself to be imaginative enough to accept and embrace the individuality of each employee, securing their full commitment and drawing upon what functional sentiments and mannerisms can be found of use amongst the intricacies of their personalities and attitudes. What this means, however, is not a new phase of anti-authoritarian work practices in which individuals can relax and express their own uniqueness and changeability in their labour. Rather, it represents a bolder and more methodical move by capitalism to intrude upon the private space of the worker and utilise whatever it finds there to boost marketability, growth and profit while at the same time presenting itself to its workforce in the positive light of 'not taking itself too seriously'. Of course, post-1968 capitalist organisations often demand that the worker at least attempts to be 'authentic' (see Cederstrom and Fleming, 2012) and embrace the new formally informal structures and practices to the extent that she opens up to disclose some hitherto mysterious 'inner self'. Cederstrom and Fleming suggest that some of these organisations are attempting to infantilise their workforce as a means of extending control in the hope of extracting yet more surplus value.

It is clear that some labour market sectors are indeed extending the demand for emotional labour and intruding further and further into the employee's private space. However, many of the shop-workers we have encountered operate on the very bottom rung of neoliberal labour markets (Winlow and Hall, 2006, 2009a). They are overwhelmingly minimum wage workers suffering under the additional burden of forced friendliness that must be presented to the demanding and sometimes rude and irritating shoppers who populate their stores. It is almost tempting to say that today's Western consumers – replete with a bloated sense of self-importance conferred upon them by decades of deference and armed with the cash required to keep businesses running in difficult economic times – oppress workers in a more complete and subtle way than the old capitalists ever did.

However, those who have clearly been instructed to offer greetings to shoppers immediately as they enter the store, and to ask while serving them at the till if they have had a nice day, and if there's anything else that they can help them with, still manage to retain a degree of subjective distance. It is clear that they have been instructed to engage shoppers in this way, but they are not micro-managed by superiors keen to ensure that they stick to the script and really give it their all. 'How's your day going so far?', one imagines, is supposed to be delivered in a Californian drawl, perhaps accompanied by a magnificent set of pearly white teeth encased in an empathetic and heart-felt smile. Some of those shop workers who offered this solicitation to us in the shopping centres of northern England somehow didn't quite pull it off. Of course, there is no reason why they *should* pull it off, and no reason at all why they should attempt to close the gap between themselves and the store's customers with such fake sincerity and inappropriate intimacy, other than to follow the orders given to them by their bosses. In this context, and in response to the shop worker's request for information, is there an appropriate response that doesn't immediately attempt to close off the possibility of similar questions? Do we not overwhelmingly offer an awkward and rather terse 'fine', perhaps while blushing a little and avoiding eye contact? The knowledge that neither party really cares is repressed, and disbelief in the derealised performance in which one is an actor is permanently suspended *despite* this shared knowledge. Breaking the rules like the child who reveals the Emperor's nakedness would not radically disrupt the falsity of the protocol and transform the social milieu, as ethnomethodologists once thought. Because postmodern subjects know that they only act *as if* the Emperor is naked and do not really believe it, the act of symbolic rule-breaking simply confirms the rules and adds to their reproductive potential as the actors reject the rule-breaker and congratulate themselves for resisting being driven to such boorish and ultimately pointless gestures.

The entirely understandable desire of store workers to engage only minimally with these unseemly directives contributes something to the shopping centre's post-social aspect. In a very important sense they are perfectly entitled to congratulate themselves for not going crazy and managing to hide behind a veil of minimal engagement, because, everywhere one looks in the shopping centre Wonderland, things are not as they appear. What looks like a brick wall is in fact made from fibreglass. In the Irish theme pub, where we stop off for a pint, what appear to be original old oak barrels are plastic reproductions. Similarly, what looks like the friendly bonhomie of shop workers is in fact something else, but what is even more uncomfortable is when these shop workers deliver their script to shoppers who enter too faithfully into the interaction. This is especially true of older shoppers who have some vague recollection of a really existing Symbolic Order (see glossary), when it was possible to believe that people who request information about your health and wellbeing may be genuinely interested in your response. We have witnessed this on a number of occasions. The naïve shopper might make an equivalent request for information, or generally structure their interaction with the disaffected shop worker as if they were not a minimum wage worker who would in fact prefer to be somewhere else, and as if there might be the beginnings of a genuine friendship that moves beyond the formally informal relationship of customer/worker. Often, the shop worker who experiences this kind of reaction immediately drops the cheery façade, even on pain of dismissal. The discomfort is almost palpable as the worker struggles to fight free from the intrusive interaction they have inadvertently brought upon themselves. In time, too, the shopper may awaken to their own naïvety, a realisation that is far more difficult and painful for the self to accept.

We often see something similar as older shoppers attempt to choose from the array of beverages available in ubiquitous corporate coffee bars. Accustomed to only one choice of coffee – black or white – and unsure what to do or how to act, they throw themselves at the mercy of harried baristas dashing around behind the counter. Almost inevitably the queue behind the older customer issues a collective sigh as they realise their order may take longer than they imagined. We saw lots of older people in the chain coffee bars of shopping centres. It soon became clear that not all older people are unaccustomed to the services of Starbucks or Costa. Indeed, some older people, especially in the de-industrialised areas of the north, appear to use these commercial outlets as a meeting place of sorts. They can often be seen perched awkwardly on the arse-shaped stools for some reason favoured by corporate managers, appearing strangely out of place and out of time in these bright, efficient commercial surroundings. As we investigated further a depressing conclusion dawned upon us: they had nowhere else to go. The old community spaces that welcome retired people have either disappeared or are no longer financially feasible, and therefore not part of the plan for the continuous restructuring of our towns and cities. Some of the old men may head for the pub or the working men's club to read the paper and nurse a pint until it goes flat, or even the library if it has not been closed down, but where else is there for the old who do not wish to retreat into the depressing solitude of the home? In many cases, these shopping centres are now located at the very centre of their world. Retail outlets are often built upon cheap ex-industrial sites, and one of the outcomes of this process is that they often sit quite close to neighbourhoods that were once inhabited by the industrial working class. The presence of these older people was never really part of the plan dreamt up by the management consultants employed by global retail corporations to give these non-places an 'identity'. Business is not so good that they can afford to turn away paying customers, but these old and often rather frugal customers are certainly not the park's target demographic. They don't buy much, and they linger over their coffees while reading the newspaper or chatting. They appear to be in search of the social, and they appear to carry with them a residual desire for the old ideals of public space. They want to feel a part of a world that accepts and values them, and to engage with others in an open and mutually beneficial manner. Some yearn for a genuine conversation freed from the restraints imposed by the environment they inhabit. In truth, this is precisely not what is for sale; there is little here for them beyond an over-priced mug of tea and the mild comfort of being around other people. For others who populate the retail park, they represent an uncomfortable reminder of finitude, as if they carry the stain of the real world.

The phoniness of intersubjective encounters in the shopping centre reflects a desire to keep the other at a safe distance and to defend the sanctity of the inner self. The bogus conversation functions primarily to enable the subject to engage only minimally and therefore retain all that is private. The imponderable abyss of the other contributes to the drive to seek out post-social space, for while we might immediately sense the shopping mall or the gated community to be ahistorical, sterile and consumerised, it also offers the subject a sense of separateness that can briefly quieten the enduring sense of absence and the emotional disquiet that lies just beneath the surface. Genuine, uncontrived social encounters are understood by the post-social subject as too raw, too intrusive and therefore too threatening. The sterility of the post-social space and the shallow conventions that govern intersubjective encounters grant us the comfort of knowing that the other will be prevented from drawing too close. We come to value these places principally because they retain the suggestion of a really existing social life, but without the messy obligations of genuine sociality. It is not that we hate the other. In fact, we are often perfectly happy to tolerate, accept, and indeed celebrate, otherness. All we ask is that their otherness keeps its distance.

If the occupant of the gated community is attempting to retreat from the social, this retreat also signifies a retreat into a subjectivity that exists beyond the reach of the network of social agreements, obligations and rituals that once structured traditional community life. The post-social spaces of the shopping mall and the gated community are not simply creations of a dynamic marketplace capable of intruding upon our subjective life and inspiring a powerful desire to purchase its objects and services. Despite what much of this literature suggests, these places are not simply the products of the capitalist ogre seeking only to penetrate and colonise all dimensions of a resistant social life. While there is clearly some opposition, most occupants of our increasingly consumerised and privatised cities do not bristle with indignation at the rise of shopping arcades and the privatisation of public space. Nor do they denounce those who seek to buy flats and houses in gated developments. Rather, as we have already suggested, the ideology of liberal capitalism congeals in our neurological circuits (see also Hall, 2012c) and in so doing grounds our experience of social reality and shapes our desires and drives. *We become simultaneously the subject preferred by liberal capitalism, and the subject who prefers liberal capitalism as the least worst of all possible worlds.* The more 'radical' amongst us maintain a degree of subjective distance from the dark heart of capitalist enterprise, believing ourselves to be separated from its ideology and fully capable of seeing in stark relief the obscene drives and the often horrific outcomes of its global project. But in no way does this separation and knowledge threaten the stability of capitalism itself. In fact, the opposite is true. As Žižek (2009a, 2011) has claimed, our conscious separation from capitalist ideology and the increasingly common criticisms of global capitalism that whirl around our technologically enhanced cultural spaces essentially have an immobilising effect. Once the emancipatory moment of realisation passes – once we know that capitalism is ecologically destructive, horribly unjust, deeply exploitative, and so on – all that remains is a residual disgust that mixes with obdurate cynicism to produce the dull interpassivity that continues to characterise the end of history. The desire to actually intervene in the world in order to set straight these injustices is replaced by mere distaste and withdrawal, which occasionally precipitate meek protests that come and go without ever coalescing into a political project with discernible historical momentum. In this sense, contemporary capitalism releases into the world knowledge of its own horrors. It encourages us to laugh at crass consumerism and the bland homogenisation of corporate culture. It encourages us to be appalled at the exploitation of developing countries and the elite's corrupt business practices, and it does this precisely in order to release the disgust, rage and dissatisfaction that might have otherwise developed into a revolutionary politics. It knows that knowledge of its practices doesn't prevent us from utilising its markets. We complain incessantly about the homogenisation of our high streets, but we continue to shop there. We know that the cheap goods we desire are made in sweat shops in the developing world, but we continue to buy them. We know foreign holidays are contributing to the destruction of our environment, but we continue to fly. In our media culture, our critique is staged for us by representatives of global capitalism; the system picks up signals from our weak protests and makes minor adjustments to its political system, advertising them loudly to maintain its image as the one and only progressive way of life, the true passage from tyranny to democracy and unlimited freedom – progress is often slow, but we will get there in the end. Cleverly, it diverts dissent from politics, builds it into its commodities and sells it back to us (Hall et al., 2008). We are encouraged to believe that the system as it exists will be held to account at some stage, and of course emphasis is placed upon the apparatus of open democracy to do this effectively. But when nothing happens, when capitalism continues to roll onwards from one destructive crisis to another, we simply grumble about the failure of our politicians or complain that our democratic institutions are not fit for purpose and require further fixing. The absence of a genuine alternative and the desire to construct one is palpable, a total vacuum in which no form of political life can survive. Liberal intellectuals do us all a disservice by fabricating new forms of communal and political life – in cyberspace, in the post-industrial urban wastelands, in night-clubs, on campuses (Maffesoli, 1995; Lash, 2010) – that are nothing more than apparitions brought into being by their own desperate wishful thinking and compulsory optimism.

The assumption that 'the people' are 'appalled' at the rise of post-social space is too simplistic, and in an important political sense both premature and far too optimistic. Social science is shot through with a pernicious myth that those judged to be excluded look at the rise of consumer spaces in disgust, keenly aware that such places have not been built with them in mind. We see this in Salford, with the rise of the Salford Quays development that adjoins a number of marginalised former working-class neighbourhoods. It's true that those trapped in decaying neighbourhoods with high crime rates and other social problems are likely to interpret the imposition of the Salford Quays development upon their lifeworld essentially as an act of symbolic violence. It seems to speak not to aspiration and self-improvement but to absence and want. Such ostentatious wealth so close to such obvious poverty functions not to encourage dynamic market engagement but rather as a constant reminder of what is available but forever out of reach. Despite being depicted as a regeneration project, the poor of Salford receive no material benefit from such massive infrastructural investment. Money has not spilled out of the Salford Quays into the surrounding neighbourhoods (see Henderson et al., 2007). And perhaps more to the point, there is a sense that, even if local inhabitants wanted to stroll around the mall, many would be prevented from doing so by the legion of private security guards keen to exclude those populations judged to be dangerous, unsightly, poor or problematic in some way.

With this in mind, it is entirely reasonable to argue that the inhabitants of Salford's poorer boroughs resent both the development and the people who work there and use its services. But this is not the end of the matter; resentment does not preclude desire but is built upon it. The true wellspring of the local population's pain is their inability to access what is available in the Salford Quays (see Jeffery and Jackson, 2012); they are not ethically opposed to the existence of such places. What the poor of all Western cities want is not the destruction of these places and the development of something more in keeping with romanticised middle-class assumptions of what the poor's needs, tastes and dispositions should be. Why should we assume that Britain's poorest communities would actually prefer wide tree-lined boulevards, or that they would prefer to give their custom to a Green Party-approved artisan working with locally-sourced materials? The liberal left's evangelical desire to help the poorest means that they refuse to see the truths that structure these communities and neighbourhoods. They must keep on believing that individuals are not animated by the congealed ideology that they actively solicit in the absence of an alternative (see Žižek,

2006a, 2007, 2009a; Johnston, 2008; Hall, 2012c), that an organic politics can grow from the spark of humanity even in the most brutalising or symbolically arid environments, and that the majority of individuals in our most marginalised populations are entirely unlike the bourgeois elite insofar as they are driven by a commitment to equality rather than self-advancement.

Rather than wanting to transform shopping malls and gated communities into the ersatz organicism that satisfies the compulsory optimism of the troubled metropolitan middle classes, local marginalised populations prefer instead to *transform themselves* and their identities into the subject who is capable of effortlessly breezing into the shopping mall and purchasing its goods and services. This is, after all, what the modern subject has always been encouraged to do, and what the postmodern subject has learned to do in a mode of accelerated proliferation. While the liberal middle classes can consummately repress and sublimate their nostalgia for the impossibly organic into the wishful thinking that permeates all dimensions of their cultural field, the marginalised are haunted by their tacit resignation to the fact that for all but the most creative, confident and enterprising this required subjective change may never be possible. This knowledge tends to be repressed in the absence of suitable channels of sublimation, producing not wishful thinking but residual, unfocused, inarticulate anger and dissatisfaction.

Similarly, the major issue the poor have with the rise of gated communities is not that they are negatively stereotyped by the rich who then deny them access. Rather, they themselves want to emulate the rich, imitate them by adorning themselves with their major forms of cultural and symbolic capital and become capable of occupying these spaces. It is not simply that they desire the forms of anxiety that drive the rich to retreat into gated communities. The desire to occupy this non-place reflects a basic acceptance of capitalism's ethico-political horizon. To over-simplify for the sake of brevity, occupying the gated community suggests that one has the material capacity to invest in such a purchase and that one is actually in possession of material items or forms of status that others might want for themselves. It reinforces the suggestion that the subject who occupies the gated development fully deserves the envy of the other, and it is this receipt of constant signs of envy from outside that, more than anything else, convinces the gated-community's subject that it is fully alive in the world of *amour propre* that characterises advanced consumer capitalism.

Liberal-left academics too often refuse to acknowledge the capacity of capitalist ideology to infiltrate the very core of the subject. Never stopping to consider the possibility that they might be wrong, they have spent years trying to convince themselves and everyone else that there is no such thing as a dominant ideology but only a relatively autonomous and resistant plurality. They prefer instead the comfort of imagining that poor people are a noble and hardy breed whose members stick together through thick and thin. They prefer to believe that 'the people', and more so the marginalised, can yet prove themselves to be the *condottieri* of social transformation, the creators of a new reformative politics rooted in equality and justice. This is very convenient, of course, because while 'the underclass' make all the sacrifices and take all the risks on the road to Utopia the middle classes can sit waiting for Godot and occasionally interjecting with some encouraging commentary. But the poor, and other exploited groups in the social mainstream, are not immediately in possession of an alternative ideology that articulates and politicises their antagonism to embedded privilege and corrosive hierarchy. The sad fact of the matter is that they are not appalled by inequality; rather, they yearn to be magically transported to the position occupied by the 'winners' (see Hall et al., 2008). Of course, if they had the capacity to suddenly leap to the top of the pile, inequality would not worry them too much. Inequality is only a problem for those who fail to reach the top. This is capitalism's current ideological triumph, a condition of existence that middle-class liberals will not even acknowledge, let alone contest in any real political sense of the word. Even the poorest remain bound up in the ideology of compulsory competitive individualism and just desert for effort. There is no organic desire for equality or to submerge the interests of the self in the interests of one's community. Until an alternative ideology can be created that encourages the people to be something else, to move away from capitalism's injunction to be profoundly self-interested, positioning an entirely different set of values at the heart of culture and politics, there can be no return to history.

So, we claim that most post-political subjects secretly and abjectly desire the sterility of the shopping centre and the privacy and solitude of the gated community. Inevitably these fail to live up to our expectations, but for the moment this leads only to a desire for more refined and authentic-looking versions of artificial sociality to accompany the ever more realistic versions of virtual reality produced by computer games engineers. Every dimension of life should drip with the symbols of desire, but remain bereft of any real political and social substance at its core. We might be at first appalled by the Ballardian horror of the shopping centre, but there still exists a degree of comfort there, a recognition that in this non-place the obligations of the social and political are effectively and permanently suspended. Similarly, we may be lonely, yet we still immerse ourselves in the forms of comportment, the post-social behavioural protocols and the various symbolic devices that enable us to ensure that a respectful distance is maintained between ourselves and those others who might have once formed part of a rewarding social network. We might crave genuine intimacy and the emotional support that accompanies it, but we find ourselves unable to sacrifice the peculiarly hollow yet seductive prize of late-modern freedom to the obligations that might accompany a genuine relationship.

Do we not find the next step in the atomisation and commercialisation of the social and the late-modern subject in the growth of dating agencies that promise to take the risk out of dating? Instead of the adventure and openness that should accompany a genuine romantic encounter, the love-lorn consumer will be matched with someone who meets an objective set of criteria laid down by both parties. And, as numerous sociologists have recognised, is this same process not at work in the obvious disposability of many contemporary romantic relationships? Just as we want love without the associated risks, we want love without fully opening ourselves up to the deep commitment that should accompany enduring romantic relationships. We might also speculate that we want the benefits of the loving relationship without any of the commitments. We want the promise of the full commit-ment and devotion of the romantic other without fully giving of ourselves in the same way. While yearning for the clarity that accompanies a really exist-ing symbolic order, we cannot relinquish our attachment to the privatism of subjectivity. We want to believe, but we cannot do it in the truest sense of the word. We can only choose to believe, when it suits us to do so. We want to experience the comfort of full absorption into the new identity of the couple, but increasingly it seems that we cannot fully expose ourselves to the threat of rejection or the risk that our feelings or interests may be abused in some way. The decay of our symbolic order means that, despite wanting those things that come with submission and commitment, we must always seek to hold something in reserve, to be forever mindful of our own interests, to be loved, like the primary narcissist, more than we are willing to love in return. In true love, we tend to construct the world from a decentred point of view, and doggedly pursue love despite intermittent pain and disruption. True love stays the course. It is this that appears threatened by the retreat into subjectivity. As Alain Badiou (2012b) suggests, love these days is under threat and needs to be reinvented.

Conclusion

What we have attempted to do in this chapter is to suggest one or two ways in which we might conceive of a world in which the social no longer appears to be fully operative. We have endeavoured to advance our thesis relating to the decline of symbolic efficiency by offering one or two practical indica-tions of how we might begin to see the outcomes of this process at work in contemporary urban space. But what is there here that relates directly to 'social exclusion'?

Firstly – as we have now stated repeatedly – in important ways *we are all excluded from the social*. If we take 'the social' to be a network of figuration and obligations that bond people together, a source of systematised meani that creates truths and compels us to accept its structuring logic, our experience of post-political reality registers a fundamental change that has taken place, a change that deprives us of the cohesion and continuity of all social relations and meanings. In this regard, what we have attempted to do here is expand and redefine the concept of social exclusion so that it speaks more directly to the current conjuncture and the forms of individualism and atomisation that are an obvious part of our experience of everyday reality.

Secondly, 'social exclusion' is an issue that relates closely to the transformation of our cities. The staggering growth of city-dwelling populations globally is an effect of the fundamental changes in political economy that we addressed in the early chapters. Even the embattled post-industrial cities of the West, some of which have undergone significant population declines, are being continually reconfigured to reflect the new requirements of capital and profit accumulation. The loss of industrial labour and productive work as a major social institution in the West continues to be a key issue for the social sciences, principally because no alternative forms of labour have come close to filling the gap in the economic and social dimensions. What we attempted to do here is extend the critique of exclusion in line with some of the theoretical observations we made in the last chapter to include other changes in the organisation of city space. We have also sought to move beyond the standard account of 'social exclusion' that settles simply on the poor as the vilified other excluded from the benefits of consumerised urban space. While it is true that consumer spaces often refuse admittance to those who display the external signifiers of economic marginality, this is certainly not the main issue at stake. Too often accounts of this kind settle on an image of the poor as victims of regressive changes in urban governance and fail to fully account for our subjective responses to these changes or the broader politics and socioeconomic change that underlie them. Unfortunately, the ideology of liberal capitalism extends well beyond the borders of the shopping arcade. We should remind ourselves that if the 'socially excluded' were to magically switch places with the elite, little of substance would change in our experience of everyday reality. For critical academics, the sudden re-inclusion of the excluded should not be the primary ethico-political goal, principally because the drive to divide and to exclude remains unaddressed and therefore the process of reincorporating the excluded has no logical end. Rather, our basic long-term goal should be to create in reality a collective life in which culture is enriched, the drive to exclude does not exist, and all are valued, respected and able to participate in economic, political and social life. That might be impossible too, and past attempts have badly failed, but without such a vision there is nothing to which we can look forward other than serial crises, failed reformism and further social disintegration.

9

Excluded From What?

Labor is pulverized into every pore of society and everyday life. As well as labor power, the space-time of labor also ceases to exist: society constitutes nothing but a single continuum of the processes of value. Labor has become a way of life. Nothing can reinstate the factory walls, the golden age of the factory and class struggle against the ubiquity of capital, surplus-value and labor, against their inevitable disappearance as such.

Jean Baudrillard, 1993: 45

In previous chapters we suggested that the exclusion of the Western poor from civilised social life may not be as straightforward as we have tended to assume. Rather than being entirely separated from liberalism's market logic and the central tenets of its ideology, the 'socially excluded' continue to be *overdetermined* (Althusser, 2005) by the ruling ideology. As we saw in previous chapters, it is a mistake to assume that the social is reproduced in today's non-places, or to suggest that the excluded occupy a new organic space beyond the social, and that the values, goals, desires and drives of the mainstream no longer hold in the ghettos of North America, the banlieues of France and the sink estates of Britain. The marginalisation of the poor does not result simply from an inappropriate mainstream classification of cultural otherness. Instead, the reality of these marginalised populations reflects a much broader and deeper social transformation. It is crucial that we acknowledge that, despite being cut-off from traditional employment, the identities, cultures and politics of this group can *only* be understood in relation to the dominance of liberal capitalism. We will not recap key elements of our thinking here, but simply note that the 'exclusion' we see in impoverished areas of our cities does not suggest something *going wrong* with capitalism; instead, this marginality is deeply indicative of a capitalist labour market that no longer has any direct and immediate need for these populations. Even if capitalism were to immediately break out of its present downward spiral, and be judged once again the very engine of prosperity for all, this would

not result in a return to full employment in the 'real jobs' that offer workers a stake in their society and a sense of self-worth and social value. The
capitalism of today does not need an expansive and fully tenured Western
industrial workforce. Its needs are limited to a small number of workers in
its knowledge economy, an assortment of downgraded institutional administrators in the private sector and what remains of the public sector, and an
army of disposable workers in its service economy. At the same time, capital
is identifying new ways of appropriating value that should compel us to ask
searching questions about the status of 'the social' and its symbolic order.

If the first major presupposition of the social exclusion discourse is that
the Western poor are fully excluded from mainstream society and economy,
Chapters 6 and 7 attempted to qualify this claim by identifying a little more
closely the economic position of the Western poor. In the pages that follow
we will extend our critique to include the second major presupposition of
the social exclusion discourse: that 'the social' remains operative in an era
of historical stasis, privatism, cynical individualism and dominant consumer
culture. In addressing this point we will take a brief look at the provocative
critical theory of Jean Baudrillard before moving on to explore the model of
ontology presented to us by Slavoj Žižek, whose philosophy of *transcendental materialism* (see glossary) in particular helps us grasp the transformed
relationship that exists between the subject and the shared social space of
culture and politics.

The dead politics of 'class'

> Today the masses are a mute referent, tomorrow, a protagonist of
> history; but only when they speak up will they cease to be the 'silent
> majority'.

> (Baudrillard, 1983: 2)

Critical theorists working in a variety of intellectual traditions have for
many years sought to identify the fundamental basis of our shared social
life. Baudrillard (1983) declared 'the end of the social' at the start of the neoliberal era, and offered three clear ways of conceptualising this fundamental
and historic termination. Firstly, we can suggest that the social never really
existed as such. Rather, what we understand to be a shared social life of fixed
meaning was always a simulation. When, during the final third of the twentieth
century, our economic and cultural life became noticeably more complex, the
simulation of traditional sociality no longer elicited faithful commitment. At
this stage, we are forced to consider the possibility that our commitment to
the social and its rules always involved a relationship with a fabrication, a
mere imaginary space of reference.

Secondly, the social continues to exist and now 'invests everything'. Our sense of the collapse of the social is rather a reflection of our mass exclusion from its traditional logic and associations. Here Baudrillard (ibid.) claims that we should engage with the social as a *residue*; it is that which is left over as 'the symbolic order is blown around'. On this point he also pre-empts his later and more detailed analysis of symbolic exchange and death. Deep in the 'pure excrement' of the social as residue, we are also surrounded by death: by dead labour, dead languages and grammars, subject to terrorist bureaucracies. We can no longer claim 'that the social is dying, since it is already the accumulation of death'.

Thirdly, the social once existed but it no longer does so. The traditional relationships between the state and civil society, and between the social and the individual, have been destroyed by a new era of 'abnormal uncertainty' (Baudrillard, 1999), in which culture is immediately translated into sign and exchange value and in which the sign is both the signifier and the signified (Baudrillard, 1981). In the social transformations that took place from the mid-1970s onwards, everywhere exchangeability was undermining the coordinates of a really existing social order, pushing us towards a *simulacrum* in which reality as such no longer mattered and could no longer be determined. With postmodern consumerism, we do not consume the material object, we consume its symbolism within a broader system of objects that contains 'the idea of a relation', that is 'no longer lived, but abolished, abstracted and consumed' (ibid.: 5). Pre-empting the autonomous Marxists to some extent, Baudrillard directs our attention to the rise of the consumer economy, with its excess of symbolism, and claims that the consumption of symbols transforms consumption into a kind of labour, a *task* involving the active manipulation of signs as the individual attempts to invest her existence with meaning (see Baudrillard, 1998).

The extinction of 'the masses' is crucial to Baudrillard's analysis, and it is his assessment of the transformation of the political potential of this group that is most relevant to our analysis of contemporary social exclusion in the West. Baudrillard deals with this directly in *In the Shadow of the Silent Majorities* (1983), but we also see throughout his work traces of the impossibility of a genuine political intervention against the post-industrial symbolic order (see Baudrillard, 1975). Baudrillard's dark pessimism suggests that 'the masses' can no longer be the vehicle of emancipatory politics. The rise of postmodernism ensured that 'the masses' were reduced to an extinct volcano, once possessing the raw power to intrude upon the world and transform the existing order of things but now merely a collection of atomised, cynical consumers, ignorant of history and unconcerned about their collective interests. For Baudrillard, all social, political, cultural and economic processes are incorporated within the commodification of signification and the signification of commodities, reduced to mere semiotic equivalence. Politics, like everything else, was now simply something to be consumed.

Baudrillard's work is often deliberately opaque, and throughout it he often appears to arrive at contradictory conclusions, especially at the inter-section of his social and political theory. Still, *In the Shadow of the Silent Majorities* offers a reasonably straightforward linear history that concludes with the death of 'the masses' and their political potentiality. The growth of industrial technologies, media cultures and consumerism during the 1960s had put an end to the old world of Fordist factory production, always a key seedbed for radical proletarian politics. Work spread outwards and away from the factory, dematerialising in an increasingly mediated cultural space. The workers had been turned into consumers, and they refused to acknowledge their abject status as exploited units of production. Rather than possessing the potential to recognise their shared status and common interests, they began to perceive themselves as individuals separated from all forms of modernist universalism, their status a reflection of their new social role as consumer rather than their traditional role in relation to an outmoded means of production. Of course, Baudrillard concludes that the new worker-consumer is no better off, and certainly no freer. His servitude continues through the sad malaise of anti-utopian postmodernism, his disaf-fection and atomised individualism expanding the cracks that were already splitting apart the social. Anonymous and controlled by means of consumer symbolism, the postmodern worker-consumer lapsed into a prolonged state of indeterminacy, ambivalent about and alienated from those others who might have once joined together to end exploitation and create a new poli-tics of value and meaning.

Baudrillard was certainly one of the first to outline these historic trans-formations, and many others would follow. Importantly, in the wake of Baudrillard's critique, those leftist social theorists capable of admitting they could be wrong were forced rapidly to update their analyses. The power and scale of new media ensured that they could no longer be viewed as a mere aspect of 'superstructure'. The forms of dematerialised exploita-tion that were developing so rapidly in Western societies required hard thinking and new ideas. Many on the left held out the prospect of new forms of political universality returning to transform postmodern capital-ist realism, but Baudrillard simply did not see it that way. The process of change was complete and irreversible. The social and its collective political identities were no longer operative. If progressive politics were to return, it needed to operate on a different plane and change entirely its mode of engagement.

There is much in Baudrillard's account that is of explanatory value. Cer-tainly, the death of traditional forms of labour and the rise of new media cultures and associated forms of lifestyle consumerism did indeed corrode traditional forms of collective identity, and the cumulative effect of these processes has truly transformed our experience of social life. It was now unlikely that the most exploited and alienated social groups could join together to pursue political projects addressing inequality and injustice. Liberal-postmodernism's individualisation bomb destroyed the very foundations of traditional leftist politics. From the 1970s onwards socialist and social democratic political parties could do little but accept individualism and the 'lifestyle diversity' of the postmodern post-political population. The left began to champion pluralism and difference, seeking progressive political movement in the form of the *tranquil acceptance of otherness*. For the new left, equality ceased to be a dour, old-fashioned economic issue. Equality could also be understood in cultural terms, perhaps suggestive of a new cultural oneness of mutual tolerance in a realm that transcends economic relations, a culture entirely devoid of discrimination, in which all are free to construct identities and forge relations as they see fit. The old leftist narrative, built as it was upon universality, solidarity, mutual interests and sameness rather than difference, no longer drew an audience. Consumerism and its ideology encouraged difference and a solipsistic focus on our own individual uniqueness. We were encouraged to explore our individuality and openly express our own idiosyncratic selves. And of course, we could accomplish this difficult task by shopping at Gap, or any of the other high street retailers who had successfully commodified the symbols of individualism. The allure of affirmative recognition of stylish individuality seemed to persuade postmodern consumers to block bland homogeneity and mass production from their minds.

As we have suggested in earlier chapters, this move away from the traditional leftist themes of solidarity and universality severed the relationship between left-of-centre political parties and their old core constituents in what remained of traditional post-industrial working-class communities. It also seems that Baudrillard's thesis on the extinction of 'the masses' has been at least partially proven. There is, amongst a broad range of informed commentators, a general agreement that, in the place where 'the masses' once stood, there now stands a disunited rabble of consumers who no longer recognise or care about their historic relation to each other in a political constituency. Trade unions have lost much of their power and, as we discussed in the previous chapter, they are increasingly reviled by painfully pragmatic private sector workers dedicated to the uninterrupted provision of services and the smooth running of the neoliberal capitalism on which they depend. There exists no obvious and organised political mass to carry forward the collective concerns of exploited workers, the unemployed and the underemployed. The politics of labour is now replaced by advocates who fight for the rights of the underdog consumer to win a better deal from the giant corporations that dominate our high streets. Advancing the rights of workers seems like a dead cause, a cause of the twentieth century rather than this one. The common view appears to be that at least there is a chance that we might secure greater 'value for money' in the act of consumption.

New political movements suggest a partial political re-engagement, but these groups have little purchase with the mass of low-wage workers who keep neoliberalism's expansive service sector ticking over. Groups such as Occupy, who appear determinedly 'anti-capitalist', display all the hallmarks of a post-political movement with no obvious progressive ideological strategy beyond a determination incrementally to reform and improve what already exists. In effect, they ask liberal-capitalist power to rehabilitate itself, to act as a knowing moral agent, as they put their faith in the system's democratic institutions, rather than attempting to step forward and enact their vision of a better world. We might also draw from one of Baudrillard's intellectual enemies (see Bourdieu, 1977, 1987), and suggest that Occupy is structured by an essentially liberal-progressive middle class *habitus* that, to low-wage workers and the populations of economically excluded locales who have seen nothing but regression for over 30 years, cannot but seem rather ridiculous (Treadwell et al., 2012). If Occupy's *vanguardist* discourse is to be successful it must traverse the huge cultural chasm that separates them from the dispersed, cynical and apolitical ex-working classes. Setting up tents outside a major tourist attraction, and expecting the law to respect their right to do so, is unlikely to prompt a political about-face from those in government. Aside from failing to clearly articulate an alternative to liberal capitalism, can we not say that Occupy fundamentally misunderstood the true nature of their opponent? Does not such peaceful democratic protest backfire as it merely confirms the openness and vitality of parliamentary capitalism? Should we really be surprised when Occupy protesters are beaten and abused in Zucotti Park while the working classes sit and watch it as entertainment on their TVs? This leads us back to the kernel of Baudrillard's thesis: *there can be no progressive politics without 'the masses'.*

If Baudrillard's 'masses' possessed a political power that resides in their commitment to collective identity and acknowledgement of shared interests and needs, postmodern worker-consumers now appear to be consummate individualists, immediately dismissive of the collective identities that might cramp their style, and worried only about their individual and familial needs. The solipsism of consumer culture encourages all to be pragmatic and individualistic, to believe that each individual is unique and totally separated from the herd of others who appear dedicated to the same task. This situation has brought into being the novel and paradoxical form of *reflexive inertia*, where impressions of progress and stasis exist together, but in which no one is willing to acknowledge sameness, or waste their energy pursuing a cause that no-one else appears to care about. The cynical individualism we see in others buttresses our own, encouraging the development of a culture in which few appear willing to act, to pursue a genuinely alternative course or to sacrifice their immediate interests to pursue a long-term political goal. Is this not what we see with the contemporary Western concern with recycling? Are we not acting in relation to a fetish, wanting to do our bit despite knowing in our heart that, without a decisive political intervention in the global economy that allows us to tell corporations to actually stop doing certain things, or even replace them with public enterprises, our activity is ultimately meaningless and futile?

Despite the power and profundity of Baudrillard's analysis, it's worth briefly considering whether his bleak, intelligent pessimism might have led him to overlook the possibility of new forms of collectivism arising, not from within the media matrix he describes but from our unavoidable continuing attachment to the material world. Despite embedded individualism, reflexive impotence and interpassivity, might a genuine Event not fundamentally transform our perception of shared social experience? In Badiou's (2002) philosophy, the Event is equivalent to Lacan's (1997) 'quilting point', a point at which everything gathers to disturb the established order of things. The Event reveals to us the inability of the previous status quo to explain the new reality. Our passage through the Event compels us to construct new accounts of the world, and this process can lead us to look back at our pre-Event selves and ask: what led us to live like that, to believe in those things and behave in that way? Badiou's philosophy is always mindful of the operation of power and the reality of inequality and injustice, but his analysis of the Event displays an enduring optimism that is radically different from Baudrillard's desolate postmodern landscape of simulacra and exchange cast in death's long shadow. Badiou's optimism is not the wide-eyed, baseless, 'happy' optimism of popular liberalism, the flag-waving, count-your-blessings optimism that steadfastly refuses to see the reality of the world. Instead, Badiou wants simply to hold out the possibility that our understanding of the world as it is can be transformed radically by our immediate experience. We can, upon experiencing a genuine Event, look back at our lives from a new perspective, which compels us to construct an account of ourselves in the light of some newly revealed reality. The self-immolation of Mohamed Bouazizi in 2011, an Event that related directly to his experience of corruption, injustice and humiliation at the hands of local officials in Tunisia, is a perfect case in point. That Event led many in Tunisia to see the world from a radically new perspective. Power that had previously been considered embedded and unchallengeable could no longer be accepted by the Tunisian people. This one Event refocused the minds of individuals across the country. The powerfully symbolic suicide of one man was understood as a symptom of a deeply unjust system that could no longer be countenanced. People who had simply accepted the status quo were suddenly and radically politicised, seeing their own struggles and humiliations in relation to Bouazizi and his powerful symbolic act. The Event itself ensured that a world that could not change now had to change. So began the Arab Spring.

Badiou's (2012a) most recent work continues to display deep insight and remains hopeful that an equivalent Event might transform what appears to be the immoveable reality of contemporary parliamentary capitalism in the West. For example, Badiou sees in the riots and protest of 2011 a raw potential he believes will eventually concentrate at particular points and secure a genuine return to history. On the other hand, Baudrillard's work on the death of the social is a coldly prescient analysis of the disappearance of collective life and its political potential. Perhaps we can still believe that a return to history is indeed possible, even though we remain mired in a deeply cynical, apolitical and thoroughly consumerised social and cultural space. Can we undergo a radical shift that compels us to abandon cynical competitive individualism and our desperate fixation on consumerist status symbols?

In the fourth year of a global crisis of neoliberalism, few compelling signs that this 'other way' is possible still exist. At the moment, a yet more authoritarian version of liberal capitalism or even the rise of new nationalisms perhaps seem more likely than a move to a social and economic system that includes and values all. Perhaps the likely outcome is the gradual disintegration of what currently exists, the painful withering away of modernity's partial achievements. But the fact remains: as we approach the limit to rapid economic growth, the world as it is cannot go on forever (Žižek, 2011). Such uncertain portent raises the crucial question: for 'social exclusion' to mean anything, there must exist a social from which people can be excluded. There are many compelling accounts of the death of this social, or at least the erosion or disappearance of those things that make social life real. We should therefore open ourselves up to the suggestion that what we see in the growth of structural poverty and obdurate marginality is not a process that *excludes* these groups from the social. To shed more light on this possibility, we should begin to think more carefully about the historic transformations occurring in the economy and politics, transformations that at the moment ensure we stay marooned in the present forever.

In the rest of the chapter we outline what we regard as the most compelling theoretical framework for understanding the death of the social. Ultimately, our goal is not to identify the redundancy of the social exclusion discourse, and nor is it to identify more precisely who is excluded from the social and why. Rather, answering the questions Baudrillard posed by drawing on the work of Slavoj Žižek, we will suggest that, in crucial ways, *we are all excluded from the social*. All that was vital, positive and integrative about modern, post-Enlightenment sociality is retreating from view. Postmodern capitalism erodes the substance of collective social life and in its place installs nothing of consequence, leaving only an empty space in which solipsism, envy, privatism, cynicism and competition reign. This is not simply a matter of rising individualism enabled by technology and globalism, although that is certainly important. It is the *decline of symbolic efficiency* – our refusal to consciously believe and to invest in truth – that makes the most fundamental contribution to the creation of a world in which 'the social' is no longer operative as such and the individualism described above is the inevitable default position. 'The social' has become a derealised (see glossary) play in which we take on the role of ourselves. This sense of derealisation, that 'the social' is effectively staged and deprived of meaningful substance and genuine commitment, pushes the subject closer to the incommunicable horror of the Real (see glossary), from which immersion in hyper-individualism and consumer culture's surrogate social world is the sole respite. The content of the modern symbolic order (see glossary) is revealed as always having been a myth: our identities a mere contrivance, our relationships structured upon falsehood, and our personal histories a story of enslavement structured in relation to this myth. As we retreat into subjectivity (see glossary), dreading the over-proximity of the other, we catch sight of the absent centre of political ontology (see Žižek, 2009c) in the awkward post-social encounters in the non-spaces of the shopping mall or the gated community, in the reduction of modern community life to contrived and essentially sociopathic displays of 'neighbourliness', and beyond the dead eyes of shop workers as they ask us about our day. In order to bring back the positive substance of the social, we need to return to politics, and in order to do that we first need to believe and to display absolute faith in an ideological truth.

The weight of knowledge is unconscious

Perhaps one of the most influential tropes of modern philosophy has been Descartes's cogito: 'I think, therefore I am'. At first glance, Descartes essentially appears to be suggesting that it is the human capacity for rational cognition that defines our species. This fundamental ability to think and to calculate one's relationship with the world around us informed much of the philosophy that developed from the European Enlightenment. As we acknowledged in the Chapter 3, the English liberals were greatly influenced by Descartes's simple maxim, and placed the rational, calculative, asocial subject at the centre of their political philosophy. The influence of Hume, Locke, Bentham and Hobbes can be seen in the classical economics of Ricardo and Smith, whose work in turn provided the basis for the early neoclassical economists and the monetarists and free marketers of the mid to late twentieth century. This model of the human subject structures the economic field, and it dominates politics and social understanding. Despite playing a huge role in shaping the world around us, the social sciences and humanities have tended to take Descartes's cogito as a point of departure, subjecting it to withering criticism and demanding a more concerted analysis of the relationship between the subject and the objective world that surrounds it.

The crucial background here is Descartes's (see 1998[1644]) fundamental philosophical scepticism, his incessant questioning of reality and his drive to discover what we can truly know for sure. His procedure begins with the assumption that everything is false, that nothing can be relied upon. But, as he notes, in order to think his immediate social experience false, he must first be able to think, to rationally begin and then develop a thought procedure of this type. In his search for a philosophical truth that might illuminate our understanding of the reality of human experience, he eventually grasps that he must indeed be something that is capable of thought; this 'self-evident truth' becomes his 'first principle of philosophy'. Understandably, modern sociologists, social psychologists and philosophers were far from convinced. For the most part the social sciences and large parts of the humanities argued that Descartes's division between the 'I' of the cogito and the external world it inhabits is too simplistic: the 'I' is overly subjective, too rational, too separated from the messy business of everyday life that exerts a broad range of pressures upon our identities, our decision-making processes, our political orientations and our socially-influenced tastes, values, goals and ambitions.

We may immediately feel that these criticisms are correct. Descartes is essentially presenting the subject as entirely autonomous and this seems too simplistic. Many on the modern left, for example, would attempt to decentre Descartes's subject and understand it in relation to a dominant and penetrative ideology; others sought to identify the role of the unconscious in shaping what we subjectively understand as rational, calculative decision-making. From the 1980s, and following the interventions of the early postmodernists and poststructuralists, language and discourse became increasingly important to our understanding of the subject. Here, according to Foucault, the subject was determined as an effect of discourse, forced always to think in relation to external language and grammar. Of course, many of these developing philosophical discourses were drifting perilously close to the other extreme – the total determination of the subject by non-subjective processes, the self as merely an effect of something else. Derrida (1991) is the key intellectual figure here, and his poststructuralism continues to exert a significant influence on the humanities and social sciences. His work, perhaps more than any other, suggests a subject entirely determined by language, completely without the characteristics of the subject identified by Descartes. If the possibility of change existed, it was in the transgressive and transformative power of language and discourse. In many respects, the philosophy of the subject has oscillated between these two extremes, between the autonomous individual on the one hand and the objectively determined individual on the other.

In keeping with sociology's interminable and sterile analysis of the agency/structure relation, one might be persuaded that the correct approach is to construct a middle path, one that retains the realm of the subject yet acknowledges its complex relationship with the objective world that surrounds it. Characteristically, Žižek's intervention here is rather counter-intuitive, yet it is one that reflects accurately a commitment to Hegel's dialectics. For

Hegel, the antithesis always lies immanent within the original thesis. The job of the dialectician is to tease out the complexities of the initial engagement in the hope of then establishing a truthful negation of the negation. So, rather than following the fashion and abandoning the subject to language, or attempting to chart some middle course that endeavours to retain both subject and object, Žižek attempts a rather heroic yet transformative defence of Descartes's cogito, which involves a radical recontextualisation of the subject in relation to the objective world of the everyday. Below we offer a very basic summary of Žižek's analysis of the postmodern subject as a means of addressing the decline of symbolic efficiency and the death of the social. We must stress that this is a grossly simplified account of Žižek's ontology, offered specifically in the hope that it might help us to grasp the fundamental emptiness that lies just beneath the surface of our experience of the social.

The hole in the middle

Žižek's defence of the cogito is prefaced by the claim that the 'I' of the cogito, the 'I' that thinks, calculates and decides, is in fact a void, deprived of all content. If the 'I' of the cogito has the capacity to think, it has no thought to wrestle with, no comprehensible structure that might allow it to grasp the essence of its being. What does he mean by this? We must begin with the common philosophical trope of the 'state of nature', a state in which human beings exist without culture, a state in which we are merely a part of the objective world, with no subjective cognitive processes that might allow us to understand ourselves or our experiences. In this 'state of nature' there can exist no subjectivity as such. Rather, we are alive in the Lacanian Real, subject to inexplicable and incommunicable experiences, entirely without the capacity to apply meaning. Our experiences of this world are so disturbing, so unfathomable, that we retreat from it. This retreat is a retreat first into madness, equivalent to Hegel's 'night in the world', a realm of total loss and profound negativity. In order to escape the incessant pain of this madness it becomes necessary to construct a 'state of culture', an essentially mythical world of imagined meanings that are used to explain and systematise our subjective experience of the world around us. We have now moved from a raw 'state of nature' to a more recognisable 'state of culture', or more precisely a *Symbolic Order* (see glossary), which allows the creation of social life to take place within its structure of communicable meanings and committed relations. It is in the passage from the 'state of nature' to the 'state of culture' that Žižek positions subjectivity. For him, subjectivity remains forever tied to the sense of loss and profound negativity that defines this transition. Once we arrive in a 'state of culture' we are presented with the substance we can use to 'fill up' the void of subjectivity. We are encouraged to find meaning in religion, commit to tradition and submit to the rules of our community. Now, the 'I' of the cogito is no longer a vacuum, but a space in which we can build relationships, commitments and social identities. However, the removal of these things from the subject, or the removal of the big Other's (see glossary) endorsement of them as meaningful and valuable, immediately exposes the subject to its own nothingness.

The establishment of a 'state of culture' now enables the subject to make sense of the world around it. The subject is compelled to subscribe to the rule of the big Other, which, in Žižek's philosophy, is best understood as the mythical embodiment of the Symbolic Order. In order to occupy an order of shared meanings and associations, we must *act as if* this big Other really exists and determines the things in which we should believe. Of course, the big Other and the entire Symbolic Order exist only as long as we *act as if* they exist. The substance of the Symbolic Order is always built upon a falsehood, an illusion, but our commitment to it is crucial if we are to maintain a reasonably civil social space. Crucially, in the Symbolic Order, the subject is always the subject of ideology. There is no fundamental truth in the imaginary ego, or the associations and meanings that the Symbolic Order encourages the subject to develop. Ideology congeals in our neurological circuits and structures consciousness, fashioning the way we think and feel about our world and our place within it. We will return to this point at the end of the chapter.

Without the ideological illusion we are compelled to face the terror of our own nothingness. Without the symbolic realm, 'reality' disappears; the world we see before our eyes cannot be understood and organised into some kind of comprehensible and communicable order of symbols. The subject's desire to free itself from the finitude of the body collapses and it returns to its brute corporeal reality, becoming once again a mere *thing* reacting to the incomprehensible Real. Therefore, if we refuse to accept the rule of the big Other and the structure and content of the Symbolic Order, we are denied access to its meanings and drift perilously close to the deep negativity that forever underlies the subject. We should not reduce ideology to that which prevents us from grasping the reality of our situation. Properly understood, ideology is a framework of meaning that allows us to explain and understand 'reality' as such. This ideology congeals within the body's flexible and adaptable neurological circuits (see Johnston, 2008; Hall, 2012a; 2012c), ensuring that the subject is never the fully conscious subject of rationality, but neither is it an automaton constructed purely in relation to the objective world around it. Rather, an *ideology of the social* structures our engagement with the world around us and encourages us to draw upon its meanings in order to gain a subjective sense of order and understanding.

Of course, if the subject is to be successfully installed in the Symbolic Order it must receive a reasonably stable and well-organised socialisation. During this prolonged period of social training, the child is encouraged to submit to the laws and expectations of the surrounding culture. Children learn to invest meaning in the world around them and to internalise and systematise these meanings so that they can make sense of themselves and their place in the world. This ideology of the social is in part communicated, regulated and terrorised by our ferocious super-ego, the aspect of our psyche that attempts to control and channel the raw self-interested drives of the id and ego while imposing upon us a range of demands that are often contradictory or incompatible with our social identity. For Žižek, the super-ego should not be understood simply as the ethical psychic instrument that regulates the subject and its social behaviour. Rather, the super-ego pressures the subject to submit to its injunctions and, because the ideology of our social life always contains within it an obscene underside of hidden meanings and inducements, these injunctions can involve empathy and altruism but also hate and antagonism. Of course, acting and thinking in relation to hate and antagonism can be one of many ways in which we 'follow the rules' of our immediate community.

So, the super-ego acts as the voice in our heads that encourages us to submit to the complicated rules of the Symbolic Order while at the same time trying to *make acceptable to the social* the raw drives of the id and the self-interested demands of the ego. Commonly understood, it acts as the nagging voice of conscience that encourages the properly socialised subject to withdraw from harmful activities, constantly reminding it of the forms of approbation that await it if it continues onwards. However, as we have already discussed, the post-modern super-ego now issues a revised order to seek out new subjective pleasures. The transformed super-ego reflects the ideology that structures consciousness, imposing upon us injunctions that are functional to the way we live now in late-capitalist consumer culture. It reflects a near universal commitment to conspicuous consumption and competitive individualism, which in turn reflects the basic needs of capital to accumulate and grow.

The postmodern refusal

Žižek has often drawn upon the old parable of the Emperor's New Clothes as a means of displaying the effects of postmodernism upon the Symbolic Order. Throughout modernity we were encouraged to submit to the rule of the big Other and accept collective identities and the myths of our shared cultural life. In this mode the Symbolic Order is fully operative, and we were actively encouraged to utilise its systems of shared meanings in order to develop an individual social identity (see also Simondon, 2007; Stiegler, 2011). We were cast out into a sea of individuals who all immediately accepted the fundamental falsehood, that the Emperor was wearing the most magnificent sartorial ensemble ever created. We were so committed to a shared understanding of the world that we could not bring ourselves to acknowledge the truth. It was not that we didn't know that he was naked. Rather, our commitment to our shared symbolic life was such that we refused to accept this truth. However, according to Žižek, postmodernism has actively sought to attack the shared meanings of the Symbolic Order, challenge modernist idolatry and expose the mythical basis of supposed modernist truths. For the archetypal postmodernist, nationhood is a myth. There is no god (although, once we consciously accept this, we are then given licence to 'believe' in such a being if we rationally choose to do so). Our identification with histori- cal communities and their traditions, like our social identities as 'man' or 'woman', are mere social constructions and contain no truth as such. Even post-Enlightenment science, as a field of supposedly objective analysis, is reduced to the sad status of a mere story we tell ourselves about ourselves, its primacy over other accounts of the world secured simply by the social construction of status hierarchies that organise truth-claims. The boundless abstraction and relativity of postmodern theory suggests a desire to strip away meaning without any great desire to install something else in its place. It encourages us to face up to the fundamental artificiality of defunct mod- ern belief systems and accept the impossibility of ever accurately identifying 'truth'. If we collapse the diversity of postmodernist thought back down into its basic politico-philosophical foundation, it appears to represent a general drive to evacuate the Symbolic Order and to force the subject to face up to the raw freedom of its own nothingness.

Postmodernism's fundamental politico-philosophical drive takes different forms within the distinct disciplines of the social sciences and humanities. In its more abject, asocial form, it structures those accounts in the fields of social policy and criminal justice that identify the essential totalitarianism of the 'law'. How can the law determine what is right and wrong, structured as it is in relation to entrenched privilege, the vacuity of 'democracy' and a partial conception of morality? Public morality is a mere social construction that incorporates all of the bigotry, falsehoods and petty-minded parochial concerns of the social. In relation to what fundamental, unchallengeable truth is public morality structured? What is the real authority in the law that requires us to accept its boundary decisions on, for example, sexual conduct? Why shouldn't young people under the age of 16 be fully entitled to actively engage in life-enhancing sexual activity? Who is to say that is it fundamen- tally wrong to enter a sexual relationship with one's brother or sister? Why shouldn't consenting adults be free to engage in sexual congress in what is deemed to be public space? Why should other occupants of that space be concerned or minded to object? Their restricted, old-fashioned view of what is right and proper in relation to sexual conduct is unnecessarily restric- tive and develops from commitment to a myth (e.g. the admonishments of the clergy, or unthinking submission to tradition). In order to progress as a collective totality, we must overcome these absurd social conventions in order to occupy a purer space of new freedoms. In this sense, postmodern- ism reanimates asocial libertarianism and fits neatly with the doctrine of neoliberalism: nothing exists beyond the immediate freedoms of the subject and no legitimate authority exists that can justifiably curtail those freedoms. By extension, of course, if nothing is sacred there is nothing that cannot be enjoyed, and nothing that cannot be sold on commercial markets.

In sociology, we see this drive most clearly in the celebratory accounts of the 1980s and 1990s that addressed the new freedoms opening up as the modern structures of class, ethnicity and gender appeared to crumble. People were freed from the hierarchical powers that intersected to structure an oppressive, totalitarian order that demanded submission. They were now free to determine social identities for themselves as a result of entirely 'subjective' decision-making. The rise of postmodernism encouraged the subject to flee from the terrorising influence of a really existing Symbolic Order to embrace the freedom of ultimate self-determination, to centre subjectivity and social life around 'the care of the self' (Foucault, 1988) and the allegedly 'cultural' mutual-interest group (Rose, 1999). On the surface of things, we appear to have freed ourselves from modernist social forces that impinged upon our subjective flourishing and free associations. However, in casting aside modernist accounts of truth that demanded our allegiance, we also relinquish the very things that enable us to live reasonably civil, organised and fulfilling lives; Foucault's self-carers degenerate into commercialised narcissism and Rose's ethical groups eye-up each other suspiciously as they tender their functionality to the shrinking consumer-service economy and their compliance to the agents of governance. We cannot help but cast out the positive content of modernist belief along with that which has been defined as false and oppressive. Now, adrift in the postmodern, we are all cast as the uncultured child who publicly announces that the Emperor is in fact completely naked. The child is no longer entangled in the falsehoods of the Symbolic Order and sees immediately the Emperor's unclothed state. Of course, once the child has burst the bubble of artificiality, everyone is now free to consciously accept what they in fact knew all along. Once disbelief was systematically suspended, but now belief is systematically suspended.

The 'freedom' that we adopt when our commitment to the Symbolic Order is relinquished returns us to the void of subjectivity. This is a raw freedom of isolation and profound negativity. If the actually-existing modernist Symbolic Order offered us a mythical framework that allowed us to make sense of the objective world that surrounds us, conscious recognition that this Symbolic Order was always a fake relieves us of the responsibility to believe. Of course, if we believe in nothing, if we immediately judge the content of the dead Symbolic Order to have been a ruse that deprived us of our freedom, how are we to construct a comprehensible model that might enable us to grasp the reality of our being in relation to the objective world that surrounds us? What use is a freedom without a framework that enables us to grasp the nature of freedom itself? What is the point of raw self-determination if we have no basis to determine a beneficial social outcome of our decision-making? What use is choice if we have no framework for understanding what might be the right choice? This liberal-postmodern refusal to submit to the rule of the big Other has had a profound effect upon our shared social life. As Jameson (1992) has acknowledged, we have become separated from our own history, and begin a journey along a restrictive path that leads only to possessive individualism and the deep cynicism that accompanies it. Postmodernism seeks to expose the world to the truth – that there is no god, that our cultures and traditions are structured in relation to a fundamental falsehood, and that we are free and ultimately alone in the world. Postmodernism thus ensures that there can be no faith in any final adjudicating authority that might tell us what to believe in and how to act.

What is the status of the social?

In the preceding pages we have offered a very basic sketch of Žižek's account of the decline of the Symbolic Order. What does this tell us about the current status of the social? First, we should conclude that the substance of faith is increasingly withdrawn from our social experience. The symbolic efficiency provided by the big Other has been removed as postmodernism has sought to free itself from history in order to occupy an open space of indeterminacy. Postmodernism has freed itself from the tyrannical rule of the big Other, but this act of regicide means that those minor social activities and know-ledges that were once taken as articles of faith are now thrown back into the void and vaporised. During the modern era, it's likely that we would have immediately accepted the medical prognosis of a doctor. The big Other had determined that this individual was deserving of respect and was the holder of hard-earned hidden knowledge, and so we were content to yield subjective control of the medical process to the professionals who would then take decisions on our behalf. Now it's more likely that we assume that the doctor in front of us to be tired and over-worked and prone to mistakes. And why should we believe, just because she has on a white coat and wears a stethoscope around her neck, that she is infallible? Aren't the prescriptive practices of doctors polluted by the interests of the pharmaceutical industry? Might there not be a cure to be found outside of the formal 'scientific' medi-cal profession? Why should I believe in the healing power of a tiny white pill rather than the healing power of crystals, chanting, positive thinking or anything else from the proliferating side-stalls of the postmodern market-place that have arisen to address our increased proximity to the Real? Why should we immediately invest the legal system with such respect? Behind all of the sub-regal pageantry, behind the wigs and the robes, sits a bigoted old fool with limited social experience passing judgement on the choices of individuals he knows nothing about. Why must we respect marriage? It's an archaic tradition that denies individuals their subjective freedom. And then, more fundamentally, why should I submit to conventional morality? I am an individual with my own irrefutable sovereignty. The boundaries of my behaviour should not be determined by idiotic others acting in relation to blind prejudice, some hazy faith in a non-existent god, out of some ridiculous attachment to convention, or out of pure spite and a desire to intrude upon my own private desires and spaces.

Those social conventions that could once be relied upon now appear less stable and secure. It is almost as if a semblance of the original convention still exists, but its substance has been withdrawn, lending a kind of brittle, insubstantial and anxious engagement with social reality. One might immediately assume that this is a pointless catastrophist digression, and that the social clearly continues to exist. After all, don't we only need to look out of our windows to see that a social world of rules, laws and obligations continues to exist? However, this is simply an external control system managed by proliferating little others (see glossary) designed to manage excessive competition, not a 'state of culture' in which the superego and the desire for sociability rule (see Stiegler, 2011; Hall 2012a; Winlow and Hall, 2012a). Underneath the fragile functionality of the everyday, the downfall of the big Other is felt as a loss (Žižek, 2007, 2009c). While we have freed ourselves from its totalitarian rule, we secretly yearn for some authority that will decide and force us to live by its decisions. The indeterminacy of the postmodern is alienating rather than pleasurable, and we fantasise about the return of a transcendent power that will demand we subscribe to a new order of fixed meaning. This enduring desire for clarity and unequivocal truth, the desire to once again become a true subject of belief, is now clearly exhibited across contemporary Western societies. Of course, once we set about the task of demolishing the Symbolic Order and rid ourselves of blind faith, we can only reconstruct our allegiances in a rational, calculating manner that tends to remove the essence of belief itself. We yearn for the restoration of transcendent authority that will force us to submit to belief and relieve us from the torment of indeterminacy, but no such authority can exist within the current coordinates of the postmodern. It may well be, as some clear-sighted Continental philosophers maintain, that the ultimate outcome of postmodern cynicism is the construction of new transcendental religious commitments, structured as a response to the fundamental pain of raw subjectivity existing too close to the Real.

More practically, in the absence of a transcendent authority, our increased proximity to the Lacanian Real compels us to at least attempt to fill the vacuum left by the death of the big Other. For Žižek, we can see this process in the construction of myriad little others that attempt to impose a framework on what is right and proper in relation to activities across a broad range of fields. These little others often take a supposedly democratic form, and the 'truth' of the little other is the democratic 'truth' of amalgamated viewpoints from the diverse constituencies of postmodern 'multicultural' society. Consider, for example, some of the genuinely perplexing ethical problems we face today. If we have no faith in God, and if there exists no truth as such, how are we to construct strategies relating to genetic engineering? Who will determine the boundaries relating to what is and what is not acceptable in this crucial field of scientific research? In order for any movement to occur we must construct a new authority that takes up the mantle of the now deceased big Other and attempts to set down rules. This often involves a new tyranny of committees. We see the rise of a new 'post-bureaucratic' bureaucracy as deeply indicative of capitalist realism. Neoliberalism purports to despise the waste of modernist bureaucratic institutions, especially those of the social democratic welfare state (see Whitehead and Crawshaw, 2012). But anyone who works within neoliberal institutions these days will no doubt acknowledge the new avalanche of bureaucratic tasks that descend from some imprecise position above to define the depressing logic of the daily grind.

This new tyranny of committees reflects, we believe, an essentially ethical drive to determine appropriate conduct. But the new rash of little others that tries to maintain a semblance of the old social order amidst the postmodern is doomed to failure. They can never be elevated to the role of the big Other, and the endlessly sceptical postmodern subject is immediately in possession of tools capable of deconstructing and dismissing the little other and its judgements. The composition of the committee of the little other, despite its attempt to be democratic and integrative, always omits some constituency or other. Its prognostications always appear subject to some corrupting influence. But it seems as though the establishment of these little others at least lends the remains of the social some residual semblance of order and symbolic consistency, even though the subject engages with the authority of these structures grudgingly and without true belief.

The fundamental issue we have discussed here is whether liberal-postmodernism's success in destroying the tyrannical old order – the big Other comprised of modernity's primary ethico-cultural and ideological forces operating together as an organising socio-symbolic order – has set the subject 'free', or even potentially 'free'. Optimists argue that today's advanced global communicative networks transcend old borders to offer a cosmopolitan free space in which individuals can creatively and autonomously construct identities and seek sociability with like-minded others (Lash, 2010). Others, even more optimistic, see the disembedded postmodern 'multitude' as the site for the birth of new radical, transformative politics that will lead to a new socioeconomic order (Hardt and Negri, 2000). We suspect that all this is premature. Baudrillard was right that the old Marxist critique was simply not radical enough. In the late capitalist era individuals are trapped in the tyranny of exchange-value, greater than the tyranny of production and use-value, a system of abstract equivalences that structures the capitalist market and has its cultural analogue in consumerism, a regime of tightly controlled sign-objects that has succeeded in commercialising every aspect of human relations from politics to sexuality. Baudrillard's infamous pessimism was tempered by a long-term optimism based on the possibility that the 'silent majority' can one day struggle free from its current inertia and return to some advanced variant of the free-flowing symbolic exchange that characterised pre-modern societies. Before this can be achieved, he argued, with what could be seen as a positive variation on Adorno's *negative dialectics* (Adorno, 1981; see also Dews, 2007), consumer capitalism's sign-object system must be driven onwards through phases of even greater perversity and emptiness to its own logical self-destruction.

In the meantime, there is little to be gained by pretending that the traditional social form still exists or that it can be revived. In Rose's (1996) Foucauldian analysis, traditional society has been 'dissociated' not into the consumer simulacrum but into fragmented and incommensurable ethico-cultural communities whose subjects are ripe for 'governmentalisation' strategies. Democracy can be furthered only when these communities firmly grasp their own freedom and shared commitments to produce their own knowledge and practices, with which they can ethically contest the authorities who attempt to normalise and govern them. These analyses come from opposite ends of a political spectrum that ranges from Baudrillard's reversed radical extremism to Rose's rather domesticated liberal-democratic culturalism. Indeed, one might suspect that Rose's (ibid.) convenient notion of a biopower regime that has recently been broken up into dissociated and customised forms to deal with incommensurable ethico-cultural groups has been contrived to avoid radicalism and universalism, both condemned as potentially dangerous by liberalism's post-war catastrophist doctrine (see Hall, 2012a). However, what they share in common is a home in the sort of hyper-Idealism that is now being recognised as a busted flush in radical philosophical circles. We have already seen in the work of Žižek that human beings are not simply cyphers in sociosymbolic or governmental biopower systems, to be seduced, absorbed, subjectified and normalised as passive victims of symbolic authorities that bear down upon them. Neither are they autonomous individuals capable of establishing a pure standpoint of critique entirely demarcated from ideology and culture. We can also see quite clearly the rapid hybridisation and absorption of Rose's supposedly ethically autonomous cultures into consumer capitalism's exchange systems as they have little choice but to struggle for the cultural and symbolic capital that can be exchanged for the economic capital (Bourdieu, 1987) necessary to ensure financial survival in a harsh and insecure post-crash economic order. This transparently active struggle by ostensibly willing agents, affirmed by voluminous data gathered by the authors over recent years, compels us to focus our attention on will and desire, and to formulate a far more active and universal conception of ideology and subjectivity.

The philosophical position of *transcendental materialism* (see glossary) can help us to move beyond liberal social science's exhausted Idealist foundations. We have written about this at length elsewhere (see Hall, 2012a, 2012c), but for our purposes here it will be sufficient to outline a few basic principles. For Lacan, the basic constitution of the human neurological system is conflict, tension and indeterminacy, which were required throughout the early and formative period of human evolution for adaptation to multiple and changing environments. Put simply, we are hard-wired for plasticity and dysfunctionality, the extreme paradox that exists as the (non)foundation of human nature. The only act determined by nature is dematerialisation of the biological proto-self into subjectivity, and our only act of natural resistance is to resist being re-assimilated back into the Real, the terrifying indeterminate void of our pre-symbolic biological being, where postmodernism foolishly seeks to send us, but where none of the irruptions sensed from internal conflicts or outside stimuli can be explained or dealt with. Notions of 'embodiment' and 'internalisation' are therefore problematic. The sheer terror of the Real compels each individual actively and positively to *solicit* incorporation into a Symbolic Order, a sociocultural organising system supplying comprehensible symbols and practices needed to deal with psychic disturbances. Put simply, the individual simply cannot tolerate Baudrillard's shifting spectacle-simulacrum, Rose's dissociated cultural milieu, Hardt and Negri's multitude, Derrida's endless subversion of meaning or any other form of fragmented, indeterminate and unstable symbolic system that threatens a regressive return to the Real. This is total anathema to the human being, and cannot act as a portal to socioeconomic transformation. The individual must belong to a comprehensible sociosymbolic order whose meanings and codes are shared with the others who are needed to ensure material and psychic survival in everyday environments.

The Symbolic Order is at root a basic survival strategy bonding together a social group around negative and positive mutual interests. The problem is *deaptation* (Johnston, 2008), where an initially functional sociosymbolic order – for instance, an ideology that grows in an environment of reduced numbers, scarcity and hostile natural threats – becomes actively counterproductive in a new environment of large numbers, abundance and domesticated nature. Transcendental materialism's radical move is thus an inversion of the normal relation between the material and the ideal. Whereas some traditional philosophies view the material as fixed and the ideal-symbolic world as flexible, and others view both as infinitely flexible and interactive, transcendental materialism views *solely* the material as permanently flexible and indeterminate, whereas the ideal-symbolic carries a tendency to dysfunctional rigidity and durability. In other words, the ideal-symbolic is the site for the reproduction of rigid ideologies resolutely defended by committed adherents *despite* the presence of radically altered underlying conditions and embryonic new ideas about how best to survive in their midst.

This supplies us with more plausible and potent conceptions of ideology and subjectivity. The subject is not created by being dragged unwillingly by some external authority – ideological state apparatuses, biopower and so on – into various symbolic systems; cultures, discourses, simulacra and so on. Nor is the subject simply a dupe of hegemony as manufactured consent. In order to escape the terror of the unsymbolised Real – the constant disturbing irruptions of the indeterminate pre-symbolic neurological system – the subject, for the sake of its survival and sanity, must actively solicit the key signifiers of an available Symbolic Order. This is primal, imperative and automatic; there is no alternative choice whatsoever, and once the subject has been through the identification-socialisation process the resultant identity is consolidated in the neurological circuits. Sociosymbolic systems are mechanisms of determinacy and entrapment, not playgrounds of indeterminacy and freedom; to achieve freedom the subject must tear itself away from its emotionally-grounded commitments and embark on a difficult journey back through the distressing indeterminacy of material being to seek an alternative sociosymbolic order. Without immersion in such an order, which is what the death of the social really means, the individual exists on a bed of unhappiness and anxiety, which can receive temporary relief only from a constant procession of temporary pleasurable sensations; the post-social world and the abject subject of consumerism are made for each other.

The current dominant and inflexible sociosymbolic system is based on the principles of neoliberal market-capitalism, and its hegemonic ideology is diffused and reproduced by the corporate mass media. However, acting in conjunction with consumer culture, the mass media's strategic ideological form is more than the standard political disinformation and myth designed to manufacture consent on behalf of the status quo. It preys upon the absolute compulsion felt by the human being to solicit a Symbolic Order that represents and organises some sort of social world in which identity and belonging can be found and consolidated. The mass media and consumer culture operate together to construct not a hyperreal *simulacrum* but a fully-blown *surrogate social world* (Hall et al., 2008), membership of which the individual – now devoid of alternative sources of identity, which have been destroyed by neoliberalism's cultural and economic convulsions in the late twentieth century – actively solicits. Baudrillard's (1994, 1998) formulation of the simulacrum was convincing in that its initial stages are reflection, perversion and pretence, but unconvincing in the final step into a hyperreal realm that is unrelated to reality. In fact the strength of the consumer culture that dominates late capitalism is its relation to reality, insofar as the human being experiences it as a seductive and compelling struggle for identity and distinction in a competitive world that nonetheless solicits the individual's commitment; it magically combines the escape from the terrifying Real with the indeterminate freedom the Real offers by suspending the individual between the Real and the Symbolic in a systematically impoverished Imaginary (see glossary) 'social world' disconnected from the two. Certainly, we have found nothing in our years of research in this surrogate social world to support Deleuze and Guattari's (2004a, 2004b) hope that it is a site that engenders the types of differences that might produce multiple symbolic challenges to the dominant consumer-capitalist order; our research suggests that it produces the sort of isomorphic, competitive differences that *faithfully reproduce* – in the senses of representation *and* forward momentum – the dominant order (Hall et al., 2008). The individual, over and above support from family and professional institutions, simply does not want to remain faithfully committed to the 'real' social world, with all of its real obligations, sacrifices, prohibitions and protocols, and feels neither excluded from it nor the urge to be re-included. As we discovered in our exploration of the *non-place*, consumer culture's surrogate social world, with its flimsy and retractable relations, hedonistic fantasy adventures, endless new sensations, off-the-peg identity symbols and electronic social networks, offers far less onerous passages into identity, belonging, security, excitement and success. The crucial problem is, of course, that it does not actually exist.

10

Conclusion

The poor you have always with you?

This book began with the simple intention of rethinking the problem of social exclusion right down to the fundamental concepts that make up social science's domain assumptions. For us, this vital field of intellectual inquiry has become bogged down in a paradigm dominated by dour policy analysis to the extent that it is now difficult to discern any genuine dialectical movement in our understanding of advanced marginality. Even those crucial studies that reveal the brutal reality of life on the margins (for example Nightingale, 1993; McAuley, 2007; LeBlanc, 2009; Briggs, 2011) and those key texts that identify the repressive nature of neoliberal governance (Lea, 2002; Wacquant, 2007, 2009; Wiegratz, 2012) seem to have lost the capacity to drive new intellectual agendas that can move beyond descriptive accounts of the suffering of the poorest, their objective conditions of existence and the constant failures of welfare support systems. What counts as critical analysis tends to limit itself to endless descriptions of the obscenity and absurdity of neoliberalism's political system, which rests on the colossal assumption that liberal-democratic politics as it stands has the latent capacity – if only we could get 'our people' in charge – to manage global capitalism on behalf of the poor; if this colossal assumption is wrong, then it is colossally wrong. This short book did not set out to provide the definitive answer to that fundamental question – although we hope that it will encourage others to address it – but to introduce from cognate fields one or two new ideas that might make some small contribution to the reanimation of social science's stalled intellectual dialectic.

We wanted to abandon all the usual protocols and approach the intellectual problem of social exclusion from a slightly different perspective that might give us a glance at its conceptual underbelly. We saw little point in simply wading into the tedious and apparently interminable slanging match between left-wing and right-wing liberals who appear incapable of saying anything new that might drive a more productive discussion. There are more than enough books out there that contribute to a strident critique of Charles

Murray and an accompanying account of the aggressive labelling processes of the social mainstream and its representatives in the press and in politics. Instead we have tried to dig underneath these issues to offer some intellectual nourishment for those who feel that the sense of urgency that should accompany the analysis of social exclusion is beginning to wane, and that our hope of one day making genuine social inclusion for all a reality might, ultimately, be futile.

Much of what we have discussed might be considered tangential to the study of social exclusion, but this would be to make the elementary mistake of ripping away too forcefully the foreground of poverty, unemployment and marginalisation from its essential contexts of history, culture and political economy. This artificial and unproductive separation is the product of post-war liberalism's *catastrophist* belief that substantial intervention in these deep contexts is no longer possible because it will inevitably turn politics into a totalitarian threat to individual freedom (see Pitts, 2008; Hall, 2012a).

Therefore, for us, in the absence of a critical reappraisal of domain assumptions it makes little sense to address the minutiae of 'social exclusion' without an accompanying account of those forces that create the ground upon which it exists as an actuality – in this case a concatenation of socioeconomic and cultural forces affecting the reality of people's everyday lives – and changes its form. This is a mistake that is made regularly in the social policy literature that addresses social exclusion. In this literature we see critiques of an assortment of chiefly political and managerial processes that lead to deeply regrettable social outcomes or fail to remedy specific aspects of the 'problem', but the fundamental issues that frame contemporary social exclusion are, in almost all cases, entirely absent. For us, the Fabian gradualism that appears to structure this discourse is patently incapable of making even the slightest dint in a neoliberal order that will continue to redistribute wealth from the middle and lower orders to the super-rich, and continue to exclude a growing number of people from the process of wealth-creation itself, until it meets a significant impediment or determined opposition capable of knocking it off course or otherwise forcing change upon it. A tweak here and a tweak there, even a more concerted attempt to reintegrate the poor by means of 'third way' social administration and haphazard 'third sector' philanthropy, is capable only of temporarily mitigating capitalism's very worst effects. This approach cannot prevent the accumulation of harms that neoliberal capitalism's unforgiving economic logic, supine politics, pseudo-pacified relations and envious, competitive subjects will always produce in abundance. In this book we have tried to suggest how the current conjuncture's dominant liberal culture has redefined idealism and pragmatism to realign the usual opposition between them. Now, those who adopt the 'pragmatic' position of slightly modifying the existing system's socioeconomic framework are redefined as the idealists. Conversely, in this current period of economic crisis and rapidly approaching environmental change, to believe that the current order can continue indefinitely should be defined as idealistic – even insanely so – but, instead, it is defined as pragmatic as we seek individual solutions tailored to the system's 'problems' as they crop up. To adopt such a position means turning away from a reality judged too traumatic to be faced head-on, and falling victim to the belief that any attempt to change it will succeed only in making things worse.

However, if we restore those two terms to their denotative meanings, it becomes clear that to adopt the real 'idealist' position and petition for genuine socioeconomic change is to abandon collective fetishistic disavowal and recognise the task that lies before us. It is to face up to a historical situation that demands the attenuation of consumer lifestyles, the democratic control of investment and the global flows of trade and capital, and the concerted attempt to narrow the huge gap between rich and poor (see Žižek, 2008b, 2011). It is vital that students interested in contemporary marginality understand that the socioeconomic divisions and poverty that are such striking features of the present are an inevitable outcome of a poorly regulated global capitalist economy whose politically-driven trajectory since 1945 has taken us to a destination where the system no longer needs an industrial workforce in the West, or at least in nowhere near the numbers and settled communities it once did. With an EU area such as Wales currently returning an *official* unemployment figure of 55.2 per cent (walesonline.co.uk), it is vital that those students understand the crucial changes that have occurred in capitalism's tumultuous post-war phase, and what those changes have meant for our shared social life. Students must also be willing to consider the position of the West's poorest in relation to fundamental changes that are taking place upon the political field and to ask if liberal democracy in its current form is capable of addressing the collective problems we face (Žižek, 2008a; Badiou, 2009; Dean, 2009).

Our book is motivated not simply by a desire to bring new life to the academic analysis of social exclusion. 2011 was a year of radical political disturbances across Europe, North America and parts of the Arab world. Despite what many of our colleagues on the liberal left think, in most instances these events did not signal the return of genuine politics, a step on the teleological path to democracy and the birth of a new desire among the people for equality and social justice. What they did suggest quite clearly is what many urban ethnographers have known for years: dissatisfaction and inarticulate rage gather in abundance in places of economic exclusion. For the moment, this dissatisfaction cannot be objectified and politically articulated in order to drive a new politics of emancipatory change (see Winlow and Hall, 2012b). Instead, after collectivist politics had been torn to shreds by the combined forces of neoliberalism and liberal-postmodernism, dissatisfaction continues to be endured by the subject who cannot yet produce an account that connects it to the dissatisfactions of others who occupy a similar structural and historical location, a specific socioeconomic and political *place* in capitalism's world.

The subjectivisation of harm and exploitation is a process that reflects the triumph of political and economic liberalism in breaking apart working-class community, its organisations and its political project of solidarity. As we suggested in our discussion of Baudrillard, despite the forlorn attempts of an army of liberal theorists to turn in their imaginations today's harm-less friendship groups into tomorrow's political collectives, a gas cloud of monadic consumers occupies the space where the grounded 'masses' once stood. This change in the basic composition of the social has had a sig-nificant impact on the ability of everyday working people to recognise their mutual interests, form affective bonds beyond the micro-level and enact political change. But this does not mean that the triumph of neoliberalism is complete and can no longer be challenged. The resuscitation of liberal capi-talism after the 2008 crash means that for the meantime the current divisive socioeconomic hierarchy will continue to be reproduced. The post-political austerity strategy timidly adopted by Western governments will inevitably inflict yet more harms and indignities on populations. Wages will fall, prices will rise and more people will find themselves unemployed, underemployed or their work and lives becoming increasingly precarious in some other ways. The sheer scale of inequality in the post-political present is supported and made possible by the huge successes of a liberal ideology that shapes the field of culture and transforms our subjective sense of being-in-the-world. Even many of the West's poorest citizens do not begrudge the wealthy their riches. Rather than wanting to see these groups brought down to earth with a crash, the poor often instead prefer to imagine their own elevation to the position of the super-rich. While many academic liberals believe the poor to be magically politicised against all the odds, an Aristotelian political natu-ralism that does not sit well in the present conjuncture, the poor are largely depoliticised and do not actively wish to rid the world of inequality. Their ultimate dream is to join the class of exploiters and to become the benefi-ciaries of liberal capitalism rather than its victims.

This is not a moral critique of the poorest. It is, rather, a sad recognition on our part based on years of gathering empirical evidence. We must stress that it reflects the daunting ideological triumph of liberal capitalism and its attendant hegemonic cultural forms rather than the moral or intellectual failures of the poor. We have of course tried to address the effects and out-comes of the end of politics in marginalised neighbourhoods, but we have also attempted to suggest how politics might return. We have no desire to indulge in the wishful thinking that is so common on the political and academic liberal-left; in the medium-term such compulsory optimism is far more dangerous than realistic pessimism because it can allow underlying conditions to degenerate further and host more extreme forms of abjec-tion and regressive political. Instead, if progress is to be made, we must address the reality of marginality with honesty. We must think clearly and unsentimentally about the fundamental changes that need to be made to reduce inequality and to provide working-aged populations with reasonably remunerative, satisfying and valued occupations. The hegemonic support to genuine socioeconomic inclusion must be founded upon the abandonment of the dewy-eyed romanticism that too often accompanies accounts of marginalised community life and the subsequent unseating of the neoliberal ethic of possessive, competitive individualism and conspicuous consumption, to be replaced by a culture that elevates altruism, mutual recognition and, above all, solidarity and the celebration of ordinary people to the pinnacle of the value-system. Only then can we begin to plot a productive path away from the harsh reality of contemporary social exclusion.

We touched briefly upon Badiou's analysis of politics and the Event, and this seems to us to be one way in which we might grasp the fundamental changes that can develop out of what might initially seem relatively small disruptions. More generally, the poor must become aware that their parlous economic position does not simply result from bad luck and inability, and that the incredible, ostentatious wealth of the rich is not simply a reflection of their remarkable good luck and ability. The poor must once again begrudge the wealthy their privileges, and see the present allocation of wealth, resources and status as deeply unfair; if a politically-significant majority of the excluded poor and precariously included middle-income groups continue to admire and defer to capitalism's oligarchs and believe in their supine politicians, no change will be possible. The excluded must also understand their pressures and dissatisfactions in relation to the injustice that is structured into the core logic of the current socioeconomic system. It is not simply that there are rich and poor; rather, some are rich precisely because some are poor. Rather than battling for 're-inclusion' expressed as upward social mobility and cultural recognition in the hierarchy as it stands, as the dominant ideology compels us to do, it might be more fruitful for the poor to move forward together as a class, and to see their troubles as equivalent to those of their neighbours. They may then be in a position not to think but to know that a more just world is possible if resolute action is taken and personal sacrifices are made.

This might seem rather naïve to the post-political sceptics and cynics of the pragmatic liberal-left, and our account will appear hopelessly 'ideological' to many of the supposedly objective social scientists of the 'social exclusion' discourse. That's fine. Our critics in Britain can keep on believing that the liberal-democratic political system will eventually ensure a more just division of liberal-capitalism's spoils, or that 'government' will eventually listen to the voices in the 'multitude' and implement the types of policies likely to make a real difference to people's lives. Our critics in America can pray that Barack Obama's recent re-election indicates a popular political swing to the left, and that in time corporate interests, driven forward relentlessly by capitalism's potent libidinal logic, can once again be domesticated and hauled back into line by liberalism's political system. Our point is simply this: if we are serious about preventing the manifold harms of exclusion in their entirety, it is clear we need a fundamental reorganisation of the global political economy from its financial core, along the lines currently being discussed by some of today's more imaginative political economists (Keen, 2011; Mattick, 2011; Stiegler, 2011; Varoufakis, 2011).

What the riots and protests we saw in 2011 indicate is that social exclusion left unchecked will eventually become an issue of such importance that it threatens to destabilise the entire edifice of Western parliamentary capitalism. As we have repeatedly suggested, fundamental change is not yet possible because the absence of clear ideological alternatives has allowed liberal capitalism to continue onwards and reinforce its image as the 'end of history', despite the relentless growth of inequality and socioeconomic redundancy throughout the neoliberal period. However, if we acknowledge in the huge growth of city populations globally, and the fact that a growing proportion of the global population now live in slum neighbourhoods, we can begin to see the crucial importance of social exclusion as a field of study. We agree with Slavoj Žižek's prediction that social exclusion will grow to become one of the defining issues of this century, and, as such, its realities and subjectivities must be talked about in far more honest and revealing terms. Those working in the field must work collectively to ensure that the study of social exclusion and its effects becomes central to both our academic disciplines and to the governments and bureaucratic organisations we work alongside.

Perhaps this book's most important original contribution has been to attempt to theorise the post-political marginalised subject. As we have said, too often analysts of social exclusion refuse to engage with the complexities of subjectivity, or they reduce the essence of subjectivity to the disapproving gaze of the other. Borrowing from the work of Slavoj Žižek, we have attempted to make sense of the historic changes that have resulted in the decline of symbolic efficiency and the rise of what we have called the 'post-social' world. We have looked in detail at postmodernism's attack upon belief and the rise of cynicism and atomisation. But rather than simply offer an abstract philosophical discussion of subjectivity, we have attempted to mobilise these ideas and put them to work as explanations of Britain's drab and monotonous post-political urban experience. We focused mostly on the commercialised centres of Britain's towns and cities, but we have also attempted to apply this intellectual framework to ex-urban commercial sites and to the growing ubiquity of post-social 'gated communities'. We have done this at least partly because social exclusion is tied to the transformation of cities in various ways, but mostly because these key sites seem to indicate a historic collapse of actually-existing social life. The substance of genuine social experience appears to have been evacuated from the enterprise zone, the shopping arcade and the gated enclave. What remains is simply the functional symbolism that enables monadic individuals to keep the other at a safe distance and negotiate shared space in the absence of effort, obligation and sacrifice. And of course, if we can no longer talk of 'the social', then what sense does it make to proceed with an analysis of 'social exclusion' that refuses to acknowledge these broader and deeper changes? What we have tried to do is extend the analysis of 'social exclusion', so that we can begin to think in new ways about social, political and economic change and address the possibility that, in important ways, we are all excluded from the social.

Be careful what you wish for

It has in recent years become something of a cliché for leftist theorists to return to Fredric Jameson's (2003) observation about it being easier to imagine the end of the world than the end of capitalism, but the apparent impossibility of genuine historical change in politics and economy tells us a great deal about the problems we face in creating a more just and equitable world. We can catch a glimpse of Jameson's thesis in a new genre of disaster movies that draw upon plausible scenarios in order to drive forward a narrative of planetary destruction or threats to the survival of our species. Of all the disaster films we have sat through in the last few years, two stand out. In Roland Emmerich's *The Day After Tomorrow*, our reckless exploitation of the natural environment reaches a tipping point. Temperatures across the global north dip radically and human life can no longer be supported across large expanses of the northern hemisphere. In *2012*, by the same director, seismic events transform the planet and survivors must clamber aboard one of the specially designed pods capable of sustaining human life until the Earth's surface stabilises. Despite the fact that, in both films, a huge proportion of the Earth's human population is wiped out, they manage to end on an upbeat note that is worth investigating a little further.

These days we can of course quite easily imagine the end of the world. We are now regularly exposed to news stories about Earth-bound asteroids and about the inevitable transformation of our natural environment. We see tragedies unfold across the world as a result of tsunamis, earthquakes, floods and droughts. Of course, the shocking nature of much of this material reaffirms our commitment to the present and produces only a fetishistic response that acts to prevent a genuine encounter with the reality of staggering environmental change and its potential repercussions for humanity. So, our anxiety about global climate change results in recycling projects and campaigns to buy sustainable consumer products; a small charitable donation frees us of the obligation to think too deeply about the suffering of others affected by catastrophic events. If these things are inevitable and await us in the years to come, should we not just lay back a little, accept the world as it is and commit ourselves to enjoying life as much as possible while we are here? If a cancer patient is dying there's no point in cutting back on the cigarettes. In that case, perhaps we should not delay buying that new SUV? Of course, the current nature of geopolitical power and global political economy mean that any attempt to genuinely intervene in the world to ensure that the worst effects of climate change are avoided remains impossible. Instead, all that can be done is encourage states to opt in and accept emissions targets and commit to renewable energies. Either that or we can draw upon the legendary ingenuity of the market to fix the problem; after all, melting ice fields are already revealing new opportunities to extract gas and other fossil fuels, and these new markets might yet drive the global economy back to growth, and in so doing produce the investment capital needed to encourage the development of new technologies that might allow our species to survive and prosper in a radically changed environment.

Consciously, we know that in the anthropocene era our natural environment is changing rapidly, and, with the assistance of vivid cinematic renderings, we are perfectly capable of imagining the end of the world. But an end to capitalism – merely one of many ways of organising an economy after all – seems impossible, especially after the abject failure of communist central command economies. China shows us that even today's communist rulers need capitalism, and the world's most imaginative thinkers struggle to imagine a world beyond it. As we have already suggested, all conceivable socialistic alternatives are either tainted by the symbolism of tyranny and evil, or otherwise seem entirely devoid of those things that make life worth living. All we can imagine, if we really push ourselves, is a variant of capitalism, perhaps a version of capitalism that is adequately controlled by the liberal-democratic state, or a capitalism destabilised by the emancipatory potential of new information technologies, new consumer cooperatives or an endless drip-feed of 'transgressive' sub-cultures that challenge vested interests. But a world in which the profit motive is no longer crucial to the system of socioeconomic organisation? For most, every attempt to dream this new world inevitably ends in a nightmare of totalitarian brutality or widespread desperation and starvation. What this suggests is that capitalism has appropriated all of those things that we consider to be positive and useful, to the extent that it becomes impossible to imagine them without also imagining capitalism. We then begin to see these things as an outcome of capitalist political economy, as if the magnanimous free hand of the market utilised by spirited entrepreneurs, rather than our own exploited labour, has itself bestowed upon us the gifts of civilisation. What by and large we cannot countenance is the painful reality that we might have to get by with less, that whatever new power fills the void left by the exit of capitalism would decree an end our profligate consumer lifestyles. Despite the likely protestations of the ethical consumers of the middle class, a world without foreign holidays, iPads and the other accoutrements of a socially included lifestyle fills the mainstream Western population with dread. It is almost as if we imagine that, were the end of the world to come, capitalism would somehow survive, or that the survivors of the catastrophe would begin the process of rebuilding civilisation by first of all ensuring the right of all to trade, accumulate surpluses and make capital investments in the pursuit of personal profit.

This inability to imagine a world beyond capitalism is what Mark Fisher (2009) has usefully called 'capitalist realism'. We have tried to suggest throughout this book how capitalist realism came about and what it means for the future of global 'societies'. In this regard, our goal has been to draw upon the philosophy of transcendental materialism in order to offer students an up-to-date account of ideological control and subjectivity in the post-political present. Here ideology congeals in our neurological circuits to ensure that we encounter and emotionally commit ourselves to the dominant ideology as pure common sense, as a timeless fact of life that must be accepted. But of course, and as we have tried to stress, Žižek's analysis of the decline of symbolic efficiency does not close off the possibility of genuine change. The advanced self-interest we see around us in contemporary popular culture is not at all a timeless fact of life, written into our very DNA as an immutable bio-evolutionary drive, a reflection of a species that ultimately remains genetically predisposed to selfishness. Despite the failures of previous ill-conceived attempts to do so, it is always possible to be something else, to transcend the ideology of liberal capitalism and replace institutionalised selfishness with genuine community, to replace enmity with solidarity, and exclusivity with inclusivity. We do not really need Žižek to tell us that; we know it to be true because we keep bumping into people who are far less selfish than others, although we also observe that, on the whole, the latter tend to enjoy far more financial success, social status and cultural influence.

What is useful in the disaster movies we mentioned above is their depiction of the world after these epochal events. In both *The Day After Tomorrow* and *2012*, despite huge loss of life, it is possible to identify a marked positivity about the outcomes of change. Both films contain in their final scenes distinct overtones of the blossoming of a new reality rooted in social justice, acceptance and mutual recognition. It is almost as if our collective passage through the destruction of the late-modern way of life enables us to look back with honesty and shock at the hubris, greed and institutionalised envy that characterise both our lives today and our shared history under neoliberalism. After the traumatic event has occurred, we can see that our petty squabbles and desperate desire to amass status through the accumulation of consumerism's symbolic objects is rather absurd. It is almost as if we had been possessed by some daemonic spirit that compelled us to turn away from the ultimate reality of human social life: that, ultimately, we rely upon each other and need mutual support and recognition to live reasonably civilised lives together. The catastrophic event means that the scales have fallen from our eyes and we see both the stupidity of our shared past and the future necessity of acceptance and solidarity. Both films then close with clear indications that a new day has dawned and that the survivors will move forward together towards a more equitable social order in which the petty concerns of the past no longer dominate our lives. If we are to solve the problem of social exclusion, we need a similarly transformative event to occur across the West, an event that allows us to see the absurdity of the present order and the absolute necessity of creating a more just and equitable world for ourselves. Our great hope is that we do not have to pass through destructive environmental change or violent social upheaval to make that happen, that we can construct and hone new social analyses and political discourses well enough to *imagine* the gravity of the trauma and its aftershock and seek civilised ways to socioeconomic transformation before it happens. Until we can do that, the reality of permanent socioeconomic exclusion in the atomised post-social will remain with us.

Glossary of Terms

Big Other – this is Lacan's term for the network of social institutions, customs and laws into which the individual is socialised. It has no substance other than the symbolic and is therefore a sort of collective lie, fiction or illusion that is nevertheless necessary for the survival of a coherent social world. Nobody really believes in the big Other, which is not surprising because it has no independent existence, but all members of a symbolically established community are compelled by everyone else's subscription to its rules to *act as if* they believe in it, and thus by way of coherent social action it becomes real.

Biopolitics – in basic terms this simply refers to the politics of the body. However, it is important to note that throughout this book, and especially in Chapter 5, we connect biopolitics to post-politics. Žižek (2008a: 34) suggests that 'it is clear how these two dimensions overlap: once one renounces big ideological causes, what remains is only the efficient administration of human life … almost only that. That is to say, with the depoliticised, socially objective, expert administration and coordination of interests as the zero level of politics, the only way to introduce passion to the field, to actively mobilise people, is through fear, a basic constituent of today's subjectivity'. For a different reading, see Agamben (1998).

Critical/ultra-realism – this is premised on the belief that social science can undercut ideology and represent the real world with enough accuracy to appeal to underlying core sentiments of good and evil shared by all human beings. Our commitment is to explaining the world as it is, warts and all. To do this effectively, we must rid ourselves of the entirely unproductive optimism that refuses to acknowledge the genuine hardships experienced by a growing proportion of Western populations.

Derealisation – in psychology and psychoanalysis this phrase is used to communicate a sense of detachment, a sense that the real world we experience is somehow false or staged and the subject can watch himself playing a role in it.

The Imaginary – is one of Lacan's three orders, and is best understood as the realm of narcissistic identification, where the ego splits and identifies with some spectral counterpart in the external world. It is connected to the Real and the Symbolic, but acts as the realm of connotative meaning, of signifieds and signification, so it is a private space of susceptibility and self-deception, whose malleable but insistent desires can be easily seduced and lured by external mediated images; unlike the Symbolic (see below), which is social and potentially political because it is structured by comprehensible and communicable symbols.

Jouissance – the French word for enjoyment, but accompanied with sexual connotations. For Lacan, especially in his later work, the term is often used to refer to those pleasures that exist beyond the pleasure principle and consequently involve an element of pain. *Jouissance*, therefore, denotes excessive or unbearable pleasures.

Little other – After the death of the big Other (see above), there exists no authority capable of determining appropriate social protocols or establishing meaning or truth. One of the outcomes (see also the Other of the Other, p. 179) of the historic decline of symbolic efficiency is the drive to establish an expanding network of new, rational bureaucratic authorities which together attempt to take up the mantle of the big Other. These are little others, but they cannot exercise convincing authority and are therefore destined to fail as the subject is condemned to greet the proclamations of all little others with cynicism, scepticism and enduring disbelief.

Master Signifier – to be brief, the Master Signifier refers only to itself. It is a powerful organising abstraction – such as 'nature', 'commodity', 'money', or, in pop culture, 'cool' – that structures our immediate understanding of the symbolic order and its content. The dominance of the Master Signifier effectively renders its prescribed meaning the only one of any consequence, and it fixes the context in which associated meanings can develop in its shadow. As Lacan (1997: 297) observes 'the relationship between the signified and the signifier always appears fluid, always ready to come undone'. It is the Master Signifier that fixes meaning in place.

Neoclassical right – we use this phrase as a means of capturing the reality of much contemporary rightist thought. It is 'neoclassical' because it revives classical liberalism's selfish, calculating rational subject as its model of subjectivity and the ideological foundation for its political and economic thought. This neoclassical right is quite different to the traditional right-wing conservative parties that were once powerful Britain and America. For example, in Britain the contemporary Conservative party has completed abandoned one-nation Toryism and is now a party dominated by the attempt to advance the interests of global neoliberal capitalism.

Postmodern/liberal left – we use these terms interchangeably throughout the text, but in most cases we are referring to the same people, processes and ideological approaches. It is our contention that at the start of the neoliberal period the traditional left – with its deep, structuring commitment to equality and social justice – effectively lost out to a new leftist discourse that discarded the symbols of the traditional left and replaced them with a general acceptance of capitalism and its harms and injustices. Rather than arguing for systemic change, they instead argued for better management of the economic and political systems with a view to ameliorating its worst aspects. Integral to this new liberal left was a concern with rights and freedoms and a faith in the legal system to defend individuals from exploitation and injustice. The discourse of the new liberal left is expressed clearly in Tony Blair's 'third way' politics, an approach to economic management and statecraft that had much in common with Bill Clinton's presidency of the United States at around the same time. They believed that the liberalisation of capital would create economic growth, which would in turn boost tax revenues, which could in turn be used to provide forms of social security that would alleviate poverty and sustain inclusivity. We also claim that this left liberalism, and the left-liberal analyses that are so common in the social sciences, is far more closely connected to the reproduction of global neoliberalism than its key protagonists are willing to countenance.

Post-politics – we talk through precisely what we mean by this phrase in Chapter 5, but very briefly: post-politics is simply the form of politics that follows the end of genuine political engagement. For us, genuine politics involved a degree of ideological commitment. Post-politics is the politics of now. Post-politics is the reduction of politics to mere representation and administration. These days, our politicians appear to have no clear ideological commitments beyond improving what already exists. For a more detailed elaboration, see Žižek (2008a), Rancière (2010a) and Badiou (2009).

The Real – for Lacan, the Real is one of the three orders (see also The Symbolic and The Imaginary) that constitute the psyche. It defines and shapes our pre-symbolic subjective psychological experience, a milieu of conflicting and unexplained stimuli and drives – powerful feelings that cannot be put into words. The word is capitalised to distinguish it from mere 'reality', which tends to occupy the symbolic realm. For Lacan, the Real exists beyond symbolisation. Quite literally, we have not got the words to describe it. Imagine being faced with a phenomenon that impacts on your senses to leave you feeling completely agog, entirely unable to explain or understand it, no matter how hard one tries. This suggests an encounter with the Lacanian Real. See Taylor (2010) and Fink (1996).

Repress/repression – this is a very basic psychoanalytic concept that refers the attempt to force subjective desire or traumatic memories from consciousness.

These desires remain in the subconscious, and can 'return' in altered form to intrude upon consciousness, identity and social behaviour.

Subject/subjectivity – we use this phrase in the traditional philosophical sense to denote the unique, internal, non-objective life of the individual. Using Žižek's transcendental materialism as a guide, we describe fundamental changes in the nature of human subjectivity throughout the book.

Sublimation – for Freud, sublimation is a process in which amorphous libidinal energy is channelled into socially acceptable activities such as artistic or intellectual endeavour. Sublimation is not simply an 'escape valve' for excess sexual energy that might cause excessive behaviour or, if repressed, neurosis, but the fundamental means by which a 'state of nature' can be converted to a 'state of culture'. It is thus essential for the journey of socialisation from the Real through the Imaginary to the Symbolic during the Oedipal phase.

Symbolic Order – for Lacan, the Symbolic Order defines our experience of everyday social life. In order to make sense of social reality, and subscribe to the normative meaning of symbols, we need to pass through a period of socialisation that encourages understanding and the acceptance of symbolic meaning. The Symbolic Order is therefore simply the social world of communication – including but not restricted to language – that allows us to understand the world around us. The law forms part of this symbolic order, but here 'the law' is not simply a reference to the formal laws created by liberal democratic legislatures. The law is used to capture all rules and conventions that are the products of the big Other (see above). Drawing on the work of Žižek, for us the very principle of the necessity of a Symbolic Order has been challenged by the rise of postmodernism and the onward march of liberal capitalism. One key aspect that suggests the decline of the modern Symbolic Order relates to the associated decline of symbolic efficiency. For clear extended accounts of the Symbolic Order, read: Bailly's (2009) *Lacan*, Taylor's (2010) *Žižek and the Media*, Dean's (2006) *Žižek's Politics*, and Fink's (1996) *The Lacanian Subject*.

Symbolic efficiency – symbolic efficiency relates to the general agreement that is reached about the meaning and consequence of the symbols that make up the Symbolic Order. Crucially, in order for a 'fact' to take on the appearance of truth, it must first be accepted by the big Other. When the big Other identifies something as factual, the subject is then also encouraged to fully believe in it. For example, before the rise of postmodernism, we were encouraged to take a medical prognosis at face value. We accepted that the doctor was the holder of hidden knowledge, and that their assessment should be accepted as truth. The decline of symbolic efficiency means that we no longer take such things at face value, and that there are gradually fewer symbols that we can immediately accept as basic truths. Symbolically effi-cient cultures are not rigid and incapable of producing new truths, but pan-sceptical postmodernism challenged all established forms of belief; it asks why they should be accepted over alternative accounts of meaning. We might imagine that challenging conventional understandings of the world must be a good thing, but refusal to accept established meaning ensures the gradual erosion of faith in all social institutions and conventions and the incremental advance of a culture of immobilising cynicism. Increas-ingly we greet all accounts of truth with cynicism, and it is difficult to iden-tify anything today that we can fully accept as an article of faith. But there is also an associated and paradoxical change taking place. Our inability to believe is connected to a deeper, unconscious form of belief that takes the form of a belief in our own non-belief, or a basic commitment to our own scepticism. This, Žižek suggests, signifies the return of the big Other, or what, following Lacan, he calls the Other of the Other. The decline of symbolic efficiency and the sad demise of the big Other encumbers us with an oppressive freedom in which less and less of the world around us makes sense and can be taken at face value. In order to escape this torment and to try and restore some sense of order we construct an Other of the Other that occupies the sphere of the Real (see above). For Žižek, we can see this process at work in the growth of belief in conspiracy theories. We dismiss authoritative accounts of an event, but we seem increasingly will-ing to accept alternative accounts of conspiracy and hidden power that test the boundaries of credulity. For example, we seem willing to believe in the existence of some hidden power that manipulates governments and controls the world order, even though we find it increasingly difficult to believe in more mundane aspects of the symbolic order. This paranoia is deeply reflective of our times, but, in the standard psychoanalytic manner, we should see this paranoia as an attempt to address some other issue. Paranoia is not in itself 'the illness'; rather it is a formation that reflects the subject's attempt to address the true illness. For Žižek, this common paranoia is an attempt to cope with the decline of symbolic efficiency and the death of the big Other. For clear accounts of symbolic efficiency, read Taylor's (2010) *Žižek and the Media*, Dean's (2006) *Žižek's Politics*, and Žižek's (2006b) *How to Read Lacan*.

Thymos/thymotic passions – thymos is the Greek word for passion or spir-itedness, but in Greek philosophy it usually refers to those passions that structure a desire for external recognition.

Transcendental materialism – this is a phrase used to describe Slavoj Žižek's contribution to philosophy, more specifically his foundational ontology. It relates to a model of subjectivity he develops sporadically throughout his work. In Chapter 8 we describe this model in quite basic terms. Žižek's ontology involves an attempt to fuse the German idealism of Hegel, Kant and Schelling to Lacanian psychoanalysis as a means of grasping the relationship between mind and body and the nature of human freedom. The fundamental principle is that the human being's material neurological system is flexible whilst the ideological sociosymbolic system is rigid. This reversal stands much of liberal thought on its head and challenges the Marxist notion that material conditions determine consciousness; the real problem we face is that material conditions *do not* always determine consciousness, which means that obsolete ideologies can survive past their sell-by date to cause huge problems in the present. See Johnston (2008), Hall (2012a; 2012c), Winlow and Hall (2012a) and Žižek *passim*.

Bibliography

Abramson, A., Tobin, M. and VanderGoot, M. (1995) 'The changing geography of metropolitan opportunity: The segregation of the poor in U.S. metropolitan areas, 1970 to 1990', *Housing Policy Debate*, 6, 1: 45–72.

Adorno, T. (1981) *Negative Dialectics*, London: Continuum.

Agamben, G. (1998) *Homo Sacer*, Stanford, CA: Stanford University Press.

Agamben, G. (2005) *State of Exception*, Chicago, IL: University of Chicago Press.

Althusser, L. (2005) *For Marx*, London: Verso.

Arendt, H. (1969) *On Violence*, New York: Harcourt.

Arrighi, G. (2009) *Adam Smith in Beijing*, London: Verso.

Atkinson, R. (2006) 'Padding the bunker: Strategies of middle-class disaffiliation and colonisation in the city', *Urban Studies*, 43, 4: 819–32.

Atkinson, R. (2012) 'Accommodating harm: The domestic home in criminology', in S. Winlow and R. Atkinson (eds), *New Directions in Crime and Deviancy*, London: Routledge.

Atkinson, R. and Flint, J. (2004) 'Fortress UK? Gated communities, the spatial revolt of the elites and time–space trajectories of segregation', *Housing Studies*, 19, 6: 875–92.

Atkinson, R. and Helms, G. (eds) (2007) *Securing an Urban Renaissance*, Bristol: Policy Press.

Atkinson, R. and Smith, O. (2012) 'An economy of false securities? An analysis of murders inside gated residential developments in the United States', *Crime, Media, Culture*, 8, 2: 161–72.

Augé, M. (2008) *Non-places*, London: Verso.

Aust, S. (2008) *The Baader-Meinhof Complex*, London: Bodley Head.

Babiak, P. and Hare, R. (2007) *Snakes in Suits*, London: Harper Collins.

Bachelor, L. (2012) 'City watchdog blames bonus culture for corrupting bank services', *Guardian* (5/9/2012).

Badiou, A. (2002) *Ethics*, London: Verso.

Badiou, A. (2009) *The Meaning of Sarkozy*, London: Verso.

Badiou, A. (2010a) *The Communist Hypothesis*, London: Verso.

Badiou, A. (2010b) 'The idea of communism', in S. Žižek and C. Douzinas (eds), *The Idea of Communism*, London: Verso.

Badiou, A. (2011) *Being and Event*, London: Continuum.

Badiou, A. (2012a) *The Rebirth of History*, London: Verso.

Badiou, A. (2012b) *In Praise of Love*, London: Serpent's Tail.

Badiou, A. (2012c) *Philosophy for Militants*, London: Verso.

Badiou, A. (2013) *The Logic of Worlds*, London: Continuum.

Bailly, L. (2009) *Lacan*, Oxford: Oneworld.

Bakan, J. (2005) *The Corporation*, London: Constable.

Baudrillard, J. (1975) *The Mirror of Production*, St Louis, MO: Telos Press.

Baudrillard, J. (1981) *For a Critique of the Political Economy of the Sign*, St Louis, MO: Telos Press.

Baudrillard, J. (1983) *In the Shadow of the Silent Majorities,* New York: Semiotext(e).

Baudrillard, J. (1993) *Symbolic Exchange and Death,* London: Sage.

Baudrillard, J (1994) *Simulacra and Simulation,* Ann Arbor, MI: University of Michigan Press.

Baudrillard, J. (1998) *The Consumer Society: Myths and Structures,* London: Sage.

Baudrillard, J. (1999) *Fatal Strategies,* London: Pluto Press.

Bauman, Z. (1998a) *Work, Consumerism and the New Poor,* Buckingham: Open University Press.

Bauman, Z. (1998b) *Globalization,* Cambridge: Polity.

Bauman, Z. (2000) *The Individualized Society,* Cambridge: Polity.

Bauman, Z. (2004) *Wasted Lives,* Cambridge: Polity.

Bauman, Z. (2007a) *Consuming Life,* Cambridge: Polity.

Bauman, Z. (2007b) *Liquid Times,* Cambridge: Polity.

Bauman, Z. (2011) *Collateral Damage,* Cambridge: Polity.

Baumann, B. (2001) *How It All Began,* London: Arsenal Pulp Press .

BBC (2011) 'Homelessness "rises by 17per cent in UK"'. Available at: www.bbc.co.uk/news/uk-14838969 (retrieved 27/6/2012).

BBC (2012) 'UK unemployment increases by 118,000 to 2.69m'. Available at: www.bbc.co.uk/news/business-16608394 (retrieved 27/6/2012).

Beaumont, P. (2011) 'Greek rise in homelessness creates a new poor' in *Guardian* (3/8/2011).

Beck, U. (2000) *The Brave New World of Work,* Oxford: Polity.

Beckett, K. and Herbert, S. (2009) *Banished,* Oxford: Oxford University Press.

Beckford, M. (2011) 'Gap between rich and poor growing fastest in Britain', *The Telegraph* (5/12/2011).

Bell, D. (1973) *The Coming of Post-Industrial Society,* New York: Penguin.

Berardi, F. (2009) *The Soul at Work,* Los Angeles, CA: Semiotext(e).

Berlin, I. (2002) *Liberty,* Oxford: Oxford University Press.

Boltanski, L. and Chiapello, E. (2007) *The New Spirit of Capitalism,* London: Verso.

Borabaugh, W. (1992) *Berkeley at War: The 1960s,* Oxford: Oxford University Press.

Bosteels, B. (2011) *The Actuality of Communism,* London: Verso.

Bourdieu, P. (1977) *Outline of a Theory of Practice,* Cambridge: Cambridge University Press.

Bourdieu, P. (1987) *Distinction,* Cambridge, MA: Harvard University Press.

Bowles, S. (2012) *The New Economics of Inequality and Redistribution,* Cambridge: Cambridge University Press.

Bowling, B. and Phillips, C. (2007) 'Disproportionate and discriminatory: Reviewing the evidence on police stop and search', *The Modern Law Review,* 70, 6: 936–61.

Brands, P. (2009) *Traitor to His Class: The Privileged Life and Radical Presidency of Franklin Delano Roosevelt,* New York: Anchor Books.

Briggs, D. (2011) *Crack Cocaine Users: High Society and Low-life in South London,* London: Routledge.

Brown, P. (1995) 'Cultural capital and social exclusion: Some observations on recent trends in education, employment and the labour market', *Work, Employment and Society,* 9, 1: 29–51.

Bruce, M. and Kratz, C. (2007) 'Competitive marketing strategies of luxury fashion companies' in T. Hines and M. Bruce (eds), *Fashion Marketing,* London: Butterworth-Heinemann.

Bulmer, M. (1986) *The Chicago School of Sociology*, Chicago, IL: University of Chicago Press.

Burdis, K. and Tombs, S. (2012) 'After the crisis: new directions in theorising corporate and white-collar crime' in S. Hall and S. Winlow (eds), *New Directions in Criminological Theory*, London: Routledge.

Burley, E. (2009) *Making People Behave*, Cullompton: Willan.

Butler, P. (2012) 'Homeless rise of 14 per cent "just tip of the iceberg"', *Guardian* (8/3/2012).

Bynner, J. and Parsons, S. (2002) 'Social exclusion and the transition from school to work: The case of young people not in education; employment, or training (NEET)', *Journal of Vocational Behavior*, 60, 2: 289–309.

Byrne, D. (1989) *Beyond the Inner City*, Buckingham: Open University Press.

Byrne, D. (1999) *Social Exclusion*, Buckingham: Open University Press.

Cairncross, A. and Cairncross, F. (eds) (1992) *The Legacy of the Golden Age*, London: Routledge.

Callinicos, A. (2000) *Equality*, Oxford: Polity.

Callinicos, A. (2010) *Bonfire of Illusions*, Oxford: Polity.

Camara, D.H. (2009) *Dom Helder Camara: Essential Writings*, London: Orbis.

Castells, M. (2010a) *The Information Age: Society, Economy and Culture, Volume 1, The Rise of the Network Society*, Oxford: Wiley-Blackwell.

Castells, M. (2010b) *The Information Age: Society, Economy, and Culture, Volume 3, End of Millennium*, Oxford: Wiley-Blackwell.

Cederstrom, C. and Fleming, P. (2012) *Dead Man Working*, London: Zero Books.

Cellan-Jones, R. (2012) 'Facebook valued at $104bn as share price unveiled'. Available at: www.bbc.co.uk/news/business-18105608 (retrieved 4/3/2012).

Chang, H-J. (2002) *Kicking Away the Ladder*, London: Anthem Press.

Chang, H-J. (2008) *Bad Samaritans*, London: Random House.

Chang, H-J. (2011) *23 Things They Don't Tell You About Capitalism*, London: Penguin.

Chomsky, N. (1998) *Profit Over People*, London: Seven Stories Press.

Cohen, S. (2011) *Folk Devils and Moral Panics*, London: Routledge.

Collins, M. (2005) *The Likes of Us*, London: Granta.

Croach, C. (2011) *The Strange Non-Death of Neoliberalism*, Oxford: Polity.

Currie, E. (2011) 'Failed Societies: On the Social Context of Preventable Harm in the 21st Century'. Paper presented at the York Deviancy Conference, June/July 2011.

Davis, M. (2004) *Dead Cities*, London: The New Press.

Davis, M. (2007) *Planet of Slums*, London: Verso.

De Angelis, M. (2007) *The Beginning of History*, London: Pluto Press.

Dean, J. (2006) *Žižek's Politics*, New York: Routledge.

Dean, J. (2009) *Democracy and Other Neoliberal Fantasies*, Durham, NC: Duke University Press.

Dean, J. (2012) *The Communist Horizon*, London: Verso.

Deleuze, G. and Guattari, F. (2004a) *Anti-Oedipus*, London: Continuum.

Deleuze, G. and Guattari, F. (2004b) *A Thousand Plateaus*, London: Continuum.

Derrida, J. (1991) *A Derrida Reader: Between the Blinds*, New York: Columbia University Press.

Descartes, R. (1998) *Meditations and Other Metaphysical Writings*, London: Penguin Classics.

Dews, P. (2007) *The Idea of Evil*, Oxford: Wiley-Blackwell.

Dorling, D. (2011) *Injustice*, Bristol: Policy Press.

Dorling, D. and Rees, P. (2003) 'A nation still dividing: The British census and social polarisation 1971–2001', *Environment and Planning*, 35: 1287–1313.

Eagleton, T. (2009) *Trouble with Strangers,* Oxford: Wiley-Blackwell.

Eitle, D. (2009) 'Dimensions of racial segregation, hypersegregation, and Black homicide rates' *Journal of Criminal Justice*, 37, 1: 28–36.

Elkind, P. and McLean, B. (2004) *The Smartest Guys in the Room,* London: Penguin.

Elliot, L. (2012) 'Britain's richest 5 per cent gained most from quantitative easing – Bank of England', *Guardian* (23/8/2012).

Engels, F. (2009) *The Condition of the Working Class in England,* Oxford: Oxford Paperbacks.

Evans, H. (1998) *The American Century*, New York: Alfred A. Knopf.

Farley, R., Couper, M. and Krysan, M. (2007) *Race and Revitalization in the Rust Belt: A Motor City Story*, Research Report 07-620, Population Studies Centre, University of Michigan.

Ferguson, C. (2012) *Inside Job,* Oxford: Oneworld Publications.

Fink, B. (1996) *The Lacanian Subject: Between Language and Jouissance*, Princeton, NJ: Princeton University Press.

Fisher, M. (2009) *Capitalist Realism*, London: Zero.

Fitzgibbon, W. (2007) 'Institutional racism, pre-emptive criminalisation and risk analysis', *The Howard Journal of Criminal Justice*, 46, 2: 128–44.

Fletcher, N. (2012) 'More than one in 10 high street shops left empty', *Guardian* (19/11/2012).

Follain, J. (1999) *Jackal*, London: Orion.

Foucault, M. (1988) *The Care of the Self,* New York: Random House.

Frank, T. (1998) *The Conquest of Cool*, Chicago, IL: University of Chicago Press.

Frank, T. (2005) *What's the Matter with Kansas?* New York: Holt McDougal.

Frank, T. (2006) *What's The Matter With America?* New York: Vintage.

Frank, T. (2008) *The Wrecking Crew,* London: Harvill Secker.

Frank, T. (2012) *Pity the Billionaire,* London: Harvill Secker.

Freud, S. (2002) *Civilisation and its Discontents*, London: Penguin.

Frey, W. (1995) 'The new geography of population shifts: Trends towards Balkanisation' in R. Farley (ed.) *State of the Nation: America in the 1990s, Volume 2*, New York: Russell Sage Foundation.

Friedman, M. (1980) *Free to Choose*, New York: Penguin.

Friedman, M. (1993) *Why Government Is the Problem*, Stanford, CA: Hoover Institution Press.

Friedman, M. (2002) *Capitalism and Freedom,* Chicago, IL: University of Chicago Press.

Friedman, T. (2000) *The Lexus and the Olive Tree,* New York: HarperCollins.

Fukuyama, F. (1993) *The End of History and the Last Man*, London: Penguin.

Galbraith, J.K. (1999) *The Affluent Society*, New York: Penguin.

Galbraith, J.K. (2008) *The Predator State,* New York: The Free Press.

Galbraith, J.K. (2009) *The Great Crash 1929*, London: Penguin.

Galbraith, J.K. (2012) *Inequality and Instability*, Oxford: Oxford University Press.

Gans, H. (1993) 'From 'Underclass' to 'Undercaste': Some observations about the future of the postindustrial economy and its major victims', *International Journal of Urban and Regional Research*, 7, 3: 327–35.

Garland, D. (2001) *The Culture of Control*, Oxford: Oxford University Press.

Giddens, A. (1998) *The Third Way*, Oxford: Polity.

Giddens, A. (2007) *Over to You, Mr. Brown*, Oxford: Polity.

Glynn, A. (2007) *Capitalism Unleashed*, Oxford: Oxford University Press.

Gorz, A. (2010a) 'The exit from capitalism has already begun', *Cultural Politics*, 6, 1: 5–14.

Gorz, A. (2010b) *Ecologica*, Chicago, IL: University of Chicago Press.

Gorz, A. (2010c) *The Immaterial*, Chicago, IL: University of Chicago Press.

Gould, S.J. (1996) *The Mismeasure of Man*, New York: W. W. Norton & Co.

Graeber, D. (2011) *Debt*, London: Melville House.

Graham, S. (2011) *Cities Under Siege*, London: Verso.

Gramsci, A. (1971) *Selections from the Prison Notebooks of Antonio Gramsci*, London: International Publishers.

Granter, E. (2009) *Critical Social Theory and the End of Work*, Farnham: Ashgate.

Hadfield, P. (2006) *Bar Wars*, Oxford: Oxford University Press.

Hall, S. (2012a) *Theorizing Crime and Deviance: A New Perspective*, London: Sage.

Hall, S. (2012b) 'Don't look up, don't look down: Liberal criminology's fear of the supreme and the subterranean', *Crime, Media, Culture*, 8, 2: 197–212.

Hall, S. (2012c) 'The solicitation of the trap: On transcendence and transcendental materialism in advanced consumer-capitalism', *Human Studies Special Issue on Transcendence and Transgression*, 35, 3: 365–81.

Hall, S. and Winlow, S. (2007) 'Cultural criminology and primitive accumulation: A formal introduction for two strangers who should really become more intimate', *Crime, Media, Culture*, 3, 1: 82–90.

Hall, S., Winlow, S. and Ancrum, C. (2005) 'Radgies, gangsters and mugs: Imaginary criminal identities in the twilight of the pseudo-pacification process', *Social Justice*, 32, 1: 100–12.

Hall, S., Winlow, S. and Ancrum, C. (2008) *Criminal Identities and Consumer Culture: Crime, Exclusion and the New Culture of Narcissism*, Cullompton: Willan.

Hallsworth, S. (2005) *Street Crime*, Cullompton: Willan.

Hallsworth, S. and Lea, J. (2011) 'Reconstructing Leviathan: Emerging contours of the security state', *Theoretical Criminology*, 15, 2: 141–57.

Hallward, P. (2003) *Badiou: A Subject to Truth*, Minneapolis, MN: University of Minnesota Press.

Harrell, E. (2007) 'Black Victims of Violent Crime', Bureau of Justice Statistics Special Report, US Department of Justice.

Harcourt, B. (2010) *Illusion of Free Markets*, Cambridge, MA: Harvard University Press.

Hardt, M. and Negri, A. (2000) *Empire*, Cambridge, MA: Harvard University Press.

Harris, B. (2004) *The Origins of the British Welfare State*, London: Palgrave Macmillan.

Hartigan, J. (1999) *Racial Situations*, Princeton, NJ: Princeton University Press.

Hartigan, J. (2005) *Odd Tribes*, Durham, NJ: Duke University Press.

Harvey, D. (2007) *A Brief History of Neoliberalism*, Oxford: Oxford University Press.

Harvey, D. (2010) *The Enigma of Capital*, Oxford: Oxford University Press.

Hatherley, O. (2011) *A Guide to the New Ruins of Great Britain*, London: Zero.

Hayek, F. (2001) *The Road to Serfdom*, London: Routledge.

Hayek, F. (2006) *The Constitution of Liberty*, London: Routledge.

Hayward, K. (2004) *City Limits*, London: GlassHouse.

Hayward, K. (2012a) 'Using cultural geography to think differently about space and crime', in S. Hall and S. Winlow (eds) *New Directions in Criminological Theory*, London: Routledge.

Hayward, K. (2012b) 'Five spaces of cultural criminology', *British Journal of Criminology*, 52, 3: 441–62.

Hayward, K. and Yar, M. (2006) 'The chav phenomenon: Consumption, media and the construction of a new underclass', *Crime, Media, Culture*, 2, 1: 9–28.

Heath, J. and Potter, A. (2006) *The Rebel Sell*, Chichester: Capstone.

Heilbroner, R. and Milberg, W. (2011) *The Making of the Economic Society*, London: Pearson.

Heinberg, R. (2011) *The End of Growth: Adapting to Our New Economic Reality*, London: Clairview Books.

Henderson, S., Bowlby, S. and Raco, M. (2007) 'Refashioning local government and inner-city regeneration: The Salford experience', *Urban Studies*, 44, 8: 1441–1463.

Hennessy, P. (2012) 'Britain must champion the wealth creators, say Tories', *The Telegraph* (8/9/2012).

Herrnstein, R. and Murray, C. (1996) *The Bell Curve*, New York: Simon & Schuster.

Hickson, K. (2009) 'Conservatism and the poor: Conservative party attitudes to poverty and inequality since the 1970s', *British Politics*, 4, 341–62.

Hills, J. and Stewart, K. (2005) 'Introduction', in J. Hills and K. Stewart (eds), *A More Equal Society?* Bristol: Policy Press.

Hills, J., Brewer, M., Jenkins, S., Lister, R., Lupton, R., Machin, S., Mills, C., Modood, T., Rees, T. and Riddell, S. (2010) *An Anatomy of Economic Inequality in the UK: Report of the National Equality Panel*, London: Government Equalities Office.

Hills, J., Le Grand, J. and Piachaud, D. (eds) (2002) *Understanding Social Exclusion*, Oxford: Oxford University Press.

Hobbes, T. (2008) *Leviathan*, Oxford: Oxford Paperbacks.

Hobbs, D., Hadfield, P., Lister, S. and Winlow, S. (2003) *Bouncers: Violence and Governance in the Night-time Economy*, Oxford: Oxford University Press.

Hobbs, D., Lister, S., Hadfield, P., Winlow, S. and Hall, S. (2000) 'Receiving shadows: Governance and liminality in the night-time economy', *British Journal of Sociology*, 51, 4: 701–17.

Hobcraft, J. (1998) 'Intergenerational and Life-Course Transmission of Social Exclusion: Influences and Childhood Poverty, Family Disruption and Contact with the Police', CASE, Research Paper No. 15, London: London School of Economics.

Hobcraft, J. (2000) 'The Role of Schooling and Educational Qualifications in the Emergence of Adult Social Exclusion', CASE Research Paper No. 43, London: London School of Economics.

Hobsbawm, E. (1989) *The Age Of Empire: 1875–1914*, London: Abacus.

Hobsbawm, E. (1995) *The Age of Extremes: The Short Twentieth Century 1914–1991*, London: Abacus.

Hochschild, A. (2003) *The Managed Heart*, Los Angeles, CA: University of California Press.

Hutton, W. (1995) *The State We're In*, London: Jonathan Cape.

Jacobs, J. (2005) *The Death and Life of Great American Cities*, New York: Vintage.

James, O. (2008) *The Selfish Capitalist*, London: Vermillion.

James, O. (2010) *Britain On The Couch*, London: Vermillion.

Jameson, F. (1992) *Postmodernism: Or, the Cultural Logic of Late Capitalism*, London: Verso.

Jameson, F. (2003) 'Future city', *New Left Review*, 21: May/June.

Jargowsky, P. (1997) *Poverty and Place*, New York: Russell Sage Foundation.

Jeffery, B. and Jackson, W. (2012) 'The Pendleton riots: A political sociology', *Criminal Justice Matters*, 81, 1: 18–20

Jenkins, S. (2007) *Thatcher and Sons: A Revolution in Three Acts*, London: Penguin.

Johnston, A. (2008) *Žižek's Ontology: A Transcendental Materialist Theory of Subjectivity*, Evanston, IL: Northwestern University Press.

Judt, T. (2010) *Postwar: A History of Europe Since 1945*, London: Random House.

Judt, T. (2011) *Ill Fares the Land*, London: Penguin.

Kaletsky, A. (2011) *Capitalism 4.0*, London: Bloomsbury.

Keen, S. (2011) *Debunking Economics*, London: Zed Books.

Keynes, J.M. (2008) *The General Theory of Employment, Interest and Money*, London: BN Publishing.

Kimeldorf, H. (1999) *Battling for American Labor*, Los Angeles, CA: University of California Press.

Krugman, P. (2008) *The Return of Depression Economics and the Crisis of 2008*, London: Allen Lane.

Krugman, P. (2012) *End This Depression Now!* London: Norton.

Lacan, J. (1997) *The Seminar of Jacques Lacan: Book III*, New York: Norton.

Lacan, J. (2008) *The Seminar of Jaques Lacan: Other Side of Psychoanalysis, Book XVII*, New York: Norton.

Lansley, S. (2012) *The Cost of Inequality*, London: Gibson Square.

Lasch, C. (1973) *The Agony of the American Left*, Harmondsworth: Penguin.

Lash, S. (2010) *Intensive Culture*, London: Sage.

Lazzarato, M. (1996) 'Immaterial labour', in M. Hardt and P. Virno (eds), *Radical Thought in Italy*, Minneapolis, MN: University of Minnesota Press.

Lea, J. (2002) *Crime and Modernity*, London: Sage.

LeBlanc, N. (2009) *Random Family*, New York: Harper Perennial.

Lemert, E. (1972) *Human Deviance, Social Problems and Social Control*, Englewood Cliffs, NJ: Prentice Hall.

Levinson, S. (2006) *Torture: A Collection*, Oxford: Oxford University Press.

Levitas, R. (1998) *The Inclusive Society? Social Exclusion and New Labour*, Basingstoke: Macmillan.

Lloyd, A. (2012) 'Working to live, not living to work: Work, leisure and youth identity among call centre workers in North East England', *Current Sociology*, 60, 5: 619–35.

Lloyd, A. (2013) *Labour Markets and Identity on the Post-Industrial Assembly Line*, Farnham: Ashgate.

Losurdo, D. (2011) *Liberalism: A Counter-History*, London: Verso.

Lyotard, J. (1984) *The Postmodern Condition*, Manchester: Manchester University Press.

MacAskill, E. (2012) 'Mitt Romney stands by gaffe but says case not "elegantly stated"', *Guardian* (18/9/2012).

MacDonald, R. (ed.) (1997) *Youth, the 'Underclass' and Social Exclusion*, London: Routledge.

Macfarlane, A. (1979) *The Origins of English Individualism*, Oxford: Basil Blackwell.

Maffesoli, M. (1995) *The Time of the Tribes*, London: Sage.

Malik, S. (2012) 'Peter Mandelson gets nervous about people getting "filthy rich": Former business secretary distances himself from remark that was seen as maxim for Labour's embrace of free markets', *Guardian* (26/1/2012).

Marable, M. (1993) *How Capitalism Underdeveloped Black America*, New York: South End Press.

Marcuse, P. and van Kempen, R. (2000) 'Conclusion: A changed spatial order', in P. Marcuse and R. van Kempen (eds), *Globalizing Cities: A New Spatial Order?* Oxford: Blackwell.

Marcuse, P. and van Kempen, R. (2002) *Of States and Cities*, Oxford: Oxford University Press.

Martin, D. (2008) 'The post-city being prepared on the site of the ex-city', *City*, 12, 3: 372–82.

Martin, G. (2009) 'Subculture, style, chavs and consumer capitalism: Towards a critical cultural criminology of youth', *Crime, Media, Culture*, 5, 2: 123–45.

Martin, R. and Rowthorn, B. (eds) (1986) *The Geography of De-industrialisation*, London: Macmillan.

Marx, K. (1970) *A Contribution to the Critique of Political Economy*, New York: International Publishers.

Marx, K. (1973) *Grundrisse*, London: Pelican.

Marx, K. (2008) *Capital*, Oxford: Oxford Paperbacks.

Massey, D. and Denton, N. (1989) 'Hypersegregation in U.S. metropolitan areas: Black and Hispanic segregation along five dimensions', *Demography*, 26, 3: 373–91.

Massey, D. and Denton, N. (1993) *American Apartheid*, Harvard, MA: Harvard University Press.

Matthews, R., Maume, M. and Miller, W. (2001) 'Deindustrialization, economic distress, and homicide rates in midsized rustbelt cities', *Homicide Studies*, 5, 2: 83–113.

Mattick, P. (2011) *Business as Usual*, London: Reaktion Books.

McAuley, R. (2007) *Out of Sight*, Cullompton: Willan.

McCartney, S. (2005) *The Fake Factor*, London: Marshall Cavendish.

McPherson, C.B. (1964) *The Political Theory of Possessive Individualism: Hobbes to Locke*, Oxford: Oxford Paperbacks.

Meen, G., Gibb, K., Goody, J., McGrath, T. and Mackinnon, J. (2005) *Economic Segregation in Britain*, Bristol: The Policy Press.

Mill, J. S. and Bentham, J. (2000) *Utilitarianism and Other Essays*, London: Penguin.

Milner, J-C. (2011) *Clartes de tout*, Paris: Verdier.

Ministry of Justice (2012) 'Prison Population Bulletin – Weekly 03 August 2012'. Available at: www.justice.gov.uk/statistics/prisons-and-probation/prison-population-figures (retrieved 4/3/12).

Minton, A. (2012) *Ground Control*, London: Penguin.

Mises von, L. (2007) *Human Action*, Auburn, AL: Ludwig von Mises Institute.

Moore, C. and Birtwistle, G. (2004) 'The Burberry business model: Creating an international luxury fashion brand', *International Journal of Retail & Distribution Management*, 32, 8: 412–22.

Murray, C. (1984) *Losing Ground*, New York: Basic Books.

Murray, C. (1990) *The Emerging British Underclass*, London: Institute of Economic Affairs.

Murray, C. (2005) 'The advantages of social apartheid', *The Sunday Times* (3/4/2005).

Mythen, G. and Walklate, S. (2006) 'Communicating the terrorist risk: Harnessing a culture of fear?', *Crime, Media, Culture*, 2, 2: 123–42.

Mythen, G. and Walklate, S. (2008) 'How scared are we?' *British Journal of Criminology*, 48, 2: 209–25.

Mythen, G., Kearon, T. and Walklate, S. (2007) 'Making sense of the terrorist risk: Public perceptions of emergency advice', *Security Journal*, 20, 2: 77–95.

Mythen, G., Walklate, S. and Khan, F. (2009) '"I'm a Muslim, but I'm not a terrorist": Victimization, risky identities and the performance of safety', *British Journal of Criminology*, 49, 6: 736–54.

Naylor, R.T. (2011) *Crass Struggle*, Montreal: McGill-Queen's University Press.

Nightingale, C.H. (1993) *On the Edge*, New York: Basic Books.

O'Neill, M. and Seal, L. (2012) *Transgressive Imaginations: Crime, Deviance and Culture*, London: Palgrave Macmillan.

ONS (2009) *Labour Market Statistics August 2009*, available at: http://research. dwp.gov.uk/asd/asd4/medium_term.asp (retrieved 21/8/ 2009).

Orsini, A. (2011) *Anatomy of the Red Brigades*, New York: Cornell University Press.

Pain, R. (2000) 'Place, social relations and the fear of crime: a review', *Progress in Human Geography*, 24, 3: 365–87.

Pantazis, C. (2000) ' "Fear of crime", vulnerability and poverty', *British Journal of Criminology*, 40, 3: 414–36.

Peach, C. (1999) 'London and New York: Contrasts in British and American models of segregation, with a comment by Nathan Glazer', *International Journal of Population Geography*, 5, 5: 319–47.

Pearce, F. (2012) *The Landgrabbers*, London: Eden Project Books.

Pearson, G. (1982) *Hooligan: A History of Respectable Fears*, London: Palgrave Macmillan.

Peet, R. (2009) *Unholy Trinity: The IMF, World Bank and WTO*, London: Zed Books.

Phillips, T. (2007) *Knockoff*, London: Kogan Page.

Pitts, J. (2008) *Reluctant Gangsters*, Cullompton: Willan.

Presdee, M. (2000) *Cultural Criminology and the Carnival of Crime*, London: Routledge.

Raffo, C., Dyson, A., Gunter, H., Hall, D., Jones, L. and Kalamboukaa, A. (2009) 'Education and poverty: Mapping the terrain and making the links to educational policy', *International Journal of Inclusive Education*, 13, 4: 341–58.

Rancière, J. (2004) *The Philosopher and His Poor*, Durham, NC: Duke University Press.

Rancière, J. (2010a) *Chronicle of Consensual Times*, London: Continuum.

Rancière, J. (2010b) *Dissensus*, London: Continuum.

Rand, A. (2007a) *Atlas Shrugged*, London: Penguin Classics.

Rand, A. (2007b) *The Fountainhead*, London: Penguin Classics.

Rasmus, J. (2010) *Epic Recession*, London: Pluto Press.

Reiner, R. (2007) *Law and Order*, Oxford: Polity.

Rifkin, J. (1995) *The End of Work*, New York: Putnam.

Ritzer, G. (1997) *The McDonaldization Thesis*, London: Sage.

Rose, J. (2010) *The Intellectual Life of the British Working Classes*, New Haven, CT: Yale University Press.

Rose, N. (1996) 'The death of the social? Re-figuring the territory of government', *Economy and Society*, 25, 3: 327–56.

Rose, N. (1999) *Governing the Soul*, London: Free Association.

Ross, K. (2004) *May '68 and Its Afterlives*, Chicago, IL: Chicago University Press.

Roubini, N. (2011) *Crisis Economics*, London: Penguin.

Rousseau, J-J. (1990) *Rousseau: Judge of Jean-Jacques*, Hanover, NH: Dartmouth College Press.

Rudd, M. (2010) *Underground: My Life with SDS and the Weathermen*, New York: Harper Collins.

Runciman, W. (1990) 'How many classes are there in contemporary British society?', *Sociology*, 24: 378–96.

Sahlins, M. (2003) *Stone Age Economics*, London: Routledge.

Schlesinger, A. (2003) *The Age of Roosevelt: The Politics of Upheaval 1933–1936 (Vol. 3)*, New York: Houghton Mifflin.

Schofield, P. (2009) *Utility and Democracy: The Political Thought of Jeremy Bentham*, Oxford: Oxford University Press.

Scott, J. (1996) *Stratification and Power: Structures of Class, Status and Command*, Cambridge: Polity.

Sedghi, A. (2012) 'Youth unemployment across the OECD: how does the UK compare?' *The Guardian* (16/5/2012).

Seidman, M. (2004) *The Imaginary Revolution*, New York: Berghahn Books.

Sennett, R. (1977) *The Fall of Public Man*, New York: Alfred A. Knopf.

Seymour, R. (2010) *The Meaning of David Cameron*, London: Zero Books.

Seymour, R. (2012) *The Liberal Defence of Murder*, London: Verso.

Shaxson, N. (2012) *Treasure Islands: Tax Havens and the Men Who Stole the World*, London: The Bodley Head.

Shildrick, T., MacDonald, R., Webster, C. and Garthwaite, K. (2010) *The Role of the Low-pay, No-pay Cycle in Recurrent Poverty*, York: Joseph Rowntree Foundation.

Shutt, H. (2010) *Beyond the Profits System*, London: Zed Books.

Singer, P. (2007) *Corporate Warriors*, New York: Cornell University Press.

Simondon, G. (2007) *L'individuation Psychique et Collective*, Paris: Éditions Aubier.

Sirico, R. (2012) *Defending the Free Market: Moral Case for a Free Economy*, New York: Regnery Publishing.

Slapper, G. and Tombs, S. (1999) *Corporate Crime*, London: Longman.

Sloterdijk, P. (2011) *Bubbles*, Boston, MA: MIT Press

Smart, B. (2010) *Consumer Society*, London: Sage.

Smith, A. (2008) *Wealth of Nations*, Oxford: Oxford Paperbacks.

Smith, J. (2009) *Building New Deal Liberalism*, Cambridge: University of Cambridge Press.

Sollund, R. (2012) *Global Harms*, New York: Nova Science Publishers.

South, N. (2007) 'The "corporate colonisation of nature": Bio-prospecting, bio-piracy and the development of green criminology' in P. Beirne and N. South (eds), *Issues in Green Criminology*, Cullompton: Willan.

Southwood, I. (2011) *Non-Stop Inertia*, London: Zero.

Squires, P. (ed.) (2008) *ASBO Nation*, Bristol: Policy Press.

Standing, G. (2011) *The Precariat*, London: Bloomsbury.

Sterngold, J. (2010) 'How much did Lehman CEO Dick Fuld really make?', *Bloomberg Businessweek Magazine* (29/4/2010).

Stewart, H. (2012a) 'Youth unemployment soars, and it's not just a phase', *The Guardian* (13/4/2012).

Stewart, H. (2012b) '£13tn hoard hidden from taxman by global elite', *Guardian* (21/7/2012).

Stiegler, B. (2011) *For a New Critique of Political Economy*, Cambridge: Polity Press.

Stiglitz, J. (2010) *Freefall*, London: Penguin.

Stiglitz, J. (2012) *The Price of Inequality*, New York: Norton.

Sugrue, T. (2005) *The Origins of the Urban Crisis*, Princeton, NJ: Princeton University Press.

Taylor, P. A. (2010) *Žižek and the Media*, Cambridge: Polity.

Terranova, T. (2004) *Network Culture*, London: Pluto Press.

Tocqueville, A. (1997) *Memoir on Pauperism*, Chicago, IL: I.R. Dee.

Tombs, S. and Whyte, D. (2012) *The Corporate Criminal*, London: Routledge.

Toynbee, P. (2003) *Hard Work: Life in Low-pay Britain*, London: Bloomsbury.

Toynbee, P. and Walker, D. (2009) *Unjust Rewards*, London: Granta.

Treadwell, J., Briggs, D., Winlow, S. and Hall, S. (2012) 'Shopocalypse now: Consumer culture and the English riots of 2011', *British Journal of Criminology*, 53, 1: 1–17.

Treanor, J. (2011) 'RBS bankers get £950m in bonuses despite £1.1bn loss', *Guardian* (24/2/2011).

Treanor, J. (2012) 'Bob Diamond cuts up rough as he quits Barclays', *Guardian*, (3/7/2012).

Varoufakis, Y. (2011) *The Global Minotaur: America, The True Origins of the Financial Crisis and the Future of the World Economy*, London: Zed Books.

Vinen, R. (2010) *Thatcher's Britain*, London: Pocket Books.

Virno, P. (2007) 'General intellect', *Historical Materialism*, 15, 2: 3–8.

Virno, P., Bertoletti, I., Cascaito, J. and Casson, A. (2004) *A Grammar of the Multitude*, Los Angeles, CA: Semiotext(e).

Wacquant, L. (1993) 'Urban outcasts: stigma and division in the Black American ghetto and the French urban periphery', *International Journal of Urban and Regional Research*, 17, 3: 366–83.

Wacquant, L. (2001) 'Deadly symbiosis: When ghetto and prison meet and mesh', *Punishment and Society*, 3, 1: 95–133.

Wacquant, L. (2007) *Urban Outcasts*, Oxford: Polity.

Wacquant, L. (2009) *Punishing the Poor*, Durham, NC: Duke University Press.

walesonline.co.uk (2012) www.walesonline.co.uk/news/datastore/wales-data/2012/09/12/employment-rate-rises-in-wales-to-55-2-as-economic-inactivity-drops-91466-31818785/ (retrieved 4/3/2012).

Walker, S., Spohn, C. and Delone, M. (2003) *The Color of Justice*, London: Wadsworth.

Webster, C. (2008) 'Marginalized white ethnicity, race and crime', *Theoretical Criminology*, 12, 3: 293–312.

Webster, C., Simpson, D., MacDonald, R., Abbas, A., Cieslik, M., Shildrick, T. and Simpson, M. (2004) *Poor Transitions: Social Exclusion and Young Adults*, Bristol: Policy Press.

Welshman, J. (2007) *Underclass*, London: Hambleton.

West, C. (1993) *Race Matters*, New York: Vintage.

West, C. (2004) *Democracy Matters*, London: Penguin.

Westergaard, J. (1992) 'About and beyond the underclass: Some notes on influences of social climate on British sociology', *Sociology*, 26: 575–87.

Whitehead, P. and Crawshaw, P. (2012) (eds) *Organising Neoliberalism: Markets, Privatisation and Justice*, London: Anthem.

Whitty, G. (2001) 'Education, social class and social exclusion', *Journal of Education Policy*, 16, 4: 287–95.

Whyte, W. (1957) *The Organization Man*, New York: Doubleday.

Wiegratz, J. (2010) 'Fake capitalism? The dynamics of neo-liberal moral restructuring and pseudo-development: The case of Uganda', *Review of African Political Economy*, 37, 124: 123–37.

Wiegratz, J. (2012) 'The neoliberal harvest: The proliferation and normalization of economic fraud in a market society', in S. Winlow and R. Atkinson (eds), *New Directions in Crime and Deviancy*, London: Routledge.

Wilkes, R. and Iceland, J. (2004) 'Hypersegregation in the twenty-first century', *Demography*, 41, 1: 23–36.

Wilson, R. and Pickett, K. (2009) *The Spirit Level*, London: Penguin.

Wilson, W.J. (1987) *The Truly Disadvantaged*, Chicago, IL: University of Chicago Press.

Wilson, W.J. (1996) *When Work Disappears*, London: Vintage.

Wilson, W.J. and Traub, R. (2007) *There Goes the Neighborhood*, New York: Vintage.

Winlow, S. (2001) *Badfellas: Crime, Tradition and New Masculinities*, Oxford: Berg.

Winlow, S. (2010) 'Violence in the night-time economy', in F. Brookman, M. Maguire, H. Pierpoint and T. Bennett (eds) *Handbook of Crime*, Cullompton: Willan.

Winlow, S. (2012a) 'Is it OK to talk about capitalism again? Or, why criminology must take a leap of faith', in Winlow, S. and Atkinson, R. (eds) *New Directions in Crime and Deviancy*, London: Routledge.

Winlow, S. (2012b) 'All that is sacred is profaned: Towards a theory of subjective violence' in S. Hall and S. Winlow (eds), *New Directions in Criminological Theory*, London: Routledge.

Winlow, S. and Hall, S. (2006) *Violent Night: Urban Leisure and Contemporary Culture*, Oxford: Berg.

Winlow, S. and Hall, S. (2009a) 'Living for the weekend: Youth identities in northeast England', *Ethnography*, 10, 1: 91–113.

Winlow, S. and Hall, S. (2009b) 'Retaliate first: Memory, humiliation and male violence', *Crime, Media, Culture*, 5, 3: 285–304.

Winlow, S. and Hall, S. (2012a) 'What is an "ethics committee"? Academic governance in an epoch of belief and incredulity', *British Journal of Criminology*, 52, 2: 400–16.

Winlow, S. and Hall, S. (2012b) 'A predictably obedient riot: Post-politics, consumer culture and the English riots of 2011', *Cultural Politics*, 8, 3: 465–88.

Wolff, R. (2010) *Capitalism Hits the Fan*, New York: Interlink.

Yi-Chieh, J.L. (2011) *Fake Stuff*, London: Routledge.

Young, J. (1999) *The Exclusive Society*, London: Sage.

Zaitchik, A. (2010) *Common Nonsense: Glenn Beck and the Triumph of Ignorance*, Hoboken, NJ: John Wiley & Sons, Inc.

Zimring, H. (2006) *The Great American Crime Decline*, Oxford: Oxford University Press.

Zinn, H. (2003) 'Limits to the new deal', in H. Zinn (ed.) *New Deal Thought*, Indianapolis, IN: Hackett Publishing.

Zinn, H. (2005) *A People's History of the United States, 1492–Present*, New York: Harper Perennial.

Zinn, H. (2010) *The Bomb*, San Francisco, CA: City Lights Books.

Žižek, S. (1997) 'Multiculturalism, or, the cultural logic of multinational capitalism', *New Left Review*, 225, 28–51.

Žižek, S. (1998) 'The Cartesian subject versus the Cartesian theatre' in S. Žižek (ed.) *Cogito and the Unconscious*, Durham, NC: Duke University Press.

Žižek, S. (2001) *Did Somebody Say Totalitarianism?* London: Verso.

Žižek, S. (2002) *Welcome to the Desert of the Real,* London: Verso.

Žižek, S. (2005) *Iraq: The Borrowed Kettle,* London: Verso.

Žižek, S. (2006a) *Interrogating the Real,* London: Continuum.

Žižek, S. (2006b) *How to Read Lacan,* London: Granta.

Žižek, S. (2007) *The Indivisible Remainder,* London: Verso.

Žižek, S. (2008a) *Violence,* London: Profile Books.

Žižek, S. (2008b) *In Defense of Lost Causes,* London: Verso.

Žižek, S. (2009a) *The Sublime Object of Ideology,* London: Verso.

Žižek, S. (2009b) *First as Tragedy, Then as Farce,* London: Verso.

Žižek, S. (2009c) *The Ticklish Subject: The Absent Centre of Political Ontology,* London: Verso.

Žižek, S. (2011) *Living in the End Times,* London: Verso.

Žižek, S. (2012) *Less Than Nothing: Hegel and the Shadow of Dialectical Materialism,* London: Verso.

Žižek, S. and Douzinas, C. (2010) (eds) *The Idea of Communism,* London: Verso.

Zupančič, A. (2006) 'When surplus enjoyment meets surplus value', in J. Clemens and R. Grigg (eds) *Jacques Lacan and the Other Side of Psychoanalysis: Reflections on Seminar XVII,* Durham, NC: Duke University Press.

Index